OBJECT-ORIENTED SPECIFICATION
CASE STUDIES

OBJECT-ORIENTED SPECIFICATION
CASE STUDIES

EDITED BY

K. Lano

AND

H. Haughton

Prentice Hall

New York   London   Toronto   Sydney   Tokyo   Singapore

First published 1994 by
Prentice Hall International (UK) Limited
Campus 400, Maylands Avenue
Hemel Hempstead
Hertfordshire, HP2 7EZ

A division of
Simon & Schuster International Group

Printed and bound in Great Britain by
Redwood Books, Trowbridge, Wilts

Library of Congress Cataloging-in-Publication Data

Object-oriented specification case studies / edited by K. Lano
and H. Haughton
     p. cm. – (Prentice Hall object-oriented series)
    Includes bibliographical references and index.
    ISBN 0-13-097015-8
    1. Object-oriented programming (Computer science)–Case studies.
   2. Computer software–Development–Case studies. I. Lano, K.
II. Haughton, H. III. Series.
QA76.64.O28   1993
005.1'2–dc20   93-21698
                                         CIP

British Library Cataloguing in Publication Data

A catalogue record for this book is available from
the British Library

ISBN 0-13-097015-8 (pbk)

---

1 2 3 4 5 98 97 96 95 94

Contents

Editor's Foreword

It is not uncommon for a speaker who presents a seminar on object-oriented technology, especially to experienced people from industry who over the years have seen other methods come and go, to get a question such as: 'Everyone is excited about this now, but what comes after object orientation? What will be the next major development in software?' The speaker will find it hard to resist the facile answer 'I cannot tell you, because I am working on it and it is really too hot to tell anyone'. But when pressed a little further I tend to answer 'formal methods'.

A specialist in formal methods may find such a comment preposterous, since formal methods have actually been around for a very long time, and certainly pre-date the current wave of interest in object orientation. But the specialist in object orientation would quickly counter any precedence claim by noting that object-oriented ideas too date back to a long time ago – the mid-sixties. So any such dispute is pointless. More interesting is the observation that the two disciplines share much of their inspiration: in particular both have been heavily influenced (although not originated) by the work on abstract data types.

Cross-fertilisation between the two areas is also not entirely new; at least one of the major object-oriented languages in particular claims to have been fundamentally influenced by an early version of Z. But someone who observes the object-oriented scene today cannot but be struck by the lack of rigour and formal basis of most of the work being done in this area; conversely, anyone who has tried to apply formal specifications to large practical systems has encountered the need for powerful system-structuring mechanisms, a need which object orientation addresses admirably.

It is not surprising, then, that a number of groups have started to work on unifying the two fields. What is more surprising is that much of this work is still so recent; but it is developing at a rapid pace, and creating considerable excitement.

The time was thus ripe for the present volume, which provides a remarkable snapshot of some of the best work in the field. The editors, Kevin Lano and Howard Haughton, have made sure that the book includes contributions from many of the currently active trends and several countries. Started as a collection of individual contributions, the volume evolved into a real book; the authors worked very hard to produce a coherent volume whose various parts rely on a common terminology, glossary and bibliography. They complement each other, refer to each other, and sometimes seem to argue with each other; for the reader should not expect complete agreement in a field which is still so young and open. One of the pleasures of the book is indeed to see the reasoned differences of approach between the different groups, which makes the various chapters less comparable perhaps to the instruments of an orchestra than to the successive movements of a serenade.

Enjoy the concert. The topic may or may not be 'the' next thing after object orientation (for that matter, object orientation will continue to make itself heard for a long time, so perhaps there is no urgent need for a next thing after all); but it is important and timely, and this book is the best survey so far.

Bertrand Meyer

Foreword

The history of object-oriented programming languages is an interesting one. Their genesis lies in the programming language Simula which was developed in the 1960s. While Simula was a widely admired language, it never achieved a great popularity outside some very small communities who were interested in system simulation. However, after two decades of very little activity there was a massive explosion of interest in object-oriented technology in the 1980s. It is for the historian or sociologist to provide detailed answers to the question of why it happened then, and why the subsequent growth of interest in object-oriented languages has been so rapid. My own view is that developers and researchers – perhaps subconsciously – felt that conventional third-generation language development had reached an endstop. This, allied with the efficiency problems being experienced by researchers attempting to develop fifth-generation languages, perhaps gave rise to a set of conditions in which object-oriented technology could blossom.

We now have a wide variety of object-oriented programming languages ranging from the elegant SmallTalk to the utilitarian C++, with the variants of C holding sway in industrial environments. We are also beginning to realise the major benefits that accrue from the use of object-oriented technology: re-usability, portability and maintainability.

If history repeats itself – and it looks like doing so – then what will happen is that the C variants will become the main media for developing industrial-strength software. One possible consequence of this is that object-oriented programming languages used in an industrial environment will be employed in the undisciplined way that programming languages such as COBOL and C were used in the 1960s and 1970s: with little thought to specification and design. In effect we may find them used as a superior tool for the hacker.

Happily, there is work being carried out by both researchers and industrial staff which is attempting to persuade us not to repeat the mistakes of earlier decades. Workers such as Ward and Booch who form part of the structured methods movement have been attempting to develop notations and techniques which take us from diagrammatic specifications to systems containing classes which can easily be re-used on other systems. This book represents the first substantial fruits of the formal methods school of software development. It contains excellent material describing the wide variety of formal notations that are available to staff who wish to construct the highest-quality object-oriented specifications and also some case studies which describe these notations in action. It is early days yet. However, what this volume shows is that object-oriented technology is just as amenable to a formal approach as other less powerful technologies, and that even if you decide to program in a less elegant language such as C++, you can still produce correct, high-quality software time and time again.

Darrel Ince
Open University

Preface

Object orientation and formal methods are widely regarded as two fields with significant potential for influence on the future of software engineering. This book aims to provide an introduction to the rapidly growing area at the intersection of these fields: formal approaches to system specification using object-oriented techniques.

We will cover various specification and development styles which are made possible by this combination of techniques, and hope to demonstrate the mutual benefits of combining object orientation and formal specification. There is clear potential for such benefits in the areas of re-use, software maintenance, compartmentalisation of system development, and the scaling up of formal specification techniques to large systems, particularly in the cases of distributed and communication systems. The case studies of object-oriented formal specification given in the book are intended to form templates for further applications of the languages by software engineers to industrial software development.

In the following chapters several applications of object-oriented styles of specification are presented, and associated methods of refinement and development are given. Although different varieties of object-oriented specification language are used, a common core of concepts have been accepted by all the groups working in this area: this core provides a syntax which enables the syntactic encapsulation of the states and operations of a subsystem of a specification into a single object class, which is a type, and allows inheritance and adaptation of classes, as well as the definition of generic classes. The philosophy encouraged by these styles is different from that of specification languages such as Z, as it leads to a stronger focus upon partitioning of a system and a specification into well-designed and encapsulated subsystems, upon which transformations, such as refinements, are applied as a whole. Hierarchical structuring facilities, such as class specialisation hierarchies (*is-a* relations between types of entities), and whole–part hierarchies with one system being used to implement services required by another (and being responsible for the correctness of these implementations), provide a natural means of specification decomposition.

Object-oriented design enhances modularisation of specifications: enabling separate parts of a development to be worked on separately, and to be refined independently of other parts of a specification; and it enhances separation of concerns, since the correctness of high-level parts of a specification can be proved without knowing the internal details of the lower-level specifications that implement its operations, the 'how' of these operations. Re-use is also potentially aided by the ability to specify systems using inheritance and instantiation: a design or specification can be partitioned into a number of segments, each of which can be re-used when needed, independently of other contexts which have been added to them. Moreover, the internal details of a class can be modified to improve aspects of the implementation, without the interface of the class changing, so avoiding the 'ripple effect' of maintenance. The facilities of object orientation may also allow system requirements to be expressed in a 'natural' way, close to the concepts of the application domain, and in a way which is directly comprehensible by domain experts. Formal methods, when integrated with object-oriented techniques, allow in addition the precise specification of the semantics of the methods of classes and hence the interfaces to classes.

Research into the effective application of formal methods within software engineering has led to new formal methods such as RSL [65] and B Abstract Machine Notation (AMN) [1], which incorporate strong modularisation features. In addition, there has been pressure from users of existing specification languages such as Z and VDM for extensions to these languages to support specification modularisation and structuring. The ideas of object orientation have been highly influential in proposals for such extensions – the ability to define object classes is quite consistent with the style of Z in particular, since object classes correspond to specifications at the Z level, and hence remedy an omission from Z: the ability to name and manipulate specifications as a whole within other specifications, and formally to document relationships of refinement and specialisation between specifications. In the VDM community also, several groups have independently responded to a need for object-oriented structuring facilities for large specifications, and rigorous semantic foundations for such extensions have been established.

These formal languages can contribute to the use of object-oriented techniques, in that formal specification provides a rigorous basis for validation and verification of object-oriented applications, and a disciplined approach to the development of implementations from specifications, including the possibility of mathematical proof of refinements. Such a disciplined approach is essential for the successful application of object-oriented techniques: languages alone are not sufficient for the use of object orientation in software engineering, as has been shown by a number of industrial projects [170]. There seems to be a tendency for software engineering practice to revert to the 'hack and debug' life cycle model when a new paradigm such as object orientation or knowledge-based systems arises: the justification being that the new techniques invalidate old approaches. If object-oriented techniques are to become the mainstream of the 1990s, as is evidenced by the uptake of languages such as C++ [93] and Eiffel [142], this should not be an excuse for reducing the rigour of the software engineering which is used to support them.

Moreover, the formal approach can provide a framework in which answers to deep semantic questions concerning object-oriented languages can be addressed, and solutions proposed based on semantic coherence and theoretical feasibility. Examples would be the determination of those forms of inheritance which lead to refinement and type-compatibility; and approaches to extensions to the object-oriented paradigm, such as multi-methods and modules.

The case studies in this book cover a wide range of areas of application, from operating systems to distributed telecommunication systems and databases to artificial intelligence, and describe a variety of techniques that have been found to have been of practical use in specification, development, and reverse engineering. Object-oriented specification languages are not a specialist concern, but are of application to a wide span of areas. Currently, for instance, there is a strong interest in such languages in the area of safety-critical systems, where the aim is to support re-use in order to gain improved reliability.

The case studies generally increase in complexity and in the scope of the languages concerned throughout the book, although significant specification issues will be addressed in each chapter. The orientation of the case studies will also move towards the refinement of specifications to code, as this is an area of critical importance for the practical uptake of formal methods: the ability to produce correct executable code from specifications is essential in order to reduce the cost of maintenance, and to provide a high guarantee of quality for dependable systems.

The following authors and research groups have contributed to the case studies in the book:

Antonio J. Alencar and Joseph A. Goguen
Programming Research Group
University of Oxford
11 Keble Road
Oxford OX1 3QD
UK.

Kevin Lano and Howard Haughton
Applied Information Engineering
Lloyd's Register
Croydon
CR0 2AJ
UK.

Silvio Lemos Meira, Ana Cavalcanti and
Cássio Souza dos Santos
Universidade Federal de Pernambuco
Departamento de Informática
PO Box 7851
50.739 Recife-PE
Brazil.

Gordon Rose and Roger Duke
Software Verification Research Centre
Department of Computer Science
University of Queensland
Queensland 4072, Australia.

Swapan Mitra
Applied Information Engineering
Lloyd's Register
Croydon
CR0 2AJ
UK.

Mary Tobin
Applied Information Engineering
Lloyd's Register
Croydon
CR0 2AJ
UK.

Alan Wills
Object Engineering
24 Windsor Road
Manchester
UK.

The book contains three introductory chapters giving background information on the specification languages, on existing object-oriented design and analysis techniques, and on the implementation of design and analysis techniques in the specification languages, and their place in a software development process. Each chapter in the main part of the book describes one or more case studies in a specific object-oriented specification language, and explores further issues related to the expression of design and the semantic means for functional specification in the language. Three of the languages presented are based on VDM, three are based on Z, and one (OOZE) is based on algebraic specification.

Chapter 1: Specification and Analysis Techniques in Object-oriented Methods

Kevin Lano and **Mary Tobin**
This chapter provides an overview of two widely used object-oriented structured methods, and the specification and design techniques which they support. It identifies those aspects of the methods which have been found to be useful in real-world applications. It aims to provide a source of comparison of these methods and techniques with the formal languages described in other chapters, and to make suggestions for enhancement to these languages to enable their wider uptake and practical application.

Chapter 2: A Comparative Description of Object-oriented Specification Languages

Kevin Lano and **Howard Haughton**
This chapter summarises the commonalities and differences between the languages presented in the book, at both a syntactic and a semantic level. The languages are evaluated both on the facilities they provide for object-oriented techniques, and on the support that they give to formal techniques of reasoning and refinement. Deficiencies and areas of further development are identified.

Chapter 3: Object-oriented Specification Languages in the Software Life Cycle

Kevin Lano and **Howard Haughton**
This chapter describes how the languages considered in the book can be used to support design and specification activities at various stages of the software life cycle. Particular attention is paid to refinement and to the structuring of class hierarchies to facilitate validation and re-use. Techniques such as top-down and bottom-up design are illustrated in this context.

Chapter 4: The Unix File System: A MooZ Specification

Silvio Meira, Ana Cavalcanti and **Cássio Santos**
In this chapter the MooZ language is summarised, and a detailed specification of the Unix File System is given, together with a comparison of this to 'flat' specification approaches. This specification illustrates the use of generic classes to produce a conceptual simplicity by factoring out common aspects of several specific classes. Composition and inheritance are also illustrated. A comparison with an Object-Z specification of the same system is given. Part of the MooZ mathematical library,

defined using object classes, is included.

Chapter 5: An Object-Z Specification of a Mobile Phone System

Gordon Rose and **Roger Duke**
This chapter describes the Object-Z language, and an example specification of a mobile phone system is given, utilising the facilities for hierarchical composition in the language. Instantiation, temporal constraints, composition, inheritance and aggregation are illustrated.

Chapter 6: Object-oriented Specification in VDM++

Swapan Mitra
This chapter discusses some of the important features of VDM++, a VDM-based object-oriented specification language. Inheritance and class composition are illustrated using a specification of a manipulation system for graphical figures.

Chapter 7: Specifying a Concept-recognition System in Z^{++}

Kevin Lano and **Howard Haughton**
The Z^{++} language is described and a specification of a machine learning system is given, together with a description of the process of refinement of a highly abstract specification to a form which is directly implementable in Prolog. Top-down development, instantiation, inheritance and composition are illustrated. The application of object-oriented specification techniques in supporting software maintenance activities is also discussed.

Chapter 8: Specification in OOZE with Examples

Antonio Alencar and **Joseph Goguen**
In this chapter the OOZE specification language is described, and two examples, an accounting system and a block structured symbol table, are given to show the utility of the features of the language. The case study illustrates self-reference and the use of meta-classes to specify operations affecting a set of existing instances of a class. Theories, modules, inheritance, multiple inheritance and views (refinement specifications) are also illustrated.

Chapter 9: Refinement in Fresco

Alan Wills

The formal language Fresco is described, with a focus on its practical application to the refinement of specifications into Smalltalk code, using a proof system. The close relationship between refinement and polymorphism is stressed and used as a guideline for the construction of inheritance hierarchies in the example given, a system for manipulating complex graphical figures.

Chapter 10: SmallVDM: An Environment for Formal Specification and Prototyping in Smalltalk

Silvio Lemos Meira and Câssio Souza dos Santos

This chapter describes the SmallVDM language and environment, together with an example of specification of a process scheduler in the language. Refinement of formal specifications to Smalltalk code is the focus of this chapter.

Glossary

This provides a glossary of terms from object orientation and software engineering, as used in the book.

Bibliography

This provides a bibliography for the book, as well as other relevant references to the area.

Index

This provides a cross-reference to the use of technical terms in the book.

Acknowledgements

Kevin Lano and Howard Haughton acknowledge the support of the AIE department of Lloyd's Register, and the DTI B User Trials project (IEATP project IED4/1/2182). The research for Chapter 6 was conducted at the Programming Research Group, University of Oxford, and was partly funded by the Esprit REDO project (project number 2487). Swapan Mitra acknowledges the support of the AFRODITE Esprit project (project number 6500).

Silvio Meira acknowledges the support of The British Council, IBM Brasil, CNPq and The Pernambuco State Science Foundation (FACEPE) for the research reported in Chapter 4. This research was partly conducted when this author was a Visiting Research Fellow at The Computing Laboratory, University of Kent at Canterbury, UK. Silvio Meira and Cássio Souza Santos are members of the Universidade Federal de Pernambuco, Departamento de Informática, Ana Lúcia C. Cavalcanti is a member of the Instituto Tecnológico de Pernambuco, Grupo de Ciência e Tecnologia da Computacao.

Joseph Goguen and Antonio Alencar are members of the Programming Research Group, University of Oxford.

Gordon Rose and Roger Duke are members of the Software Verification Research Centre, Department of Computer Science, University of Queensland. The financial support of AOTC (Australia) and contributions to the development of Object-Z by Cecily Bailes, David Carrington, David Duke, Ian Hayes, Paul King, Anthony Lee and Graeme Smith are gratefully acknowledged by these authors.

Chapter 1

Specification and Analysis Techniques in Object-oriented Methods

K. Lano and M. Tobin

This chapter provides an overview of two prominent object-oriented methods and the specification and design techniques which they support. It aims to give a source of comparison of these methods and techniques with the formal languages described in other chapters as well as suggestions for enhancement to these languages to enable their wider uptake and practical application.

We will concentrate on the notations and techniques that are provided for analysis, rather than for design, since we envisage the predominant use of diagrammatic notations at the pre-specification life cycle stages, with formal languages being predominately used after formalisation of a system.

1.1   Introduction

Object-oriented development is a relatively new approach to software, based on using objects as abstractions of the real world. The term *object-oriented development* has been used to cover various stages of the software life cycle, from implementation, through design to system analysis. Object-oriented technology has evolved in a way analogous to that of structured software development, in being driven largely by fundamental changes in the programming languages available.

Object-oriented programming languages (OOPLs) have three important features which distinguish them from traditional programming languages: encapsulation, polymorphism and inheritance. *Encapsulation* is the ability of an object to hide information which is internal to it from outside access. It also implies the ability to bundle data with operations on that data. *Polymorphism* allows for generic operations to take on different forms in different classes, via *dynamic binding*, where the method to be executed is identified at runtime. *Inheritance* is the ability of an object to derive its features from another object or from a number of objects.

A large number of languages have been developed which support the above features to varying degrees, ranging from Ada to Smalltalk. Object-oriented versions of more traditional languages, such as C and COBOL, are in use or under consideration.

Although object-oriented programming has become well established, it emphasises implementation issues rather than the underlying design and requirements of the system being developed. The emphasis in object-oriented technology has therefore recently shifted to these earlier stages in the software development process, with the recognition that object orientation is more than just a programming style. Use of traditional structured analysis and design methods with OOPLs has proven problematic, with clashes between functional decomposition techniques and the object-oriented approach. A number of methods have been developed to support particular OOPLs, e.g. HOOD [94] and Buhr [19] are targeted at Ada. Work has also progressed on extending traditional structured methods with object-oriented features, e.g. Ward [190] on Ward/Mellor and Hares [83] on SSADM. A third area of work has concentrated on developing methods which have the object as the underlying model (with the OOPL features of encapsulation, polymorphism and inheritance). Techniques from traditional structured development methods, e.g. data flow analysis and entity-relationship modelling, are incorporated to support the development of the object model. The following methods, which belong to the third category, will be considered in this evaluation:

- Object Modelling Technique (OMT) – Rumbaugh *et al.* [174]
- Object-Oriented Analysis (OOA) – Shlaer and Mellor [179]

The purpose of the evaluation is to provide an overview of two prominent object-oriented development methods by describing their salient features and the techniques supported. Those features and techniques which could enhance formal approaches to system specification will be highlighted.

Each method will be evaluated against three main criteria:

- support for the three complementary views of a system. These can be described in terms of how they relate to change, namely the *what, how* and *when* of change. This is similar to the three models in SSADM [57]:

    static data model – gives the structure of and static interrelationships between data (via a Logical Data Structure (LDS));

    dynamic model – gives the behaviour of a system, in terms of its component entities (via an Entity Life History);

    functional/process model – gives processes and their interfaces (via a Data Flow Diagram).

    Comparisons will be made with features of SSADM (as an example of an established structured method) to highlight commonality and differences in approach;

- coverage of the software life cycle. For our purposes, we use the following definitions for life cycle phases:

  analysis – starts with a problem statement and results in a logical model of what the required system should do.

  design – the logical model resulting from the analysis phase is refined and made more concrete, taking account of the target environment. A physical model is produced.

  implementation – the physical design is translated into a software product: it is encoded in a particular programming language and operates in a particular software/hardware environment.

- uptake of the method, as measured by the availability of training materials and CASE tool support for the method. The applicability of the method will also be considered; for which application domains the method is suitable and what (if any) constraints are imposed on the implementation environment (e.g. the method may be targeted at a particular implementation language).

References to formal methods will be illustrated throughout using Z and temporal logic for consistency.

1.2 Evaluation

1.2.1 Overview

Object Modelling Technique (OMT)
This methodology was developed at the General Electric Research and Development Center (GE R and D) in New York. Originally intended for internal use on government contracts, its success led to the active promotion of the method by General Electric. It is documented in [174]. The life cycle model supported by the method is given in Figure 1.1.

OMT adheres to the 'three views of a system' paradigm. Its static data model is termed the *object model*, its representation of system dynamics is termed the *dynamic model*, and its representation of processes is termed the *functional model*. Each model is used at every life cycle stage, to build up a set of views of a domain or of a system. There are consistency constraints between these models. The object model is given pre-eminent status, since, as the authors of [174] argue 'It is necessary to describe *what* is changing or transforming before describing *when* or *how* it changes'. It is possible iteratively to build up the system views, moving from highly abstract descriptions to levels of detail that permit conversion to code. Iteration within analysis, design and implementation stages is advised and iteration between them is not disallowed.

Diagrammatic notations are used for the three views of the system, although these can be supplemented with textual items such as function descriptions, or

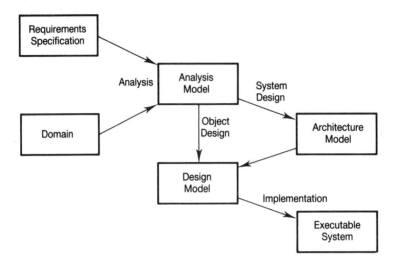

Figure 1.1: Life Cycle Model of OMT

with code items at more detailed design stages.

Shlaer/Mellor Object-oriented Analysis (OOA)
This method derives in part from the Ward and Mellor structured analysis and design method for realtime systems. It was initially applied to realtime systems, and was extended so that it could be applicable to a wide range of application areas.

It has the following life cycle model:

$$Analysis \longrightarrow Design \longrightarrow Implementation$$

The analysis stage is further divided into the following steps, each of which has a corresponding work product mandated by the method:

- overall domain identification;
- partitioning of system into subsystems;
- modelling of relationships between subsystems;
- modelling of communications between subsystems;
- subsystem access modelling;
- creation of an information model;
- creation of object and attribute descriptions;
- creation of relationship descriptions;
- definition of the required communications between objects;
- definition of event lists;
- definition of object access models;
- definition of state process table;

- creation of state model;
- creation of action data flow diagrams;
- creation of process descriptions.

The design stage uses the technique of recursive design and the OODLE notation to map the work products of the analysis stage into implementation-specific descriptions, and thence into code.

The three views of a system are supported. The static data model of OOA is termed the *Information Model*, the dynamic model is the *State Model*, and the process model is the *Action DFD*. The order of development of these models is given above. Unlike OMT, however, these models are not retained from analysis through to design and implementation.

1.2.2   Static Data Model

OMT Object Model
The notation consists of:

- boxes representing classes with a mandatory class name and optional attribute names or declarations, and optional method names and declarations;
- boxes representing objects, with a mandatory class name and optional attribute names and values;
- lines representing optionally named *associations* (relationships) between object classes or *links* (instances of relationships) between objects, with symbols to indicate cardinality (including qualified multiplicity);
- lines with a diamond representing *aggregation*;
- lines with a triangle, representing inheritance, with the class at the base of the triangle inheriting from the class at the apex;
- dashed lines representing instantiation of classes or constraints between relationships;
- bracketed textual items denoting *constraints*.

Additionally, association attributes, derived attributes and classes, distinctions between sequence-valued and set-valued links, distinctions between disjoint and non-disjoint subclasses, propagation of operations from an aggregate class to its components, and class attributes and operations are all representable in object models.

This is therefore a much richer notation than that of (SSADM) LDS and is more complex than the other notations of OMT, reflecting the emphasis of the method on this system view. The notation is also more detailed than the information model of OOA. The complexity of the notation is probably at the limit of that which is readily learnable and usable at the analysis stage.

Examples of object model diagrams are given below. Further examples, and specific techniques for mapping these models into formal object-oriented specification languages, will be given in Chapter 3.

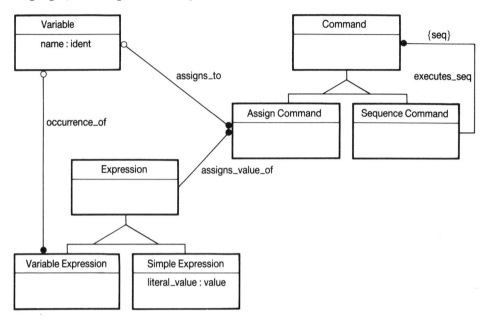

Figure 1.2: Data Model of Simple Procedural Language

Figure 1.2 shows a portion of an object model for a simple model of the syntax of a procedural language. In this example, expressions are (exclusively) either simple (with a literal value) or variables (with a link to a particular variable entity). Commands are exclusively either sequence commands or assignment commands. Non-exclusive subtypes would be represented by a filled triangle rather than an unfilled triangle. We identify that the *occurrence_of, assigns_value* and *assigns_to* associations are optional at the destination end, and are used as attributes of *Variable Expression* and *Assign Command*, so that a filled circle is placed (for example) at the *Variable Expression* end of the *occurrence_of* association.

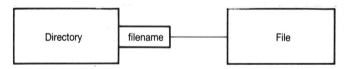

Figure 1.3: Use of Qualified Association

Figure 1.3 gives an example of the use of *qualified* associations in OMT. This qualification reduces the cardinality of the association from one-to-many to one-to-one. Formally, it can be regarded as stating that the *Directory* class possesses an attribute which is a partial injective function from identifiers to files, that is, in each directory a file can be uniquely identified by its name.

file_name : *Ident* ⤔ *File*

An example of a recursive association is given in Figure 1.4. This describes a simple graphical system involving boxes and lines, to which we will refer again in Chapter 3.

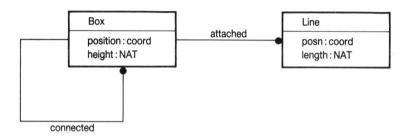

Figure 1.4: Box/Line System

The role of object classes in these diagrams corresponds to that of entity types on an LDS. For OMT, 'An object is simply something that makes sense in an application context' [174, Chapter 3], and hence objects can include 'real world' objects such as houses and cars, in addition to conceptual ones such as laws, and programming objects such as linked lists.

One distinction between this approach and 'pure' object-oriented approaches is the central role of relationships between classes, termed *associations*, in object models. Associations can have attributes and permit an abstract description of interdependencies between classes, without insisting that such dependencies are modelled in a particular way (for instance, as foreign keys or pointers to objects, as is done in Shlaer/Mellor information models). Associations have directionality, via either *role names* attached to the object classes at either end of the association (e.g. *employer*, *employed*) or naming of the association. This directionality is critical for hierarchical decomposition of the network-like object model diagram.

Two omissions can, however, be identified in the notation:

- the strong distinction between associations and attributes means that there is significant discontinuity when attribute types are replaced with a class type, and corresponding attributes by associations, during design (e.g. see [174, page 248]). In the example of Figure 1.2, for instance, the *value* type may become a complex class type;
- although OMT recognises the distinction between conformant and non-conformant inheritance (i.e. between forms of inheritance and overriding of features which do or do not lead to state and behavioural subtyping) [174, page 42], this distinction is not clearly shown on object model diagrams.

The latter shortcoming is also shared by the OOA notation.

An additional process of explicitly modelling enquiry access paths, as in SSADM, may be of use in constructing object models from requirements, and for deciding on the directionality of associations. As with SSADM, a one-to-many relationship from one entity type to another permits two forms of enquiry access: navigation from a single instance of the object class at the 'many' end of the link to a single instance of the object class at the 'one' end (provided the association is mandatory at the many end), and navigation from a single instance of the object class at the one end to a set of instances of the object class at the many end.

The notation is for the most part readily formalisable. Object classes translate to object classes in a formal language, and choices must be made over the expression of associations: as object-valued attributes of a class, or as object classes in their own right. This is a design decision, and could be delayed until after mathematical formalisation, if a formal object-oriented specification language supporting associations existed.

Aggregation can be expressed via either inheritance or recursive composition: the latter is the only possibility if the aggregation relation itself is recursive (as could be the case in the above language syntax example if we had included binary expressions, each of which has two other expressions as subparts). Constraints on object states and between associations can be expressed in mathematical or natural language, and can include temporal constraints.

Unlike SSADM and OOA, the use of separate textual descriptions for object classes (entity types), attributes and associations is not stressed; instead, as much information as possible is placed on the object model diagrams. This clearly has advantages in reducing the amount of mental effort needed in switching between different descriptions, but has the converse problem of overloading and complicating the one view. In practice, particularly in design, more detailed textual descriptions would be essential if the object model notation was to be used. The use of a formal object-oriented specification language during design, with object model documentation generated as needed from descriptions in this language, would obviate this problem. Indeed, some requirements may be more directly expressed in mathematics at the analysis stage. For instance, the requirement on a class *ProcessManager* that 'priority never increases' can be placed as a temporal constraint 'always, the value of *priority* in the next state is less than or equal to the value of *priority* in the current state':

$$\Box(\bigcirc(priority) \leq priority)$$

in the formal version of the class, as an alternative to its textual expression in the object model diagram.

OOA Information Model

This consists of boxes representing classes (which Shlaer and Mellor term *objects* – unspecified instances of classes), directed lines representing relationships, possibly with attributes, and barred lines representing inheritance. A class box is named and can possess attributes. 'Identifier' attributes, i.e. those attributes which make up a candidate key, are signalled with a * symbol. Relationships can be named. The notation distinguishes between one and many relationships, and optionality at either end of a relationship.

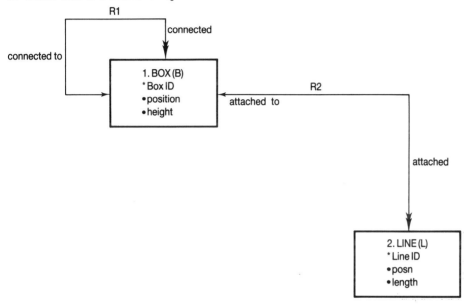

Figure 1.5: Line and Box Example in Shlaer/Mellor Notation

The example of Figure 1.4 is given in Figure 1.5 in information model notation. Unlike OMT, the only form of inheritance which can be represented is exclusive subtyping. Moreover, all subtypes of a class type must be listed on a diagram, whereas OMT allows an ellipsis notation ... to be used to express the fact that other subtypes may be defined. There is no specific representation of aggregation or methods on the diagrams. More detailed information on the cardinality of relationships and the domains of attributes must be given in associated textual object, relationship and attribute descriptions. Precise specifications of the contents of these descriptions are given. Composed relationships are directly representable, whereas in OMT they would be expressed via a constraint.

One critical problem, however, is the stress on the use of pointer attributes or object identities to express relationships between objects. Formalisation of a relationship by means of attributes of one class whose values are object identities from another class is a step completed during analysis in OOA, rather than deferred until alternative design decisions can be taken.

In general, the notation is less detailed than that of OMT. The graphical elements are formalisable.

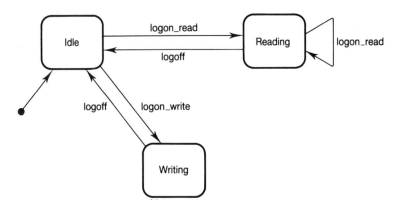

Figure 1.6: State Model for Database Manager

1.2.3 Dynamic Model

OMT Dynamic Model
The dynamic model of OMT is based upon Harel state charts [82]. These are graphs, whose nodes are state descriptions, which include a name for the state, optional internal actions (instantaneous operations) and activities (operations that take time to complete), optional entry and exit actions, and whose edges are transitions between states, annotated with definitions of the form

$$ev(attributes)[pre\text{-}condition]/action$$

This means that the event *ev* with optional parameters *attributes* can occur or be accepted if the condition *pre-condition* holds, and it then leads to the state transition indicated in the diagram, together with any associated action *action*. Precise definitions and distinctions between events, actions and activities are provided. Typically there will be one state chart for each class, with communication from class C to class D indicated by actions of the form *eventD*, where *eventD* is an event of D, attached to transitions of class C. A simple example is given by the state chart of a database management system, where the initial state of the class is *Idle*, and an arbitrary number of read access logons to the database are allowed, but only one write access. A *logoff* event clears all current logons (Figure 1.6).

The initial state of a state model is indicated by the use of an arrow leading into this initial state from a point; the final state is shown by a bull's-eye. Both states can be labelled. Continuous loops with neither start nor end can also be modelled.

Several stages in building up a dynamic model are identified in [174, Chapter 5]:

- prepare scenarios (i.e. required or actual sequences of behaviour);
- identify events between objects;
- provide an event trace diagram identifying the sender and receiver of each event and the sequence of events;

- provide a textual state description, including any characteristic activity of the state, event sequences that lead to the state, any characteristic constraints on the values of attributes of the class to which the state refers, and any events that are accepted in the state, together with the actions and following states of these events;
- provide state diagrams (directed graphs of events and states) as in the above example;
- provide a dynamic model: a collection of state diagrams which interact with each other via shared events.

Structuring of state diagrams via nesting and factoring is allowed. Figure 1.7 is an example of a dynamic model of two classes from a lift control system, illustrating inter-object communication.

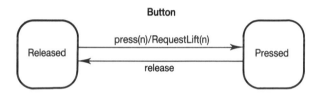

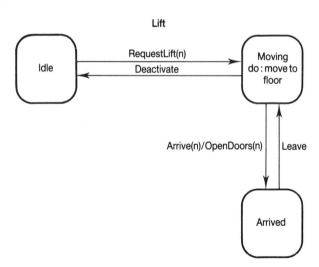

Figure 1.7: State Models for Lift and Button

A state is viewed as an equivalence class of attribute values and association values of an object class: this equivalence class being formed under a relation of 'same behaviour' with respect to the real-world situation or requirements being modelled. States define 'transitory subtypes' of the object classes to which they belong: they are not classes in their own right that can be represented as exclusive subclasses of their owning class on the object model diagram since they represent only temporary differences between objects, rather than the permanent differences represented by typing. This distinction is not clarified in Shlaer and Mellor, for instance, which supports 'subtype migration' as a concept [179, Chapter 3].

A particular semantic interpretation of events is given, which distinguishes between automatic and externally triggered events. Spontaneous actions of a class are a special case which are represented by transitions without an event name, but with only a condition and an action (see [174, page 107] for an example of the use of such events to define a programmable thermostat). There is a slight ambiguity between such systems, in which a state can contain an activity (such as *run furnace*) which can be arbitrarily interrupted by an event which is triggered by a condition (*temperature too high*), and systems in which events must wait for the activity of their source state to complete before they can fire: for example, a state with an activity *verify bank code* with two guarded eventless transitions with conditions *bad code* and *good code* respectively [174, page 177].

Formalisation of the notation requires mathematical modelling of this semantics, or an interpretation into suitable attribute updates and method pre-conditions in a specification of a class. Attempts at formalisation using Real Time Logic have been made [133], and a translation of simple state charts into CSP has been developed [58]. However, we are not aware of a full formalisation of these models when timing aspects are included. One approach is the interpretation of states as sets of object instances – that is, the set of instances of the object class which are currently in this state. Transitions upon an instance are then simply represented as a deletion of an instance token from one set and the addition of the instance token to another, with choices being made on the basis of the values of the attributes of the instance and the states of other instances. Synchronisation and communication could be modelled through the use of operations which combine the synchronised operations.

OOA State Model
This is based on Moore state models [149]. These are directed graphs, with edges corresponding to *events* or transitions between states and nodes corresponding to states. Actions are associated with each state and are performed when an object arrives in that state. (The distinction made in OMT between actions and activities is not made here.) The simple database example given in Figure 1.6 is almost identical in this notation. Again, parameters of an event can be supplied, e.g. the identity of the object(s) involved. The action of each state is indicated beneath it in pseudo-code. Unlike OMT, exit, entry and standard actions of a state are not distinguished. The generation of events for other state models is distinguished from the accessing and updating of local attributes. Although object life cycles are classified in OOA as 'circular' or 'born-and-die', there is no support in OOA

notation for representing initial or final states (as there is in OMT).

A state model is constructed for each object class: the concept of a state, as a transitory subclass, is similar to that of OMT. However, one can also instantiate state models for specific instances of an object class, to obtain *state machines* using an identical notation. In addition, *deletion* states are distinguished from *quiescent* states as termination states by the use of dashed lines for the former.

The assumptions made about time in the state models are made explicit and a specific *Timer* state model is defined to support the generation of delayed events. Subtype migration is allowed (for instance, a *MixingTank* can be *Assigned* or *UnAssigned* a load, but its identity does not change from one state to another, even though its type appears to change from one subtype of the *Tank* class to a disjoint subtype [179, Chapter 3]). In this respect, the state concept of OOA is not distinguished clearly from the concept of a subtype. Additional potential weaknesses of the method, compared to OMT, are the omission of pre-conditions from events, and the use of (possibly extensive) pseudo-code for the action of each state.

The notation and the techniques used are, in other respects, more detailed than the dynamic model of OMT. Auxiliary documentation is mandated, such as a *state transition table*, giving a precise list of the possible transitions in each state, so allowing the analyst to check for completeness and consistency of the model: that every event has a unique source and destination, and that every possible transition has been accounted for. Detailed advice on creating state models is given, and failure analysis is described. The evolution of relationships is specifically considered, together with means of resolving *contention* by mechanisms such as monitor objects.

A further diagrammatic representation, the *Object Communication Model*, is a product of the dynamic modelling process. This expresses the pattern of required and offered services between classes, i.e. the clientship relation, and allows the distinction between passive and active objects to be made. Object communication models also provide a means of representing the *layering* of a system as a hierarchy of interfaces, each of which hides information about their implementation by lower-level classes. *Thread of Control* charts can be produced from object communication models, allowing the analysis of the sequences of communications between objects which can exist in the system. These in turn allow the analysis of the duration of a particular sequence of events. Simulation of a set of state machines is also recommended as an alternative approach to analysis of communication patterns in the system. Problems associated with repetitive control are specifically considered.

Formalisation of the notation raises problems similar to those for OMT state models.

1.2.4   Functional/Process Model

OMT Functional Model
Functional models in OMT specify how operations derive output values from input values, without regard to the order of computations. They consist of data flow diagrams with directed named edges linking process nodes to process nodes or linking process and data nodes. The names of edges describe the data which is passed into or out of each process. Two forms of data are distinguished: *actor* objects which produce and consume data, and *data store* objects which store data passively.

Textual functional descriptions are allowed to supplement the graphical descriptions, and processes can be nested, as with SSADM. Bottom-level processes correspond to operations on particular classes. The rules given for identifying the associated object class of a process in [174, Chapter 6] are heuristic rather than prescriptive.

Control flow (e.g. the result of one process which determines whether another process can execute) is represented by dashed lines between processes.

Two simple examples of functional models are given in Figure 1.8 and Figure 1.9. Figure 1.8 describes a parser which consists of a sequence of operations which translate source text into an intermediate representation, using a passive data store of token definitions, and an intermediate passive data store of symbol tables which populate a repository with abstract syntax trees of the source language. The symbol table data is retained since it may be required in further operations, such as a compilation or debugging process.

Figure 1.9 describes a process of performing a query on a repository, considered as an element of a passive datastore of all existing repository instances, the extraction of information from the repository, and the storage of this result in a result repository, upon which specific result presentation operations can be performed.

The process model notation is not mathematically precise; it can only be used to define outline method definitions and to provide a view of the usage dependencies between methods (i.e. what methods of supplier classes are used by which methods of client classes). It is the least well-developed model in OMT.

OOA Process Model
The Shlaer/Mellor OOA process model is based upon Action Data Flow Diagrams (ADFD), which are graphs whose nodes are processes and datastores, and whose directed edges represent dataflows or control flows, annotated with the names of the data items flowing between datastores and processes or between processes. Each process on the ADFD is assigned to an object class from the information model. Both unconditional and conditional control flows between processes are represented, and it is possible to express the fact that the output data of one process has a different semantic meaning when it is used as an input of another. These facilities are not provided in OMT. Four distinct forms of process are identified,

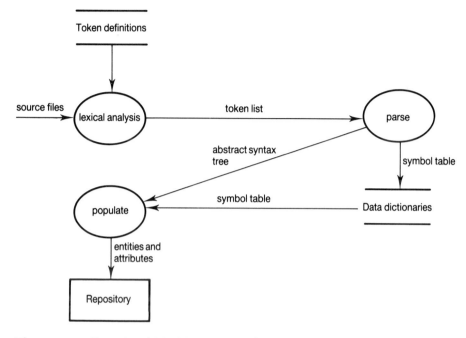

Figure 1.8: Functional Model for Parser/Populator

and the rules for assigning these processes to object classes are quite detailed.

As with OMT, however, formalisation of the process model is problematic due to the possibly informal nature of process descriptions.

1.2.5   Design Notations

In OMT, the same notational forms are used in design as in analysis, with the exception that further details can be added in object model diagrams, such as explicit representation of pointers and tables.

In OOA the use of the OODLE notation is proposed for the design stage. This consists of the following four diagrammatic forms:

- Class Diagrams, representing the detailed internal structure of a class and its methods;
- Class Structure Charts, representing the decomposition of the methods of a class, and the data which is input and output via these operations;
- Dependency Diagrams, representing the client-server and 'friend' relationships between classes;
- Inheritance Diagrams, expressing the inheritance relations which hold between classes.

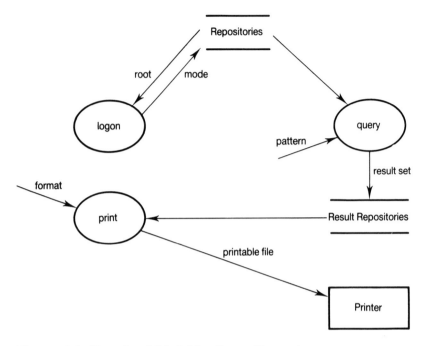

Figure 1.9: Functional Model for Query Processing

Systematic processes for translating the OOA products into design products in these notations are given.

1.2.6   Consistency Checking Between Representations

OMT
The three views of a system in OMT are required to be quite closely connected. Each event on a dynamic model is expected to correspond to an operation on the object model, and the dynamic model should be partitioned into state diagrams for each class on the object model, with states defining transitory subclasses of their associated class.

Undecomposable processes on the functional model correspond to operations on classes of the object model.

OOA
In OOA the links between the models are not stressed as strongly as in OMT, but the three views clearly allow consistency requirements to be stated and checked. As with OMT, the information model is the most significant in providing a basis for consistency checking: each object class and relationship on the information model must have an associated state model dealing with the states and events which can

occur for this class or relationship (when these models are non-trivial), and each process on an ADFD is associated with an object from the information model.

1.2.7   Rigour of Development Process Supported

OMT
Well-defined stages of analysis, system design, object design and implementation are identified in OMT, with each of these being decomposed into further stages and techniques. There are few mandated products apart from the three models. The traceability of the method is strengthened by the use of the same notation throughout the development process. However, the level of detail in the decomposition of the process and the number of intermediate products and number of mandated transformations between products are all lower than in SSADM and OOA.

OOA
The process of development in this method is more finely detailed than in the OMT method, with specific 'work products' being mandated from each analysis technique, and more precise decomposition of the stages of these processes, whereas OMT is more flexible and open in its processes.

1.2.8   Uptake

OMT
Courses on OMT are available from GE, covering design, analysis and language-specific courses for implementation. The book [174] is a thorough guide to the method and notation, and compares this notation with structured methods and other object-oriented methods.

The *ObjectMaker* tool produced by Mark V Systems supports the OMT notation and provides a repository for OMT documents. The *Object Modeller* from Versant and GE supports the notation, provides a repository and supports the use of the method.

OMT covers the whole life cycle of a system, with the exception of testing and maintenance. It has been used for the development of compilers, graphics systems, user interfaces, databases, an object-oriented language, CAD systems, meta-models and control systems [174]. It has also been used to redocument existing systems. It was used in the development of the FUSION method of Hewlett-Packard, and it is, in some respects (particularly in its data and process model notations), consistent in notation with existing structured methods such as SSADM. It seems suitable for realtime, engineering and business information system domains, with a bias towards the first and the last. It is not targeted at any particular implementation environment. The emphasis on the object model may be excessive, especially when more subtle realtime issues are required to be modelled.

The backing of a major company may be a significant factor in persuading developers to adopt the method.

OOA

Courses on OOA are available from the Project Technology company founded by Shlaer and Mellor. These cover analysis and design, with language-specific versions available for implementation. The two books [179] and [178] describe the method, with the former concentrating on dynamic modelling and the latter on static data modelling.

The *ObjectMaker* tool from Mark V Systems, the *System Developer* from Cadware and the *Teamwork* tool from Cadre all support the Shlaer/Mellor notation and provide repository support.

OOA, while focusing on analysis, covers the entire life cycle, with the exception of testing and maintenance. Specific advice is given for the treatment of large systems, with additional diagrammatic forms being required at the initial analysis stage to decompose a large system into manageable subsystems:

- Subsystem Relationship Model;
- Subsystem Communication Model;
- Subsystem Access Model.

Heuristics for decomposition are provided. The method has been used in various forms for a number of applications: banking operations, manufacturing processes (aircraft engines, circuit boards, etc.), telecommunications systems, simulation and credit card billing systems.

It seems suitable for a wide range of applications and particularly for realtime applications. Problems with the information model (i.e. lack of detail and the imposition of explicit object identities) may limit its usefulness in some cases and make it appear biased towards a relational database interpretation.

1.3   Conclusions

Object-oriented methods are still a new area; they have not yet been adopted on a wide scale nor are any industry standards emerging (although standardisation efforts in the area of tool integration and methodologies by organisations such as the Object Management Group (OMG) have taken place). There are as yet no published surveys on the take-up of object-oriented methods in industry, e.g. in terms of support via training courses, CASE tools or user groups (although [33] does include OMT in its evaluation of five object-oriented development methods). CASE tools for the two methods do exist, but they do not have the market visibility of those for structured methods. However, these methods have been used in practice and refined in the light of experience [174, 179].

OMT object model notation is highly expressive and, for the most part, readily formalisable (naturally, it is not always possible to formalise informal constraint annotations). However, the central role of associations between object classes in these models raises problems for the formalisation process, since none of the formal object-oriented specification languages which are covered in this book, or of which the authors are aware, have an explicit representation of associations between object classes. Thus, potentially premature design decisions may be forced upon the specifier. This is a problem with the formal languages, rather than with OMT.

The dynamic model notations of OMT and OOA are quite similar, although each includes features not possessed by the other. Full formalisation of these models requires more research in the expression of concurrent and dynamic properties of objects in the formal specification languages. However, information from these models can be used as input into the identification of states and methods of object classes.

The process model notations of OMT and OOA are also quite similar. Their input to a formal specification would be based upon the guidelines to process decomposition that they can provide.

Attempts at formalising OOA in the UK have uncovered some problems with the implicit semantics of the notation. One example is the apparent lack of connection between inheritance and subtyping: there need be no subset relationship between the sets of object identities of a class and its superclasses. Likewise there is a perceived lack of clarity over the queueing or discarding of requests sent to an object. There has been less work on the formalisation of OMT in the UK.

While the notations and language vary from method to method, at a deeper level the two methods have much in common. As notations for initial analysis of a system, domain and requirements, these graphical notations are of significant use in the development of the architecture of a specification. An analysis phase before the writing of formal specifications is of key importance for large systems, avoiding the need for numerous rewrites and iterations of the specification in order for it to fit the domain model or requirements more closely or to obtain internal coherence. While techniques that (in principle) allow the development of implementations that are correct with respect to formal specifications exist, the formalisation of specifications that are correct with respect to stated or implicit user requirements is still an area in which development is needed. It is hoped that an object-oriented approach, together with techniques to bridge the gap between formal and diagrammatic notations, can contribute to this area.

Chapter 2

A Comparative Description of Object-oriented Specification Languages

K. Lano and H. Haughton

In this chapter outlines are given of the syntax and semantics of the object-oriented specification languages considered in the remainder of the book together with evaluations of their approaches to object orientation and formal specification. The aim is to provide a reference point and comparison between the syntax and semantics of these languages, and to introduce the use of formal techniques in object-oriented software development.

2.1 Languages

The languages we will discuss in this and following chapters are as follows:

1. MooZ [135];
2. OOZE [3] and FOOPS [72];
3. Object-Z [24, 48];
4. Z^{++} [113];
5. Fresco [196];
6. VDM++ [52, 51].

Each of these languages addresses the problem of how to use most effectively the concepts and methods provided by the object-oriented paradigm within formal specification. Some, such as Fresco, are also concerned with using formal techniques to support conventional object-oriented languages, such as Smalltalk. However, the coverage of the languages and their relationship to mainstream concepts of object orientation differ, which may have substantial implications for their use as a means of producing high-quality applications in object-oriented programming languages. A comparison of the Object-Z, MooZ, Z^{++}, ZEST, OOZE, ZERO and

Fresco languages, based upon their treatment of two brief examples, is also given in [183]. The present book extends this comparison by the use of more substantial case studies that aim to illustrate specific advantages of the given languages.

In addition, the object-based language used in the B notation of 'abstract machines' will be discussed as a significant extension of Z in the direction of mathematical programming. In Chapter 3, we will also consider the contribution that existing object-oriented structured methods can make to object-oriented specification.

It should be noted that the languages discussed in the book are the result of relatively recent and, in many cases, ongoing research. In this chapter, discussion is based on the authors' understanding at the time of writing.

Other interesting approaches to object-oriented specification are ZERO [194], Hyper-Z [130], and ZEST [37]. The last in particular has been the subject of sustained and ongoing research and practical application, and is being used as the basis of research in a UK DTI-funded project into the use of object-oriented formal languages in Open Distributed Processing.

In the following sections a brief introduction to the syntax of each language is given, and then a set of evaluation criteria for the languages is proposed and evaluations of the languages according to these criteria are carried out. The aim is not to set one language against another, but to identify commonalities and differences which may be hidden by surface syntax, and to clarify the different areas of application of the languages.

2.1.1   MooZ

The MooZ specification language is an object-oriented extension of the specification notation Z. A MooZ specification consists of a set of class declarations that define classes which can be used as types and as generic templates for other classes, as in more familiar object-oriented languages such as Eiffel [142]. The general outline of a MooZ class is:

Class ⟨*Class-Name*⟩
    givensets ⟨*type-name-list*⟩
    superclasses
                ⟨*class-reference-list*⟩
                ⟨*auxiliary-definitions*⟩
    private ⟨*definition-name-list*⟩
      or
    public ⟨*definition-name-list*⟩
    constants
             ⟨*axiomatic-description-list*⟩
             ⟨*auxiliary-definitions*⟩
    state

⟨*anonymous-schema*⟩ or ⟨*constraint*⟩
⟨*auxiliary-definitions*⟩

initialstates

⟨*schema*⟩
⟨*auxiliary-definitions*⟩

operations

⟨*definition-list*⟩

EndClass ⟨*ClassName*⟩.

The **givensets** facet declares sets whose existence is assumed to be present, but of which no internal details need be defined, as with *given sets* in Z [182]. The use of these sets makes it possible for classes to be parameterised. Unlike the other specification languages with generic parameters, however, there is no syntactic difference between formal generic parameters and local given sets declared as types.

The **superclasses** facet declares those classes that are inherited by the present class. Multiple inheritance is allowed, and it is possible to have name clashes as a result of inheritance and multiple inheritance.

The **private** and **public** facets define those features of the class that are visible and not visible respectively to clients of the class. The interpretation is that external users of objects of a class cannot see private definitions but these are, however, visible to all subclasses. In addition, it is possible for visibility definitions to be changed by subclasses.

The **constants** facet defines functions and constants which are available for use in the class. These functions and constants are defined by means of *axiomatic definitions* in the sense of Z [182].

The **state** facet describes the constituents of the state of a class, that is, its attributes, and an invariant which is a predicate expected to be true for these variables between method invocations. The state is described by an anonymous state *schema* in the sense of Z [182], and additional constraints are given by the *constraints*.

The **initialstates** facet describes the initial state of the class. This is simply the conjunction of the initial state of this class with those of the superclasses if any.

The **operations** facet describes a set of methods which transform the state of the class, using Z-like schema definitions.

Like Z, MooZ includes a number of predefined types, but in this case specified by classes. This differentiates it from Object-Z and Z^{++} which use Spivey's [182] set-theoretic definitions of basic types and operations on these: in this sense MooZ is more consistently object-oriented than these languages.

The concept of message passing is used in MooZ. Each state component and operation of a class is treated as a message that can be handled by the objects of a class (an object can be defined by declaring a variable to be of a class type). All other definitions which do not involve state components correspond to messages that can be handled by the class. As a result of the foregoing, it is clear that different types of messages will have to be dealt with in different ways. Most significantly, because schemas can be messages, the number of ways in which these can be manipulated will now increase. Semantically, an object or class instance in MooZ is a record, as opposed to a class history in Object-Z.

2.1.2 OOZE

OOZE stands for 'Object-oriented Z Environment': it is an object-oriented language in which the specification notation Z is used in an object-oriented manner. Although the notation of OOZE is centred around Z, the underlying formal semantics and hence its reasoning system are based on order-sorted, hidden-sorted algebra. This type of semantics has been applied to algebraic specification languages such as OBJ3 [67]. As a consequence, it is possible to use the implementations of these languages (via term rewriting) to provide the means by which certain kinds of OOZE specifications can be executed as a prototype.

OOZE can be seen as extending the usual notion of algebraic specifications in that it facilitates the encapsulation of states, a property which the traditional use of algebraic specifications preclude.

The philosophy of OOZE is very much in the style of OBJ3 and FOOPS [70], in that theories can be used to provide a means of describing properties of the parameters of a class.

The general form of an OOZE class specification is as follows:

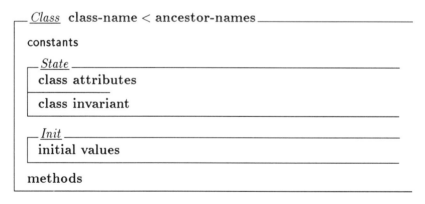

Here **class-name** is the name of the defining class and **ancestor-names** are the names of classes inherited by the class. The **constants** denote unchanging values. The facet **class attributes** defines variables whose values are of some predefined or constructed data type or of a class type. The **class invariant** is a logical property holding for all objects of the specified class. The facet **initial values** denotes the initial state of the class. The facet **methods** defines the operations that can affect the attributes of a class. These methods are described using the conventional Z schema notation. It should be noted that the methods of an OOZE specification describe conditional equations, that is, each schema (method)

operation is constrained by a pre-condition which must evaluate to true in order for the state variable updates to take place.

Method definitions can be divided into a number of cases (corresponding to distinct equations in OBJ), and delta lists are used as for MooZ, Object-Z and Fresco to identify the variables which are updated by an operation. A distinction is made between loose definitions of methods versus executable definitions.

OOZE contains a further structuring construct, known as the module. The purpose of a module is to encapsulate all classes that have interdependent relationships, or to gather together related specification components. It has been proposed by some authors as a necessary and orthogonal concept to that of the object class [185]. In OOZE the syntax of a module is as follows:

```
┌─ module-name[parameters] ──────────────────────────────
│  ┌─ Importing ──────────────────────────────────────────
│  │  imported-modules
│  │
│  ┌─ Class  class-name-0 ────────────────────────────────
│  │  ⋮
│  │
│  ⋮
│  ┌─ Class  class-name-n ────────────────────────────────
│  │  ⋮
│  │
```

As mentioned above, OOZE has been developed upon the specification language OBJ. In this respect much of the apparatus available for OBJ can be re-used at the OOZE level. In particular, the use of *theories* (a particular form of module) provides a powerful means of stating properties of class parameters. Theories can themselves be parameterised and can use and inherit other theories via the use of modules. A general description of a theory has the form:

```
┌─ theory-name ──────────────────────────────────────────
│  types
│  │  axiom-declarations
│  │  ─────────────────
│  │  axioms
```

The **types** describe the relevant data types for this theory, the signature of an axiom is denoted by **axiom-declarations**, and **axioms** denotes predicates which use the signature.

In OOZE every object has a unique identity (an identifier) that is set upon creation of an object. This identifier plays a number of useful roles, ranging from disambiguating identical attributes which may cause problems as a result of multiple inheritance and determining the sequence of allowable operations over instances of a class. The latter feature (implemented via the meta-class concept) is specific to OOZE and provides a means of reasoning about the correctness of object operations. This follows if we view an object as denoting a simple variable and method applications as operations with a predicate transformer semantics [39]. Another use of the meta-class is to identify operations which act only on certain objects of a class: this may be a useful design mechanism.

2.1.3   Object-Z

Object-Z is an object-oriented extension of the specification language Z. Like the other Z-based object-oriented languages described in this book, Object-Z makes use of many of the features of Z, including schema notation for defining operations. A general class definition has the following form:

$$
\begin{array}{|l}
\hline
\_\ ClassName[generic\ \ parameters]\ \rule{8cm}{0pt} \\
\quad visibility\ \ list \\
\quad inherited\ \ classes \\
\quad type\ \ definitions \\
\quad constant\ \ definitions \\
\quad state\ \ schema \\
\quad initial\ \ state\ \ schema \\
\quad operation\ \ schemas \\
\hline
\quad history\ \ invariant \\
\hline
\end{array}
$$

The facet *inherited classes* denotes those classes that are inherited by the defining class. The facets *type* and *constant definitions* are type definitions and axiomatic definitions which use the Z syntax for these aspects. Because of the use of reference semantics for objects, that is, variables declared to be of a class type are considered to be actually (variable) pointers to objects of the class, it is often the case that instances of supplier classes are defined via pointer *constants* in the constant definitions part of an Object-Z class. In this case the pointer constant serves as a fixed name for the modifiable object which is pointed to.

The *state* schema is an anonymous Z schema which declares the attributes of the class, and these attributes may be of a class type (implicitly they are of type 'pointer to' class). The *initial* schema defines a set of possible initial values for the attributes of the class by means of a boxed Z predicate over these attributes.

The operation schemas use the schema notation of Z to define state transitions (in terms of dashed and undashed variables). However, a Δ-list can be provided to describe the *frame* of the operation, that is, which variables of the class state it is allowed to change. The *history invariant* is a linear-time temporal logic predicate restricting the behaviour of the objects of a class.

Temporal logic provides a means of specifying certain dynamic aspects of a possibly highly complex system. History constraints can also provide a summary of intended behaviour which can then be used in proof.

Object-Z permits the redefinition of operation schemas within an inheritance hierarchy. Combining this with the fact that the features of a class are not unique to the class, it follows that renaming may have to take place on inheritance when inherited classes have features in common. A more detailed overview of the syntax is provided in Chapter 5. This language is perhaps the most mature of the object-oriented specification languages in terms of the number of applications in the language and the international take-up of the language.

2.1.4   Z^{++}

The specification and design language Z^{++} is an object-oriented extension of the Z language. Although Z^{++} has been developed upon the Z language, it also provides support for the use of temporal logic specifications. The general description of a Z^{++} class specification is as follows:

$$
\begin{aligned}
\textit{Object\_Class} ::= {}& \text{CLASS } \textit{Identifier } \textit{TypeParameters } [\text{EXTENDS } \textit{Imported}] \\
& [\text{TYPES } \textit{Types}] \ \ [\text{FUNCTIONS } \textit{Axdefs}] \\
& [\text{OWNS } \textit{Locals}] \\
& [\text{RETURNS } \textit{Optypes}] \\
& [\text{OPERATIONS } \textit{Optypes}] \\
& [\text{INVARIANT } \textit{Predicate}] \\
& [\text{ACTIONS } \textit{Acts}] \\
& [\text{CONSTRAINTS } \textit{Constraints}] \\
& [\text{HISTORY } \textit{History}] \\
& \text{END CLASS}
\end{aligned}
$$

where:

$$
\textit{TypeParameters} ::= [\text{ ``[''} \textit{ Parlist } \text{``]''}]
$$

$$
\begin{aligned}
\textit{Parlist} \quad ::= {}& \textit{Identifier } [, \textit{ Parlist}] \\
| \ {}& \textit{Identifier} \ll \textit{Identifier} \\
& [, \textit{ Parlist}] \\
\textit{Imported} ::= {}& \textit{Idlist} \\
\textit{Types} \quad ::= {}& \textit{Type\_Declarations} \\
\textit{Locals} \quad ::= {}& \textit{Identifier} : \textit{Type} \ ; \ \textit{Locals} \\
| \ {}& \textit{Identifier} : \textit{Type}
\end{aligned}
$$

$$
\begin{array}{rl}
Optypes & ::= [*] \ Identifier : Idlist \ \rightarrow \\
& \quad Idlist \ ; \ Optypes \\
& | \ [*] \ Identifier : Idlist \ \rightarrow \\
& \quad Idlist \\
Acts & ::= [*] \ [Expression \ \&] \ Identifier \\
& \quad Idlist \ ==> \ Code \ ; \ Acts \\
& | \ [*] \ [Expression \ \&] \ Identifier \\
& \quad Idlist \ ==> \ Code \\
Constraints & ::= Equation \\
& | \ Equation \ ; \ Constraints \\
History & ::= Fmla_{LTL}
\end{array}
$$

The *TypeParameters* are a list of *generic* type parameters. A parameter X can be required to be a descendant of a class A via the notation $A \ll X$ here. The **EXTENDS** list is the set of previously defined classes that are inherited in this class. The *Types* are type declarations of type identifiers used in declarations of the local variables of the object. The *Locals* variable declarations are attribute declarations, in the style of variable declarations in Z. The **OPERATIONS** list declares the types of the operations as relations between a sequence of input domains and an output domain. The **RETURNS** list of operations defines the output type of those attributes and functions of the object's internal state that are externally visible; these are operations with no side-effect on the state. The **INVARIANT** gives a predicate that specifies the properties of the internal state, in terms of the local variables of the object. This predicate is guaranteed to be true of the state of an object class instance between executions of the operations of the object instance. The default predicate is *true*.

The **ACTIONS** list gives the definitions of the various operations that can be performed on instances of the object. The input parameters are listed before the output parameters in the action definitions. *Code* includes Z schema predicates and procedural UNIFORM [207, Chapter 9] code, and both can be given a precise semantics as predicate transformers or as Z schema definitions [18]. The **HISTORY** predicate specifies the admissible execution sequences of objects of the class, using linear temporal logic formulae with operators □ (henceforth), ○ (next), and ◇ (eventually). Further temporal logic operators, such as ; (chop), * (iterate), *before* (before) and *until* (until), can also be defined. The default temporal predicate is □*true*.

Operations which are prefixed by the * symbol are spontaneous internal actions: they cannot be called by clients or descendants of the class, although they become spontaneous internal actions of the descendants in turn. They correspond to *daemons* in object-oriented terminology. Explicit pre-conditions of methods can be declared via the & syntax.

The notation is closer to that of an object-oriented language than to Z or VDM. This is intended to allow greater extensibility of the notation, to include new clauses, and was inspired by the Abstract Machine Notation of the B system [1], a language aimed at extending Z to allow machine support for refinement of specifications to code. Due to the algebraic semantics of Z^{++}, based on a category of classes with refinement as the categorical arrow, it is possible to use algebraic reasoning to prove properties of a Z^{++} specification. Thus, for example, classes can be combined via the *product* and *co-product* constructions of category theory [78]. The former refers to the notion of a class which is the most refined class refined by two other classes (i.e. it represents the greatest extent of their commonality), and the latter the class which is the least common refinement of two classes.

In addition to the algebraic semantics of the language, a model-based theory has been devised so that the combination of both semantics provides a means of reasoning about classes and class refinements. Refinement is central to any formal object-oriented approach, since the refinement relation between classes determines when the corresponding types are compatible in the sense of [142].

Problems that have been identified with the language, from the viewpoint of object-oriented programming, are the lack of object self-reference, the absence of the ability of one object of a class to refer directly to another object of the same class (instead, both objects must be manipulated by a common client object), and the forbidding of circular references between classes. Polymorphic application of methods is supported only through the possibility of explicitly casting objects into different types using refinement mappings between these types.

2.1.5   Fresco

Fresco is an interactive environment and language, based on Smalltalk [196] supporting the evolutionary development of re-usable specified, proven software components. Fresco extends Smalltalk in two principal ways:

- inclusion of re-usable 'capsules';
- provision of a specification language for verifying the code of capsules.

Fresco extends the usual notion of object/class hierarchy by employing the use of capsules. A capsule contains code, specifications and proofs, and systems are built by composing capsules. Unlike the other object-oriented extensions mentioned in this book (except OOZE), classes and types in Fresco are essentially distinct concepts. The former describes a construct for representing implementations of types and the latter the behaviour of objects when messages are sent to it. The notion of a type/class definition (TCD) provides a means of combining types and classes into a single framework. This in turn gives rise to a form of inheritance known as 'conformant inheritance', in which subclasses of a class are expected to implement subtypes (where each class is associated with a type). The notion of subtype inheritance used in Fresco can be implemented in a manner similar to that used by Milner in dealing with polymorphism [147].

The general form of a Fresco specification is:

```
ClassName
Visible operation signatures
• operation specifications
• invariants
private model variables  |  private implementation
```

The **visible operation signatures** facet describes those operations that are visible outside the class. The **operation specifications** facet describes the operations of the defining class. The **invariants** facet describes the class invariant. The **private model variables** and **private implementation** describe those features of a class type structure which are hidden from the outside world. Inheritance of a class *InheritedClass* in another class is denoted by statements of the form

$$InheritedClass + ::$$

in the inheriting class.

A Fresco specification is similar to that of a VDM specification [96] except that a few 'Z-like' features can be incorporated:

- different aspects of an operation can be described separately, such as in the separation of the cases of a successful operation execution from its error cases;
- composition of operation specifications from one or more supertype(s) and the extension of these within a class;
- composition of specifications from older and newer versions of software components, to ensure compatibility.

In order to combat the frame problem in defining the scope of changes that are consequences of an operation or method application, Fresco adopts the use of the Δ notation Δ**vars** to specify the set **vars** of variables as liable to be affected by an operation.

2.1.6 VDM++

VDM++ [52] aims to build upon VDM by providing several object-oriented design structuring facilities. A facility for the specification of dynamic behaviour of objects of a class is also provided. A class description has the following syntax:

$$
\begin{aligned}
\textit{Class-description} ::= \; &\textit{Classheader};\\
&[\textit{Instance variable part}]\\
&[\textit{Method list}]\\
&[\textit{Inheritance part}]\\
&[\textit{Synchronisation part}]\\
&[\textit{Thread part}]\\
&[\textit{Aux reasoning}]\\
&\textit{Class Tail}
\end{aligned}
$$

A class header provides for single and multiple inheritance of classes in another (via the syntax **Class** *Class-identifier* **is subclass of** { *Class-id* }*), but not for generic parameterisation. The *Instance* variable part simply defines attributes of the class, and these attributes may have declared types built out of class types using the standard constructions of VDM. However, class types themselves are referred to by the notation @*Class-id*, where *Class-id* is the name of a class. Types may be defined using a mixture of standard VDM constructs such as **Set of** X for $P(X)$, **Sequence of** X, for seq(X), and **Map** X **to** Y for $X \twoheadrightarrow Y$. Named invariants of the state can be stated by clauses of the form *invar- Iden : # Expression #* where *Expression* is a predicate over the state variables. The initialisation of a class is defined using the syntax

init- Iden : # Expression #

where, typically, there will be one named clause of this form for each state variable.

The method list defines methods of the class, either in an outline *preliminary* form or in a *full* form using the conventional VDM pre- and post-condition style, with variable modality definitions such as **rd** (read only) and **wr** (writable) taking the place of Δ-lists in Object-Z. Error clauses can also be included to specify method behaviour when the pre-condition of normal operation is violated. Methods of supplier classes can be invoked using the (message-passing) syntax:

objectname!methodname(parameters)

Each class also has a **new** method, which creates objects of that class.

The syntax for method declarations is as follows:

method-definition ::= *method-heading clause* “; ”
method-heading   ::= *method-name* “ : ” *operationtype*
              | *method-name* “(” [*par-name-list*] “)”
operationtype   ::= *optionaltype* [“**Value**” *optionaltype*]
optionaltype   ::= *type-indication* | “(” “)”
par-name-list   ::= *par-name* { “,” *par-name*}

where method names and par (paragraph) names follow the syntax for variable identifiers (beginning with a lower-case letter).

The preliminary style allows the phrases **is not yet specified** and **is subclass responsibility** in place of method definitions (the *clause* syntactic item above) to allow deferral of an explicit definition until a later stage of the development process, in the first case, or to a subclass of the current (abstract or deferred) class, in the second. Thus

calcArea : Set of @*Point   Value N*
calcArea(pointSet)
    is not yet specified;

is a valid deferred method specification – the method takes a set of *Point* instances as input and returns a single natural number, although the details have been deferred for future development.

The form of an explicit method definition is as follows:

> *clause* ::= [*method-external-part*]
> [*method-internal-part*]
> [*method-pre-cond*]
> *method-postcond*
> [*method-exception*] "; "

The *external* part has the general form

> **ext** { **rd** | **wr** } *instance-var-list* [":" *type-allocation*]

This defines variables which are externally visible at the point of call. The internal part has a similar syntax to the external part, except for the keyword **internal**, and this part defines purely local and auxiliary variables of the method.

The pre-condition part describes the condition which must hold before execution of the method – if this condition does not hold, any exception part of the method provided by the specifier will be executed. The mandatory post-condition part describes the state after execution of the method, with the hooked variable convention of VDM being used to denote the values of variables before the method is executed.

VDM++ distinguishes between *representation inheritance*, in which the state of one class becomes visible to another, but its methods cannot be used, and *behaviour inheritance*, in which methods of one class can be selectively inherited by another. The notation

> **is subclass of** { *Classname* }* *method-name-list*

is used here. An additional feature is the possibility of using indexed classes in the inheritance list, to express *aggregation* in the sense of [174]. The synchronisation part of a class definition is also optional, and can consist of either a *declarative-synchronisation-part* or a *trace-part*. The trace part uses a finite-state machine notation in place of the temporal logic of Object-Z. This includes synchronisation operators but is not more expressive than a linear temporal logic with counting and arbitrary interleaving operators. Additional means of specifying concurrent constraints and dynamic behaviour are provided by deontic logic formulae for the specification of permission and obligation relations on methods, and by the use of *thread* specifications, in the *thread-part*, for the description of process behaviour, by means of deontic logic formulae. These additional components will be described in more detail in Section 2.2.12 below. The *Aux-reasoning* part of a class provides a workspace for additional derived assertions and results about a class – the predicates here are simply VDM specification language predicates, and do not constrain the state or operations of the class, but simply provide an overview of properties for further use.

2.1.7   B Abstract Machine Notation

A brief introduction to the syntax of B Abstract Machines is given here. Full details of the language can be found in [1].

The outline form of a B abstract machine is:

```
MACHINE  M(params_M)
CONSTRAINTS  Constraints_M
CONSTANTS  constants_M
PROPERTIES  Prop_M
VARIABLES  variables_M
INVARIANT  Inv_M
INITIALISATION  Init_M
OPERATIONS
     z ← m(y)   ≜
        PRE  Pre_{m,M}
        THEN
           Op_{m,M}
        END
     ....
END
```

The machine M can be parameterised by a list of set-valued or scalar-valued parameters. The logical properties of these parameters are specified in the CONSTRAINTS of the machine. Optionally, constants, corresponding to axiomatic definitions in Z, can be declared in the CONSTANTS section. The definitions of these constants are given in the PROPERTIES section.

The variables of the machine are listed in the VARIABLES section. The constraints on the variables, including the typing of the variables, are specified in the INVARIANT of the machine. The initialisation operation of the machine is specified in the INITIALISATION section of the machine. The methods or operations of the machine are listed in the OPERATIONS section. Input parameters are listed after the name of the method in its definition, and output parameters are listed to the left of an arrow from the method name.

2.2   Evaluation Criteria

In this section we describe criteria by which the languages described above can be compared. The criteria can be viewed as a list of desirable characteristics that a language should have. The list is not meant to be exhaustive but simply represents the authors' experience in the use of object-oriented languages and formal methods plus the views of other researchers [33, 142, 163]. The criteria required are divided into three groups:

- to implement object-oriented techniques;
- for the use of formal techniques;
- for general software engineering support.

Criteria required to implement object-oriented techniques are:

- objects and methods: the ability to encapsulate state and operations on state;
- method composition and extension: the ability to extend definitions of methods to deal with subtypes and to compose methods into more complex procedures;
- data abstraction: the ability to describe high-level abstract types in the language, as distinct from individual objects;
- classes: the ability to describe the common aspects of objects and encapsulate them in a class structure in such a way that objects can be considered instances or values of a type corresponding to the class. As a result, it should be possible to create objects from a class and (selectively) set and access the values of object features via methods;
- inheritance: the ability to define a class as an extension of an existing class, where features of this new class can contain modified versions of those of the inherited class, and to identify certain forms of inheritance as representing subtyping (*conformant inheritance*);
- multiple inheritance: the ability to define a class that is an extension of several (possibly unrelated) classes;
- polymorphism of operations: the ability to define operations that act upon several distinct types (classes);
- executability, prototyping and animatability: the ability to animate or rapidly produce executable forms of specifications, to check their compliance with a user's requirements;
- compositionality: the ability to use classes as types, and to declare an attribute to be of a class type so that an object of this class type can provide services to the defining class (a *client*). Composition is a very useful structuring facility, enabling the use of a simple interface (the methods of the supplier class) in place of its complex internal implementation;
- object identity: the notion of a persistent identity for an object;
- graphical notations: the existence of graphical notations, with semantic links to the formal languages, to facilitate validation of designs against user requirements, and to assist in the development of systems.

The last item, and the means available for translating object-oriented design concepts such as aggregation and associations into formal languages, will be covered in more detail in Chapter 3.

Criteria required for the use of formal techniques are:

- a formally (mathematically) defined semantics;
- a practical reasoning system based on this semantics;

- a refinement system, allowing the systematic refinement of specifications to code, preferably in a compositional manner.

Properties of relevance to wider software engineering concerns are:

- the ability to specify concurrent behaviour and properties;
- support for generic classes: classes in which formal type and value parameters exist and can be instantiated.

In the following sections we describe how each of the languages implements various criteria.

2.2.1   Objects and Methods

All of the above languages have a concept of an object as an encapsulation of methods, functions and types together with a state that they relate to. Conventional Z does not have a syntactic construct allowing this, although a minimal extension, such as the combination of Z and HOOD, does provide this power [92]. However, the way such an object is specified differs quite markedly between the algebraic style which is typified by FOOPS and the state-based styles of the other languages. In FOOPS, a class of accounts could be specified by defining the type which the class is based on as a distinguished *sort* Acct, and then defining suitable attributes, methods and error situations:

```
omod ACCT is
 cl Acct .
 at bal : Acct -> Money .
 at hist : Acct -> LIST[Date * Money] .
 me credit, debit : Acct Money -> Acct .
 er overdraw : -> Money .

 ax bal (new (A)) = 0 .
 ax hist (new (A)) = nil .
 ax bal( credit (A,M)) = bal(A) + M .
 ax bal( debit (A,M)) = bal(A) - M  if  bal(A) > M .
 ax bal( debit (A,M)) = overdraw(M) if bal(A) < M .
 ax hist ( credit (A,M)) = app (hist(A), << today ; M >>) .
 ax hist ( debit (A,M)) = app (hist(A), << today ; -M>>)
                          if  bal(A) > M .
 ax hist ( debit (A,M)) = app (hist(A), <<today ; overdraw(M)>>)
                          if  bal(A) < M .
endo ACCT
```

The effects of the methods (me ...) are defined in terms of the changes they yield to the values of attributes (at ...). Several axioms for each method may be needed.

In contrast, Object-Z, Z++, OOZE and MooZ define methods as Z schemas, acting on the entire state of the class being defined. Fresco and VDM++ define methods via pre-condition/post-condition pairs.

The languages adopt somewhat different syntactic approaches to the solution of the 'frame problem', stating in a clear way which attributes are changed or not changed by the application of a method. Conventional Z requires that the predicate of a schema explicitly states even identity changes in state variables (although this can be made more readable by the use of the ΞS construct, stating that a substate S of the system state remains unchanged over an operation). Object-Z, MooZ, OOZE and Fresco use the notation $\Delta(v)$ to indicate that the list of variables v are liable to change in an operation, all other variables remaining unchanged. In Fresco, this leads to difficulties when several different pre-condition/post-condition pairs are used to define one operation [183]. This is similar to further problems with compositions of methods that we discuss in Section 2.2.2 below. Z++ uses a syntactic convention that any occurrence of v' for a variable v in the predicate of an operation indicates that v is liable to be changed by the method. This creates problems when class invariants are used to impose implicit state transitions in methods: that is, the text of the method action may imply that an attribute w does not change in value as a result of the method application, even though the invariant of the class logically requires some change in the value of w in order for the invariant to be preserved. A partial solution to this is provided by the requirement of internal consistency on classes in Z++, following the B AMN specification approach. This places a proof obligation on the specifier to show that the full definition of a method possesses a non-empty domain.

VDM and VDM++ use the **rd** and **wr** declarations to indicate that particular variables may or may not be modified by a method. This enables an indication of the *read frame* of an operation (i.e. those variables which can be accessed by the operation code) in addition to the definition of the *write frame* (those variables which are updated by the operation code).

In the B notation, programming language syntax for assignment is used to limit the variables changed by a statement. Thus instead of $x' = x + 1 \wedge y' = y$ it is sufficient to write $x := x + 1$ in a machine with variables x and y. In general there appears to be no single 'best' answer to the problem, as each approach has certain drawbacks and advantages. However, the various ways of solving it are all inter-translatable in principle.

To illustrate the differences and similarities between the languages, we give an example of the way in which a method is specified and applied in each language. The method is *MoveQuad* to move a quadrilateral (defined as a class with five attributes, a *position*, and four vectors each defining an edge of the quadrilateral).

In **MooZ** we have the definition:

```
┌─ MoveQuad ──────────────────────────────────────
│  Δ(position)
│  move? : Vector
│ ─────────────────────────────────────────────────
│  position' = position + move?
└───────────────────────────────────────────────────
```

If q, q' : *Quadrilateral*, then the application of *MoveQuad* to q to produce q' can be written as:

   q MoveQuad

Note that q' is hidden in this application. Renaming of variables used in a method is performed by means of the notation

   MethodName(oldname\newname)

where *oldname* is the name of an attribute declared in the schema defining *MethodName*, and *newname* is the name of an attribute which replaces it in the resulting method definition.

   In **Object-Z** the definition of *MoveQuad* is syntactically identical, but the application of the operation is written as

   q.MoveQuad

where q is a pointer (constant or variable) to an object of type *Quadrilateral*.

   If we wish to provide an actual value *value* in place of the *move?* input argument, we must perform a substitution:

   q.MoveQuad[value/move?]

Again, the resulting object is implicit. This operation involves a change to the attributes of the object referred to by q, and does not produce a new value of q. The critical semantic difference between this method specification and the MooZ specification is the use of reference semantics.

   In **OOZE** the definition of the operation is textually identical (although brackets are omitted in the Δ-list). The separation of pre-conditions from actions is enforced in OOZE, and separate choices in a operation definition are listed in separate sub-boxes of the schema defining it. A different syntax, using schema boxes with a double bar, is used for methods which are built out of other methods – these are called method expressions.

   The above method is called via the notation

   q • MoveQuad(value)

where actual parameters are associated with formal parameters in the order in which the latter are declared. This is a departure from Z, where the order of attribute declarations in a schema is mathematically irrelevant.

   In **Z⁺⁺** the typing of a method is declared separately from its predicate. *MoveQuad* is declared as follows:

OPERATIONS
   $MoveQuad : \quad Vector \quad \rightarrow$

identifying the fact that the operation expects a single argument, and returns no value. Its action is:

ACTIONS
   $MoveQuad \quad move? \quad ==>$
$$position' \; = \; position \; + \; move?$$

If $q : Quadrilateral$ is declared in a suitable class, then a method of this class can call the $MoveQuad$ method as follows:

   $q' \; = \; (MoveQuad \; value) \; q$

for a particular value $value$. This notation is valid in the case that $MoveQuad$ is deterministic. In general cases, the notation

   $q.MoveQuad[value/move?]$

is used.

In **Fresco** we can define the $MoveQuad$ operation by the pre- and post-condition specification

   $[: - position = \odot position + move]MoveQuad(move)$

where the pre-condition in this case is the default $true$. The declaration of the typing of the operation is separated from the definition of its semantics, and is given as:

   $move : (Vector)$

where the parentheses identify an input. This operation is applied to an instance f of a quadrilateral by means of promotion:

   $[\![f.MoveQuad(move)]\!]$

In **VDM++** we have the notation

$$MoveQuad(move : Vector)$$
$$\textbf{ext wr } position$$
$$\textbf{pre:} \quad true$$
$$\textbf{post++:} \quad position = \overline{position} + move$$

The fact that the attribute $position$ of the class is the only one changed by the operation is indicated by the declaration **ext wr** $position$. This operation is called via the syntax $q!MoveQuad(value)$ for a specific $q : @Quadrilateral$ and $value : Vector$.

For comparison, in the **B** notation, we would define:

```
OPERATIONS
    MoveQuad(move)      =
            PRE  move  :   Vector
            THEN
                position  :=   position  +  move
            END
```

and the operation would be called upon a 'renamed' machine instance *aa* by the notation

$$aa.MoveQuad(value)$$

These examples make it clear that only minor differences exist between the languages. All have departed from the Z conventions of Ξ- and Δ-lists as conventional schema inclusion operations. Since the state space of a class is named by the class name it would be confusing to use this as a state description in addition to a specification of a type. Separating operation typing declarations from action definitions has some advantage in allowing a user (or re-user) of a class to ignore implementation details of an operation when seeking a particular method. The use of renaming of formal parameters by actual parameters to achieve parameter passing is useful when we wish to be explicit about the meaning of particular arguments. As in Ada though, such explicitness should perhaps be an *optional* feature, since we may not wish to be aware of the names of formal parameters of a method when we apply it in a client class.

2.2.2   Combining and Extending Methods

Allowed means for combining methods vary between the languages. Object-Z provides conventional Z schema operators of conjunction $\wedge$, sequential composition ⨟ and disjunction $\vee$, and adds further operations $\|$ of parallel composition (whereby inputs and outputs of two schemas with the same basename are equated) and $[\!]$ of choice (a guarded non-deterministic choice between several schemas). The promotion construct from Z is also given a distinct notation. In MooZ, standard Z techniques for combining schemas can also be applied to method definitions, although there are conceptual differences between the way MooZ treats a method definition and the Object-Z approach: in MooZ a reference q M or C M to a method M of class C, where $q : C$, involves an expansion of the definition of M with each occurrence of an attribute v of C being replaced by q v in the first case. That is, these references are seen as the results of messages that are sent to the object q, or in the case of class aspects which are independent of state, to the class C. In Object-Z and Z^{++} they are simply accesses to schema definitions or fields of a schema, in a sense close to that of Z.

Z^{++} diverges from Z in forcing the specifier of a class to explicitly list the input and output declarations of a composite method. Whereas in Object-Z, OOZE and

MooZ one can write (essentially)

$$DownLoc \triangleq Down \wedge Loc$$

to define a method *DownLoc* in a class where *Down* and *Loc* are defined, and where these two methods may have quite different input–output typing, in Z^{++} one must explicitly give the resulting input–output modality of *DownLoc*:

OPERATIONS
$$Down \; : \; \mathsf{N} \; \to;$$
$$Loc \; : \; \to \; \mathsf{N};$$
$$DownLoc \; : \; \mathsf{N} \; \to \; \mathsf{N}$$
....

ACTIONS
$$DownLoc \; down \; loc! \quad ==>$$
$$\qquad Down \; \wedge \; Loc$$
....

One could be even more explicit and identify the specific input and output variables of the component methods that are used in the composed method.

Explicit pre-conditions or guards for methods are also absent in Z, MooZ and Object-Z, although Z^{++} allows these to be declared outside the body of the method via the notation

$$Pre \; \&$$
$$\qquad M \; x \; y \quad ==> \quad Def$$

which states that an implementation of M needs to deal only with situations in which *Pre* holds of the input parameters and object state. This is *guarding* the definition *Def* by *Pre*: we need to distinguish between guarding and *pre-conditioning* in the sense of Abrial's generalised substitution language [1]. Z expresses only the former in schema definitions of the form

$$
\begin{array}{|l}
\underline{\quad M \rule{5cm}{0pt}} \\
\Delta S \\
x : X \\
y : Y \\
\hline
Pre \; \wedge \\
Def \\
\hline
\end{array}
$$

In B, the distinction between **PRE** *Pre* **THEN** *Def* **END** and **SELECT** *Pre* **THEN** *Def* **END** (guarding of *Def* by *Pre*) is made clear in the predicate transformer semantics of these operations. They have weakest pre-conditions ($wp(\_, R)$)

$$Pre \wedge wp(Def, R)$$

and

$$Pre \Rightarrow wp(Def, R)$$

respectively, so that the former is refined by the latter (although the latter is more likely to be infeasible – i.e. impossible to execute). Typing of operations is only specified for input parameters, with implicit typing being used for outputs. OOZE enforces the separate presentation of pre-conditions for methods, although in this case the semantics is different, and refers to the possibility or not of performing an equational rewrite.

The frame problem arises in situations where methods are to be combined. For instance, if we have two schemas A, B, defining methods in an Object-Z-like language:

```
┌─ A ──────────────────────────────────────────────────────
│  Δ(x, y)
│  ─────────────────────────────────────────────────────────
│  θ₁(x, y, z, x', y')
└───────────────────────────────────────────────────────────
```

```
┌─ B ──────────────────────────────────────────────────────
│  Δ(y, z)
│  ─────────────────────────────────────────────────────────
│  θ₂(x, y, z, y', z')
└───────────────────────────────────────────────────────────
```

and we combine these via a form of disjunction which merges Δ-lists, we get:

```
┌─ C ──────────────────────────────────────────────────────
│  Δ(x, y, z)
│  ─────────────────────────────────────────────────────────
│  θ₁(x, y, z, x', y')  ∨
│  θ₂(x, y, z, y', z')
└───────────────────────────────────────────────────────────
```

which in Z means that z in the first case, and x in the second case, can change in an arbitrary manner, which is probably not quite what we wanted! This means that we must expand the definitions of the schemas before we combine them, or use an operator such as the choice [] of Object-Z to perform one or other state transition, depending on the pre-condition of this transition.

2.2.3   Data Abstraction

An abstract data type (ADT) can be viewed as a collection of sets and operations on these sets, which describe *implicitly* the effect of these operations on the sets. Although this is a narrow view of ADTs, the definition allows a large number of data structures to be specified. This is evidenced on the basis of literature in the algebraic specification world. One way to view this style of specification is as a high-level design in which decisions as to how data structures might be implemented have not been made. Contrast this with the model-based approach, as realised through the languages VDM and Z, in which it is all too easy to write excessively implementation-biased specifications. Algebraic specification of class methods can provide a simpler description of their semantics for a potential user of a method than the explicit state-based representations. They can also provide a summary of properties for use by proof tools. For example, all we need to know to reason about updates to an array object are facts of the form

CONSTRAINTS
$$\forall \; i : \; \mathsf{N}; \quad a : \; Array; \quad v : \; Value \; | \; \; a.ValidIndex(i) \; \bullet$$
$$(access \; i) \; (update \; i \; v) \; a \; = \; v \quad \wedge$$
$$(update \; i \; v) \; (update \; i \; v) \; a \; = \; (update \; i \; v)$$

without details of the internal implementation of the contents of the array, as a sequence or function.

At present, only OOZE provides a facility for specification of ADTs, and a semantics in which these specifications can be compared to state-based specifications of implementations. An attempt to include algebraic specifications is provided in Z^{++} but without semantic integration to the state-based aspects of the language [110].

2.2.4   Classes

Classes are templates for objects, and stand in a similar relation to them as types do to values of a type in conventional procedural languages. Classes are used to represent concepts from a domain, as well as units of state and related functions upon this state. They can be organised into hierarchies of inheritance, or into hierarchies based upon the client–server relation, the use of one class (the supplier) to define the type of an attribute of another class (the client).

The given languages all have means for declaring classes, but they differ in the status which is given to classes. For OOZE, the unit of modularity in the language is not the class but the *module*, which can consist of a single class, a group of related classes, or a theory defining quite general constraints over a collection of specification items. In Fresco also, the unit of modularity, type/class definitions (TCDs), is more general than the class. In Z^{++} and MooZ the type of the class is not distinguished from the class (module) which defines it. Although Object-Z, VDM++, Z^{++} and MooZ have no structure which is more extensive than the class or generic (parameterised) class, such a structure could be considered useful in grouping together related classes (such as classes which mutually use each other as clients – this is explicitly disallowed in Z^{++}). In addition, a module structure would be useful for distinguishing between import and inheritance relationships

[185]. A module extension has been considered in MooZ, and has been proposed for Z^{++} [116], but this latter extension has not yet been given a semantics.

Since the Z-based languages retain Z specification elements, such as schemas, it is possible to write entirely orthodox functional Z specifications in them without using classes. None of the languages allow nested class definitions. Z^{++} elaborates a series of operations for combining classes, and defines an *algebra of classes* similar to the algebra of relational tables proposed by Date for the relational paradigm [41]. This algebra aims to provide a powerful facility for combining and extending classes, and proof rules for refinement are supplied for some of these operations.

Class operations available in the other languages include renaming of features (OOZE, Object-Z and MooZ) and operations associated with metaclasses (OOZE), such as the specification of 'virtual containers' for sets of existing objects of a specific class by means of some predicate on these objects. Hiding of features of a class is provided by Z^{++} by a specific $\backslash$ (hide) operator, analogous to the schema operation of the same name in Z. In Object-Z and MooZ, visibility of features are controlled by declarations within classes that introduce or inherit them.

In the Object-Z and MooZ languages it seems to be possible for a class to use itself as a type of an attribute defined in the class (although semantic constraints upon this do exist [130]). In OOZE this is explicitly allowed, as are other cycles in the client–supplier relationship. Z^{++} requires that the client–supplier relationship, the inheritance relationship and the importation relationships are all directed acyclic graphs.

2.2.5   Inheritance

All the languages implement inheritance, but their defaults concerning renaming and redefinition of features of a class in descendant classes differ. Object-Z and MooZ use the Z schema conjunction construction to combine one definition of a method with a new definition in a descendant class. For example, we can define a (stateless) class *Button* in Object-Z:

$$
\begin{array}{|l}
\hline
\text{\textit{Button}} \\
\hline
\upharpoonright(\textit{Activate}) \\
\\
\quad\begin{array}{|l}
\hline
\text{\textit{Activate}} \\
\hline
\textit{acts}! : \text{seq } \textit{Action} \\
\hline
\end{array} \\
\hline
\end{array}
$$

The projection notation $\upharpoonright$(*feature list*) identifies those features (attributes or methods) of the class which are visible to clients of the class.

We can make the single method of this class more precise in descendants of the class by simply defining schemas of the same name. The predicates of these schemas are conjoined to the predicate (*true* in this case) of the existing definition of the *Activate* method:

$$
\begin{array}{|l}
\hline
\_\_ActionButton _____ \\
\quad \upharpoonright(Activate) \\
\quad Button \\
\quad actions : \mathrm{seq}\ Action \\
\quad \begin{array}{|l} \hline
\_\_Activate_____ \\
\quad acts! : \mathrm{seq}\ Action \\
\hline
\quad acts! = actions \\
\hline
\end{array} \\
\hline
\end{array}
$$

A similar process occurs with the state schema of a class: attributes defined in both the inherited and inheriting classes are merged automatically. If the specifier requires these attributes to be distinct then these must be explicitly renamed. Renaming of methods is performed via the following syntax: *ClassName*[*NewName / OldName*]. For example, the following class renames a method *On* of *OnOffButton* in order to effect an implicit conjunction of this method definition with the existing definition of *Activate* from *ActionButton*:

$$
\begin{array}{|l}
\hline
\_\_RadioButton _____ \\
\quad \upharpoonright(on, INIT, Activate, Off) \\
\quad ActionButton \\
\quad OnOffButton[Activate/On] \\
\hline
\end{array}
$$

In Z^{++} in contrast, renaming of features to avoid name clashes is implicit. The advantage of this automatic renaming convention is that the default form of inheritance is generally a refinement. The disadvantage is that this creates an extra burden for the specifier when merging is required.

The definition of a method as given in a specific class is referred to by qualification by the name of the class which defines it in Z^{++} and MooZ. In MooZ the notation for S as defined in C is $S.C$. In Z^{++} it is $C.S$. Object-Z and MooZ also allow the definition of a method in the inherited class to be used directly without qualification in the inheriting (which is not allowed by Z^{++}). For instance, schema inclusion can be used to extend a method to an extended state in MooZ:

$$
\begin{array}{|l}
\hline
\_\_MouseUpPrimed _____ \\
\quad MouseUpPrimed \\
\quad \Delta(status) \\
\hline
\quad status' \neq status \\
\quad act! = \varnothing \\
\hline
\end{array}
$$

where *MouseUpPrimed* is being extended from its definition in *Button* to a new definition in *OnOff* [183].

Initialisation schemas are a special case (since these can be considered to be 'methods' of the class of classes, rather than of individual classes). In MooZ and

Object-Z initialisation schemas of the same name are merged when the classes defining them are linked by inheritance. In Z^{++} initialisation methods are treated just as other methods, and any desired conjoining of initialisations must be explicitly performed. Indeed, even the fact that a particular method *Init* is intended to be performed at the beginning of the life of an object must be explicitly stated in the history invariant of the class by writing *Init* $\wedge$ ....

As described in Section 2.1.6, VDM++ distinguishes between inheritance of state and inheritance of methods. A similar differentiation is provided in the B Abstract Machine Notation: the forms USES and SEES of inclusion of one machine in another provide only (limited) access of the state of the used (included) machine in the using machine. The forms IMPORTS and INCLUDES allow access to the operations of the used machine, and EXTENDS allows in addition the exportation of operations of the included machine.

2.2.6   Multiple Inheritance

OOZE/FOOPS, MooZ, Object-Z, Z^{++}, VDM++ and Fresco all support multiple inheritance. Object-Z and MooZ have a different approach to multiple inheritance from that of Z^{++}, in that they require the specifier to explicitly rename methods or attributes of inherited classes to avoid name clashes. Z^{++}, in contrast, takes as the default an automatic renaming of attributes and methods which are made ambiguous by multiple inheritance: if a method m is defined in classes C, D, listed as ancestors in the EXTENDS list of a class E, then, in E, the notation $C.m$ refers to the definition of m as given in C, and $D.m$ the definition given by D. This allows flexible combination and extension of inherited versions of a method.

It could be argued that automatic renaming of same-named attributes in multiple inheritance is conceptually valid: if two same-named features are inherited from different classes, even if they originally come from the same class, then conceptually they are *distinct*: they are components of distinct concepts, and should only be identified explicitly in a specification, rather than by default.

2.2.7   Polymorphism of Operations

Object-Z uses the notation $\downarrow D$ to refer to the class whose instances are all objects which are instances of exactly one of the descendants of D. It corresponds to the deferred classes of Eiffel [142], which are considered to have no genuine instances of their own, but whose instances will always be of some strict descendant class of the deferred class, which serves to abstractly represent the commonalities of all these descendants. In Fresco and Z^{++} polymorphism is achieved by showing refinement of classes, equivalently, conformity of types. That is, proving that various types are subtypes of others.

In OOZE two notions of polymorphism exist: subsort and parametric. The former is implemented via the subsort construct of OOZE and the latter by the use of parameterised modules and theories concerning these parameters. If D is a subtype of C, then a method m of C has some interpretation method n in D, and applying n to an object which may either belong to C or to D will select the appropriate definition of m or n.

2.2.8   Executability and Animatability

There has been debate in the Z world over the benefits or otherwise of 'executing' specifications [87]. Some form of specification animation would clearly be of benefit in early validation of specifications against requirements – critical scenarios could be directly submitted to the prototype to determine if it (and hence the specification) meets the user's requirements in this case. Such an approach has been partially developed for Z, using Prolog [43], and this proved useful in uncovering errors in published Z specifications. However, there are strong limitations on the form of specification that can be animated by this method. The B notation enforces some of these restrictions from the beginning of the specification process in order to obtain translations into procedural languages. Testing techniques for B specifications are being developed, using its animation tool. OOZE also has a focus on specification emulation, via FOOPS, i.e. via OBJ and LISP which is useful as a means of conveying designs and quick validation/verification of these designs.

Work has taken place to support the transformation of Object-Z specifications to C++ code [167] and to provide animation facilities for Z^{++} specifications using menus and dialogs to represent object interactions [116]. In the B Toolkit animator and the Z^{++} animator, non-deterministic operations are 'executed' by asking the user to choose an element from the set of possibilities. Fresco has a focus on the generation of code in object-oriented languages, and allows the combination of code fragments with specification elements in class definitions. In general, direct animation of specifications is to be preferred to rapid prototyping and translation as a means of validation: any translation process carries the risk of lost correctness, and itself involves effort that can divert resources from formal concerns.

2.2.9   Compositionality

Class composition refers to the use of one class (the supplier) as a type for the attribute of another class (the client). Type constructors such as sequencing and function type constructors can be used to build complex types out of class types. All of the languages (except B AMN) implement composition in this sense. The semantics of composition varies, however, in the given languages, and the notations for invoking methods of objects of supplier classes vary from functional notations (Z^{++}) to standard Eiffel-style invocation (MooZ, OOZE, B AMN) and Z schema expressions (Object-Z, Z^{++}) to message-passing syntax (VDM++, Fresco).

In OOZE it is possible to refer to the entire set of instances of a class C by means of the notation

$$\overline{C} \bullet objs$$

and to selectively apply an operation to a subset of these instances. In each class declaration it is possible to refer to the object which is being acted upon by a particular method, by the keyword *self*, and therefore to specify an action for all existing instances of the class except the one being acted on at present. An example of this is contained in the button specification of [183]. In some respects it seems unintuitive to mix operations upon a specific object and operations upon a set of instances of the same class. In Object-Z, MooZ and Z^{++} such specifications would take place in a class which encapsulates sets of instances of the class C. One cannot perhaps rely upon the destination language having such powerful self-reference facilities as are provided by OOZE. In fairness to OOZE, the other Z-based languages run into considerable difficulties when using *promotion* to lift an operation on single objects to an operation on sets of objects of the same class. Despite much ingenuity expended on the subject [126, 202], manageable proof rules remain elusive.

The use of composition to express aggregation and relationships (associations) between classes will be discussed in Chapter 3.

2.2.10 Graphical Forms of Notation

Each of these languages supports some graphical notation to represent the overall design of a specification, with FOOD diagrams [189] being used for FOOPS/OOZE, and variations on the design diagrams of Eiffel [142] for MooZ and Z^{++}. Fresco uses a detailed graphical notation for its type/class definitions. For B, Rumbaugh's Object Model diagrams and Shlaer and Mellor's configuration diagrams have been proposed. All these notations display the dependencies between classes, and attempt to distinguish between the various kinds of dependency: use of one class as an attribute type within another, or as a generic parameter of another, and the use of one class as an ancestor of another, or as a generic template for another. Further links between structured notations and formal languages are given in Chapters 1 and 3.

2.2.11 Object Identity

There appear to be two distinct ways to treat the concept of object identity. One is to argue that it is a programming language mechanism, which should not be imitated in a specification language, but instead, represented explicitly by means of functions from object identifiers to object values, or by incorporating object identifiers as attributes of objects. The second is to retain the concept in the specification language, but to limit the use of this concept so that the problems associated with aliasing and sharing of objects which can arise through its use are limited.

The problem of object identity has been treated in a similar way by the languages Z^{++}, VDM++ and MooZ, in that objects are considered simply to be values, without a persistent identity as a necessary attribute. Instead, objects are organised into collections as the ranges of naming functions (for instance, the attribute *files* : *FID* $\rightarrow$ *File* of the Unix File System specification of [24]), or the classes of which they are instances are provided with an explicit *name* attribute, with an invariant stating that two objects with the same name have identical values for other attributes. This approach was also initially taken in Object-Z.

Object-Z has recently adopted the approach of using constant *pointers* to objects in place of object variables to access and update objects within another class. A declaration

$$\mid \; c : C$$

where C is declared as a class, automatically identifies c as a pointer to an object (and accesses $c.v$ to attributes of c are actually accesses to the attributes of the object pointed at by c). In this case the constant does serve as a name for a specified object, and this name cannot itself be changed by an operation of C. If objects are to be reassigned different names, then the pointer declarations must be as variables rather than as constants.

OOZE and Fresco, in contrast, provide built-in object identities. Built-in identities conflict in some respects with the style of Z, and lead to difficulties in reasoning about equality. Specifically, how is a statement $a = b$, for $a, b : C$, a class type, to be interpreted? Does it imply only that the values of the attributes of a and b, apart from their identities, are the same, or does it suggest that they are fully identical? This leads to the need to consider two forms of equality, a 'weak' equality $\sim$ corresponding to the first case, and full equality in the second case. In Fresco these two forms of equality are denoted by = and == respectively. In Z, the use of two different variables usually implies that these variables can be distinct in practice (the specification will have models in which the variables take different values). An explicit equality or equivalent axiom is needed to force the variables to be the same.

In this respect the idea that an object can only be named with respect to a *local* naming system is preferable: this may correspond more closely to the situation in the real world, where there is no absolute global naming system for entities, only various means of referring to them. For instance, if one observes at different times, two apparently identical cars (say Ford Capris), with identical registration plates (our default primary key or naming system), we can only assume that they are identical. An improved naming system would be needed in a situation where well-equipped car thieves were active.

Formalisation of object identity has taken place, via the use of 'dereference functions' which map object identities in an abstract set to the corresponding object values [117]. The approach of Hall (given in [183]) is an example of this.

2.2.12   Concurrency

Only Object-Z, VDM++ and Z^{++} deal directly with the specification of concurrent properties of a system. Object-Z and Z^{++} have both adopted the view that linear temporal logic is a natural approach to the specification of the concurrent behaviour of an object.

Temporal logic formulae allow the intended execution sequences (i.e. sequences of method applications) of objects of a class to be specified, in quite abstract ways. The basic temporal logic operators are □ (henceforth), ○ (next), and ◇ (eventually). For instance, in Object-Z, it can be specified that a class *SafeService*, with operations *AcceptMsg* and *DeliverMsg*, and attributes *MsgsAvail* and *items*, is 'live', in the sense of always (eventually) responding to an available message, and to a non-empty internal queue of messages, by extending the class to a class *LiveService* [24]:

$$
\begin{array}{|l}
\hline
\_\,LiveService\,\underline{\hspace{6cm}} \\
\quad SafeService \\
\hline
\quad \Box(MsgsAvail \neq \langle\rangle \Rightarrow \Diamond(\mathbf{op} = AcceptMsg)) \\
\quad \Box(items \neq \langle\rangle \Rightarrow \Diamond(\mathbf{op} = DeliverMsg)) \\
\hline
\end{array}
$$

In Z^{++}, one would write

CLASS *LiveService*
  EXTENDS *SafeService*
HISTORY
  □(*MsgsAvail* ≠ ⟨ ⟩ ⇒ ◇ *AcceptMsg*)
  □(*items* ≠ ⟨ ⟩ ⇒ ◇ *DeliverMsg*)
END CLASS

A limitation of linear temporal logic is its apparently unnatural representation of simultaneous events (modelled as two events that can occur in either order). However, a well-developed theory and tools for this language and for extensions of the language exist. It is possible to express intended constraints on the allowed sequences of methods of an object within a language without temporal logic or state machine constructs by judicious use of method pre-conditions. However, this potentially makes a specification less clear by combining two separate aspects of a method into one definition: its effect as a state transformation, and its allowed sequencing relationship in the 'execution' traces of the objects of the class. This also hinders re-use if one wishes to use the same state transition operation in new dynamic contexts.

Semantically these specification choices are also distinct. Pre-conditions for methods simply indicate that no guarantee is made about the result of a method if it is executed outside its pre-condition. However, the use of a 'blockage' specification:

HISTORY
$$\square(M \;\Rightarrow\; Pre_M)$$

for a method M states precisely that no execution sequence can contain an execution of M in a state in which its pre-condition is invalid. It is the latter form of assertion which allows true synchronisation to be specified. Thus these two specification techniques should be distinguished where possible.

One can also state that whenever a condition ψ holds, an action M should be taken:

HISTORY
$$\square(\psi \;\Rightarrow\; M)$$

In Z^{++} this can be combined usefully with methods M which are spontaneous internal actions, to define 'daemons' or partially predictable events.

In VDM++, permission and obligation statements can be used to similarly constrain the occurrence of methods. One would write

$$\textbf{per } m \;\longrightarrow\; \theta$$

to express that m cannot be executed if θ fails to hold. More sophisticated constraints over the dynamic behaviour of an object are possible through the use of history event counts

$$\#act : methods \rightarrow \mathbb{N}$$
$$\#fin : methods \rightarrow \mathbb{N}$$

which give, respectively, the number of initiations and terminations of specified methods of a class at a particular point in time.

In a stack specification, we could, for example, state that a *Pop* cannot occur unless the number of completed *Push* operations is greater than the number of completed *Pop* operations:

$$\textbf{per } Pop \;\longrightarrow\; \#fin(Push) \;>\; \#fin(Pop)$$

Other aspects of a concurrent environment, such as the list of requests for executions of specific methods being queued at a particular moment, are also treatable via the history function

$$\#req : methods \rightarrow \mathbb{N}$$

which counts the total number of requests received for each method of a specification.

Other alternatives to the use of temporal logic are Modal Action Logic [6], which has been proposed for use in MooZ and for the semantics of VDM++, and CSP

[90], which has been proposed for use in Z^{++} [114]. The use of CSP would allow more natural representation of simultaneity via the concurrency operator of the language. However, it is less declarative and abstract than temporal logic. For example, even deterministic but non-sequential processes such as

$$P = (\alpha \rightarrow P \mid \beta \rightarrow (\gamma \rightarrow P))$$

in CSP require the recursive definition of the underlying process, as a composition of simpler processes. The corresponding temporal logic description

$$\Box(\alpha \vee (\beta \wedge \bigcirc \gamma))$$

is more abstract.

Issues which are not dealt with by linear temporal logic are those concerned with dynamic aggregation of objects and sharing of one object by other objects [85]. In addition, the duration of methods would need to be modelled via the use of an explicit attribute of a class which gives the current time, and conjuncts of each method defining the time constraints which the method is expected to obey. Moreover, method execution is treated as an atomic indivisible and uninterruptible action, so that there is no way to specify situations in which several invocations of a method are concurrently executing, or in which several different methods from the same class are currently executing. Work performed in the IS-CORE project [85] has used a combination of temporal and modal logics to formally treat such issues.

A particular problem related to concurrent execution is that of the sharing of objects. The possibility of shared objects clearly leads to problems when reasoning about objects which own such values: the state of such an object may 'change spontaneously' as the result of methods executed by another owner of the shared value. One way in which this could be represented is via the use of spontaneous internal actions in Z^{++}. These can also represent the separation of control between an application and an external user. For instance, we could be interested in specifying an application which uses instances of a *Window* class, and which only needs operations of *Fill*, *Clear* and *Flash*, but in which these instances can also be modified by operations *Move*, *Resize*, *Close* and *Open* applied by an external user. Moreover, our reasoning is required to deal with these operations, in cases such as the need to prove that a warning message is definitely communicated to the user. The outline of such a class would therefore be:

CLASS *Window*
OWNS
    contents : seq *Text*;
    visible : *yes* | *no*
OPERATIONS
  ∗*Open* : →;
  ∗*Close* : →;

```
*Move  :  N N  →;
*Resize  :  N N  →;
 Fill  :  File  →;
 Clear  :  →;
 Flash  :  →
END CLASS
```

No client or descendant of this class can use the starred operations, but these operations must be taken into account if we want to prove properties such as

$$\Box(Flash \Rightarrow (visible = yes))$$

Such a class can be considered to be a specification of objects which are designed to be shared between two different clients, and these clients have access to a disjoint, but inter-dependent, set of services of the supplier.

The use of realtime logic (RTL) in conjunction with Object-Z has been proposed by McDermid [133] explicitly to constrain method duration and other realtime aspects of an object class. This involves the use of RTL formulae in the history invariant of a class. The development process advocated by [133] uses a translation from Harel statechart notation into classes and method definitions.

2.2.13 Genericity

The languages Z^{++}, OOZE, MooZ and Object-Z allow the use of generic type parameters to define generic classes, analogous to the definition of generic schemas in Z. Instantiating these parameters with specific types leads to the definition of new classes. In OOZE, parameters can be modules, typed by theories. In this case the name of the parameter is not necessarily used in the class, instead, it simply acts to import the definitions of the theory as a module. In object-oriented languages, the use of dummy instances or objects to import standard libraries such as mathematical libraries or input–output libraries has been criticised for its abuse of the composition construct [185]. The module importation mechanism of OOZE may be preferable in these cases. MooZ, Z^{++} and Object-Z need to use inheritance or composition to implement importation of method definitions from one class to another.

Statements of constrained genericity are possible in Z^{++} and OOZE. These allow the specifier to require that an actual parameter of a class satisfies certain minimal conditions: that it is a descendant of a given class, or that it satisfies a particular theory. Whilst constrained genericity is theoretically redundant, it is convenient and informative to readers of a specification.

2.2.14   Formally Defined Semantics

The languages Z^{++}, Object-Z and MooZ have been criticised from the viewpoint that they lack a sufficiently well-developed semantics. For VDM++ a semantics only exists for the part of the language which can be translated into the standard VDM specification language: this excludes aspects of the language relating to concurrent properties.

For Z^{++} a theory of subtyping or refinement has been worked out, but this appears to be poorly integrated with the facilities for handling concurrency and algebraic specification in the language. Object-Z has a well-developed theory of temporal logic specification, but again, the links between this and the semantics of sequential specification aspects are not so well developed. In addition, the use of pointers to objects in place of object variables complicates semantic issues related to aliasing (two different names for the same object). The semantics of OOZE is defined in terms of the established semantics for FOOPS and OBJ3, although research on the semantics of refinement for many-sorted order-sorted algebra is still in progress, as is work on the semantics of concurrent execution of methods. The semantics of B abstract machines is defined in terms of predicate transformers for its constructs [1].

2.2.15   Reasoning Systems

For those parts of the languages which are based directly upon standard Z, that is, for Object-Z without reference semantics, and Z^{++}, the $\mathcal{W}$ reasoning system can be used [203]. This is a natural deduction calculus in which sequents are of the form

$$Pred1 \vdash Pred2$$

where *Pred*1 is a list of declarations and predicates, and *Pred*2 is a list of predicates. For OOZE, a reasoning system based upon term rewriting is available. For VDM++, extensions of the Mural proof assistant for VDM are being developed in the Afrodite Esprit III project, to include the specification constructs which VDM++ defines on top of VDM. The B abstract machine notation allows reasoning based on predicate transformer semantics, and the B tool theorem prover has been developed to support this reasoning.

For Fresco, there are inference rules for combining separate pre- and post-condition definitions of methods, and inference rules for the promotion of an operation from a supplier to a client class.

2.2.16 Refinement Systems

Refinement to code has been an increasingly important concern in the Z world, although originally the language was used as a pure specification language, with manual coding of applications from Z documents being the normal procedure for its use. The B abstract machine notation, and associated tools, aims to bridge the gap between Z specifications and code by means of a semantically well-founded process of refinement, based upon predicate transformer semantics for code and specifications. Similar Z-based techniques are those of Morgan [150]. For pure Z, a theory of refinement has been worked out, as a result both of practical experimentation [35] and theoretical development [126]. Similarly, a theory of refinement for VDM has been established and is supported by the Mural toolset. Thus, for those parts of the object-oriented specification languages which are directly based upon their predecessors, techniques for refinement are available.

Z^{++} has a well-developed theory of refinement, based upon the Z concept of procedural refinement, and a series of rules exist for reasoning about refinement between classes built out of other classes by means of the class algebra operations of the language [115]. This theory of refinement does not, however, cover algebraic aspects of the language, and no definite decision has been made on the way in which temporal specification aspects can be incorporated: i.e. on what the definition of refinement for temporal logic specifications should be. For Object-Z, a theory of refinement for the language has been worked out, which includes the treatment of temporal logic specifications. For these, options such as *observational equivalence* versus *operational equivalence* are available as the basis of refinement definitions. Techniques for the systematic translation of Object-Z to code have been developed [167].

Z^{++} and OOZE allow the explicit assertion of refinement relationships between classes, via predicates of the form

$$C \sqsubseteq_{\phi,R} D$$

in the case of Z^{++}, where C, D are classes, ϕ is a mapping from the method names of C to those of D, and R is a predicate defining a relation between the non-method features of C and D, and via a form of module known as a 'view' in the case of OOZE, which similarly defines a mapping between the features of two classes or modules.

2.3 Conclusions

2.3.1 Summary

We have shown that all of the surveyed languages (apart from B) deserve to be referred to as 'object-oriented', according to generally accepted criteria. However, the ways in which these languages implement various object-oriented concepts differ quite strongly at a syntactic level, and their similarities are most marked at a level of inter-expressibility: it is generally possible to translate a specification from one language into a different language, even when constructs involving dynamic constraints on behaviour are concerned. Obviously, the details of the semantics may differ in subtle ways, so that a direct transliteration cannot in general be applied without additional user-guided translation.

In addition, languages without multiple inheritance or without generic parameters are not effectively able to imitate the design of specifications written using these facilities [141].

2.3.2   Areas of Further Development

It is clear that the languages do not deal with the full range of issues which can be required to be treated in formal specifications. For example, the model of time used in those languages which treat timing issues is still discrete, rather than realtime. Moreover, treatment of non-functional issues is still limited. None of the languages appears to have an integrated approach to the use of diagrammatic informal notations with formal notations, an issue which could significantly affect their uptake and usability. Similarly, tool support is provided only by research prototypes. Specific problems related to the semantic model of the language have been identified for the use of modularisation facilities for VDM [154].

Refinement, and notations for explicitly documenting refinement, are central to the Fresco, OOZE and Z^{++} languages. This is an area which is critical for practical application of formal specification languages, and more attention is needed to extend the reasoning support for refinement to deal with concurrency and timing issues.

Chapter 3

Object-oriented Specification Languages in the Software Life Cycle

K. Lano and H. Haughton

In this chapter we give analysis, design and specification techniques using object-oriented specification languages. Examples are also given to show how the object-oriented specification languages described in this book implement these techniques and can be used throughout the software life cycle.

3.1 Life Cycle Model

A *life cycle model* is a specification of the sequencing of processes and products involved in the development of applications. Effectively, it is a software process model, addressing the questions 'what shall we do next?' and 'how long shall we continue to do it?' [15]. Examples are the waterfall and spiral models. The *development method* used in forward engineering is to some degree orthogonal to the life cycle model chosen, since some development methods prescribe a corresponding life cycle model, whilst others can be adopted in any life cycle adhering to certain criteria. Moreover, methods may be designed only for a certain part of the life cycle, and therefore need to be supplemented by other techniques to cover the whole of a life cycle.

Formal methods have often been limited in their coverage of the software life cycle, with the most successful methods (or notations, more precisely), VDM and Z, being used mainly in the early stages of a development process: specification of requirements and functional specification, although only after initial domain analysis and requirements-capture processes have been performed. More recent approaches, such as OOZE, B AMN and Fusion, have aimed instead at a wider coverage of the life cycle, to support the use of rigorous techniques throughout the development process.

Formal object-oriented specification languages are potentially applicable throughout the software life cycle: as with object-oriented programming languages, they can support a clear expression of designs and, in addition, a precise description of functionality, at a number of levels of abstraction. Non-formal methods exist for the development of object-oriented systems [33]. Attempts to enhance these with mathematical semantics and reasoning techniques have been made [34], which could potentially lead to formal specification techniques supported by diagrammatic notations. We believe that such an integration of formal and informal notations is an essential support for development and validation of specifications, particularly at the domain and system analysis and requirements-capture stages of the software development process, and this chapter will give examples of the ways in which these forms can be used together.

The concern of the object-oriented development approach is to create generalised, adaptable and re-usable systems. This is consistent with the aim of formal specification to create abstract functional specifications of a system, in a form which enables formal verification and which supports validation. In so far as object-oriented programming is programming with abstract data types [93], the use of very high-level data constructs and of abstraction from implementation concerns is compatible with object-oriented methods. In contrast to Z and VDM, object-oriented specification languages allow explicit encapsulation of state and associated methods into a class, and hence extend the amount of specification information which can be formally represented, rather than informally in textual annotations. In addition, they support compartmentalisation of proofs, since only properties of classes used directly or indirectly in a given class will be relevant for the proving of properties about that class. Some aspects of object orientation, such as message passing as the paradigm for communication between objects, will not be directly relevant to a specification language, since one of the purposes of a specification language is to abstract away from possible implementations in order to gain generality and re-usability, in addition to clarity of expression.

In the following sections we will give examples of techniques using object-oriented formal specification languages throughout a life cycle process which contains phases of requirements-capture, domain analysis, system analysis, specification, design and implementation. An outline of such a process is presented in Figure 3.1.

3.2   Using Formal Specification Languages

In Chapter 1 we described two of the main object-oriented analysis and design methods in current use, together with simple examples from these methods. In these methodologies, as with traditional structured methods such as SSADM [57], requirements-capture and domain analysis is performed by the abstract modelling of the existing (possibly manual) system, and of the business requirements of the new system, in notations which are intended to be clear to both the client and the analyst. Such notations are now being integrated with formal methods in a number of projects and research directions [33, 63, 164, 165], and would provide a useful supplement to formal techniques at the earlier stages of the life cycle. Specific ways in which these notations can be used together are given below.

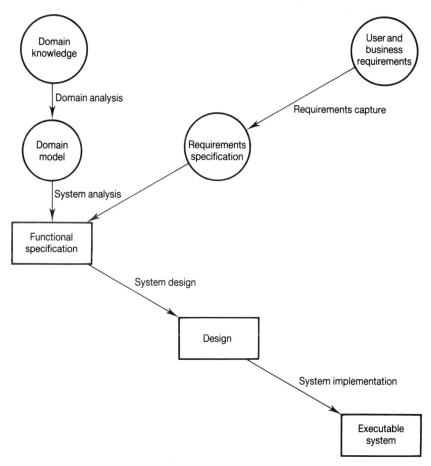

Figure 3.1: Outline Context for Object-oriented Development

Following the model for structured methods given in Chapter 1, we will consider the following three forms of system description:

- static data modelling;
- function/process/data flow modelling;
- dynamic and concurrent behaviour.

The elements of such descriptions will be textual (as in SSADM entity and attribute descriptions), diagrammatic and formal. All these forms of description can be used, with a tendency towards more formal descriptions as the software process progresses, and with processes of translation from informal and semi-formal descriptions to formal descriptions being used at the early life cycle stages and processes of generation of diagrammatic and textual forms from formal descriptions at the later stages.

3.3   Requirements Analysis

3.3.1   Identifying Objects and Classes

One of the critical problems involved in creating an object-oriented design is in identifying the features (attributes and methods) of classes plus the relationships between them. Intuitively, whenever we think of an entity (i.e. any real-world facet: a house, car, person, etc.) we naturally associate that entity with what may be termed attributes, that is, characteristics which are persistent and necessary for the identification of the entity. For example a description of a person might include, among others, attributes such as age, sex, height, name and address. The attributes are, in most instances, permanently associated with the person (although their values may be changed by operations or *methods*). Clearly the mental process just described can be applied to identifying attributes of classes from a variety of domains, as part of the wider process of software design.

At the same time that we make an association of attributes to an entity we also have in mind a number of events which can change the value of these attributes. In many cases there may be more than one event which can change a particular attribute. In the case of the person entity the events are fairly obvious: birthday, gaining height, moving house etc. In general, for every attribute of a class we can associate a set of events (possibly empty) which we call methods, that update the attribute. These methods can be:

1. Observers: in that they provide information on the current value of an attribute;
2. Constructors: in that they create elements of the attribute type;
3. Destructors: in that they destruct elements of an attribute; or
4. Rearrangers: in that they change the way in which we can view an attribute.

Having identified an object class with its possible features, we might want to refine the class so as to reflect certain types of domain issues. For example, we may place further logical constraints on the attributes of a class in order to make the class fit more closely to the domain concept which it is modelling. This is an instance of class *specialisation*.

3.3.2   Creating Systems of Objects

At this stage we should also identify any relationships or dependencies between object classes. Consider the entity *Book*, having attributes *title, isbn, author, date, publisher*. The attribute *author* can be defined to be of type *Person*. In this case we say that the book and person classes are related via a client and server relationship, where the person class provides information (concerning person features) to the book class. Operations on books do not need to know all the internal details of people, but only selected aspects of them. The client/server relationship in object-oriented terms is called composition or vertical inheritance. The term vertical is used because the client does not acquire any more attributes or methods of its own but can be provided with such features via a server class: there is a hierarchical relationship between the two classes which reflects their relative position in a hierarchy of subsystems. In such cases the client has no direct access to the features of its server, so increasing the extent to which loose coupling is used in the specification.

There is a dual to the notion of vertical inheritance, which is known as horizontal inheritance or simply inheritance. In this case the using class has direct access to the features of the used class and it is not necessary to declare a variable to be of a class type (as in composition). Conceptually it is often considered to imply the existence of an *is-a* relationship between the two classes: if A inherits from B then every instance of A is an instance of B. However, this is only formally true in certain circumstances, essentially when the inheritance relation is a refinement. Inheritance has also been used as a simple module-importation mechanism, and there is a strong case for separating these two uses [185]. Clearly there is also a need to separate the concepts of composition and inheritance. Imagine, for example, that we had used inheritance to describe the book class as being an extension of person. Clearly this would have made no sense, based on our understanding of books!

The process of inheritance invariably involves adding additional information regarding new features of a class. For example, if we extended the person class to that of a working person class, we might choose to include new attributes such as salary, job-title, place-of-work, etc. Corresponding new methods might also be defined for the new class. Conceptually, what we are trying to convey is the fact that a person and working person may be regarded in different ways, as instances of different classes or concepts, as well as the same. However, we are also doing more than this. That is, by employing the use of inheritance we are in fact defining re-usable components in our design.

Is-a relationships are often asserted on the basis of the static aspects of an object class alone, without concern for dynamic behaviour. We could name such a general relationship by the term 'specialisation', and require that this be implied by subtyping, but not conversely. An example of this situation is the specification of geometric shapes defined in [183].

The entities considered are: *Quadrilateral, Parallelogram, Rhombus, Rectangle* and *Square*. Intuitively, one might expect that the inheritance hierarchy is such that *Parallelogram* inherits from *Quadrilateral*, *Rhombus* and *Rectangle* inherit from *Parallelogram*, and *Square* inherits from both *Rhombus* and *Rectangle*. Indeed, if one considers only the state components of the corresponding classes, then the inheritance hierarchy of this form is also a subtyping hierarchy. That is, the state of *Rhombus* is more restrictive than the states of its ancestors, and so forth. Therefore, the specialisation relation between these concepts follows the above pattern.

But in the object-oriented paradigm, concepts are represented both by a certain state and by characteristic operations over this state. The combination of these aspects is significant for determining refinement (i.e. subtyping). In this case, for example, we might consider operations of *Shearing* a quadrilateral through a specified angle, and an operation to determine the *Angle* of any shape which is at least a *Parallelogram*.

Unfortunately, the *Shear* operation does not preserve the property of being a *Rhombus* or a *Rectangle*, so for no proper descendant of *Parallelogram* is it an appropriate method. This means, in addition, that there is not a simple refinement relation between *Parallelogram* or *Rhombus* or between *Parallelogram* and *Square*. In practical use, one could not safely use an instance of the *Square* class as an instance of *Parallelogram*, since applying a non-trivial *Shear* operation to this instance would result in a violation of the invariant of *Square*. Instead, the OOZE specification of the problem in [183] considers the following hierarchy: *Quadrilateral*, inherited by *Parallelogram* and *ShearableQuadrilateral* (i.e. the *Quadrilateral* class with the method *Shear* added), and with *Rectangle* and *Rhombus* inheriting from *Parallelogram*, *Square* inheriting from *Rectangle* and *Rhombus*, and *ShearableParallelogram* inheriting from *ShearableQuadrilateral* and *Parallelogram*. Viewed in this way, every inheritance relationship is also a refinement relationship, and hence, type-compatibility is correctly expressed in the class hierarchy. The ZEST specification in [183] similarly factors out the *Shear* operation into the *QUADRILATERAL* class, and uses a *PARALLELSHAPE* class as a supertype of the non-shearable shapes *RHOMBUS*, *RECTANGLE* and *SQUARE*.

Related to inheritance is the process known as multiple inheritance, where several classes can be inherited in some other class. Clearly as human beings we often engage ourselves in activities requiring the use of multiple inheritance. In certain cases we might even inherit two similar attributes from two distinct classes. Whereas in the real world this poses no problems, the same is not necessarily true in object-oriented development. For example, in the case of object-oriented languages which do not automatically create unique identifiers for their features, inheriting two like-named features might make execution of methods impossible. This case of inheriting like-named features occurs even in the process of single inheritance where a method may have been redefined and later inherited by some class. In such cases care must be taken to ensure that features are renamed, if necessary, in order to avoid any semantic problems.

Similarity relationships between concepts can be expressed by means of inheritance by linking two classes representing these concepts by direct or indirect inheritance relationships. Relationships between classes which involve hiding or removing some features should be distinguished from relationships in which all the facilities of one class remain available in the other. If, for example, we want to express the idea that an *Extendible_Polygon* (with an *Add_Vertex* method) is similar to a

Rectangle (with no such method), we must use an intermediate class *Polygon* and inherit this in both classes. In general, the common parts of meaningful classes should be examined to determine whether they should themselves exist in a class hierarchy.

This far we have discussed a process of identifying the features of classes and describing the relationships between classes. It may be possible, however, to normalise the classes further, in order to eliminate redundant information. The main steps involve the following analysis:

1. If several classes have similar methods we can factor out these methods, with their associated attributes, and form a new class. The original classes will now inherit this class;

2. If there are methods which are used by only a few classes, and are similar in nature, we can create a general operation and refine it in each relevant class.

Structuring a hierarchy of classes in a way which facilitates re-use and adaptation of these classes is a key problem both within applications and within libraries of re-usable components: even the libraries for Eiffel have required restructuring to (1) rationalise the use of names for methods, so that analogous methods for different data structures have the same name [143]; and (2) to reduce the number of inheritance links which involve deletion of features [26].

3.4 From Analysis to Specification

In this section we give examples of the way that analysis models formulated in OMT can be mapped into formal object-oriented specifications or formal object-based specifications. Z^{++} and B Abstract Machine Notation (AMN) will be used as the formal languages, with some examples being expressed also in Object-Z.

3.4.1 Formalising Object Model Notation

Each component of OMT Object Model Notation will be considered in turn, together with the choices that exist for their formalisation.

Attributes. For Z^{++} (or Object-Z) the attributes of a class C on a Object Model Diagram become attributes of the formal object class C expressing this class. Domains which we do not wish to detail further can be defined as *given sets* in Z terminology [182] and refined later as needed. For B AMN, the currently existing instances of a class C on an Object Model Diagram are represented as a variable $cs \subseteq CS$ in a *abstract machine* C. CS represents the set of all *possible* instances of C, cs is the set of object identities of existing instances. Attributes $at : T$ of the OMT class become variables at of C which are of a suitable function type $cs \rightarrow T'$.

Associations. An association can be modelled in the following ways. If we have a pair C, D of classes, with an association $r : C \leftrightarrow D$ without attributes between them, then for Z^{++} or for Object-Z there are two main possibilities:

1. Form Z^{++} or Object-Z classes for each OMT class involved in the association, and a class E encapsulating a system involving a set of instances of C and a set of instances of D, and an attribute which is a relationship between these sets, with the cardinality constraints given by the diagrammatic notation. For example:

```
CLASS E
OWNS
    cinstances  :  P(C);
    dinstances  :  P(D);
    rinstance  :  C  ↔  D
INVARIANT
    dom  rinstance  =  cinstances  ∧
    ran  rinstance  =  dinstances
END CLASS
```

if r is many-to-many. Use of generic classes could be made to express general forms of association: C and D in the above class could be replaced by generic class parameters X and Y of E. This would be similar to the use of the generic *Table* class in the MooZ specification of Chapter 4.

Cardinality constraints can be expressed by additional conjuncts of the invariant. For instance, if we had used the constraint that the cardinality of the relationship was always 2 at the D end we would conjoin the predicate

$$\forall\ c:\ C\ |\ c\ \in\ \text{dom}\ rinstance\ \bullet$$
$$|\ rinstance\ (\!|\ c\ |\!)\ |\ =\ 2$$

to the invariant. In this representation it is possible to express tertiary relationships and the constraint that one relationship is an inverse to another. It avoids the need to explicitly consider object identities or to decide if one class is hierarchically superior to (i.e. a client of) another.

2. Form a Z^{++} or Object-Z class for each OMT class involved in the relationship, and define an attribute of one class which effects an *enquiry access path* [57] derived from the relationship r. This path corresponds to the way that navigation from one entity instance to an r-associated entity instance or set of r-associated entity instances will be required in the final system. For example:

```
┌─ C ──────────────────────────────────────────────
│ ┌────────────────────────────────────────────────
│ │ att₁ : T₁;
│ │ ...
│ │ r_D s : P D
│ └────────────────────────────────────────────────
└───────────────────────────────────────────────────
```

in the case that we have a one-to-many OMT association $r : C \leftrightarrow D$ from C to D, and we do not need to navigate from instances of D to instances of C. Here there is no indicated ordering on the elements of D associated with an given instance of C: if an ordering was indicated, the translation would use $\text{seq}(D)$ in place of $\mathbf{P}(D)$. Note that the inverse enquiry access path, from an instance of D to an instance of C, will only exist if the association is mandatory at the D end, and would in this case be modelled as a C-valued attribute r_C of D.

It is clear that if enquiry access in both directions along an association is required the former approach must be taken, and the latter approach is also ruled out if we require expression of global constraints on r and other associations, such as inversion constraints.

For B, only the first approach is possible. We have the formal representation:

```
MACHINE System
SETS
    CS;  DS
VARIABLES
    cs,  ds,  rinstance
INVARIANT
    cs  ⊆  CS  ∧
    ds  ⊆  DS  ∧
    cs  ∩  ds  =  ∅  ∧
    rinstance  :  cs  ↔  ds
END
```

with cardinality constraints being expressed through further invariant conjuncts, as with Z^{++}. It is also possible to separately specify the sets of instances of C and the sets of instances of D, in distinct machines of these names, and to use the INCLUDES or USES facility to incorporate both machines into a machine which deals only with the association elements:

```
MACHINE System
INCLUDES
    C, D
VARIABLES
    rinstance
INVARIANT
    rinstance  :  cs  ↔  ds  ∧
    cs  ∩  ds  =  ∅
INITIALISATION
    rinstance  :=  ∅
END
```

In OOZE, or in an Object-Z-like language which allowed recursive class types, there would also be the possibility of representing associations via attributes of each class which refer to elements or sets of elements of the other. Maintaining the consistency of the association would then be a problem, as it is in the implementation of associations by pointer attributes in an object-oriented programming language [174]. An example of such a representation is given in the Fresco specification in Chapter 9. Object identity equality $==$ and *self* are used to constrain one attribute (implementing one half of an association) to be the inverse of another (implementing the other part). In OOZE, a set of classes with mutual references to each other would be placed in the same module to indicate that they should be re-used together, rather than individually.

If the association itself has attributes, then for Z^{++} there are again two possibilities:

1. The association elements can be represented as an object class:

    CLASS R_{link}
    OWNS
        $linkedC$: C;
        $linkedD$: D;
        att_1 : T_1;
        .....
    RETURNS
        Cof : $\rightarrow$ C;
        Dof : $\rightarrow$ D
    ACTIONS
        Cof $c!$ $==>$ $c!$ $=$ $linkedC$;
        Dof $d!$ $==>$ $d!$ $=$ $linkedD$
    END CLASS

    where the attributes of the association are att_1, ... These elements are then combined in an overall class as for case 1 above:

    ```
     E
      cinstances : P C;
      dinstances : P D;
      rel : P R_link
      ...

      {r : R_link | r ∈ rel • Cof r} = cinstances  ∧
      {r : R_link | r ∈ rel • Dof r} = dinstances
    ```

    in the case that the link is many-to-many;

2. An intermediate class type can be created and used as the value of an attribute of one or another class, again, depending on the form of the association and the required enquiry access paths:

```
CLASS C
OWNS
    rDs  :  P  R_link_to_D;
    ... attributes of  C ...
END CLASS

CLASS R_link_to_D
OWNS
    linkedD  :  D;
    att1  :  T1;
    .....
END CLASS
```

The latter representation is simpler, but does not permit the expression of global constraints on the association, or an enquiry access path from instances of D to instances of C.

As an example of the second approach, consider a domain where we are defining entity types *House*, *HomeOwner* and an attributed association *Ownership* between them (Figure 3.2).

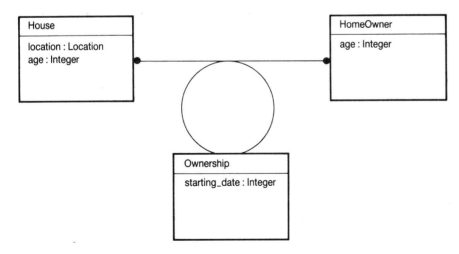

Figure 3.2: Home-ownership Representation

This situation can be formally expressed by the classes:

```
CLASS HomeOwner
OWNS
    ownerships  :  P  Ownership;
    age  :  Z
END CLASS
```

```
CLASS Ownership
OWNS
    starting_date  :  Z;
    house_owned  :  House
END CLASS
```

```
CLASS House
OWNS
    location  :  Location;
    age  :  Z
END CLASS
```

In the diagrammatic model there is the implicit possibility of accessing sets of home owners from a given house, and of sets of owned houses from a given home owner; only the second possibility is expressed in the formal model. This, and the necessity of making similar decisions in specialising the domain model for practical specification and implementation, is one reason we recommend delaying full formalisation of domain models until after requirements have been captured.

For B AMN, we must adopt the first approach, and treat the association as a new class type *CDLINK* with set of existing instances *cdlinks*:

```
MACHINE System
SETS
    CDLINK;  CS;  DS
VARIABLES
    cdlinks,  cs,  ds,  linkedC,  linkedD,
    att₁ ...
INVARIANT
    cdlinks ⊆ CDLINK ∧
    cs ⊆ CS ∧
    ds ⊆ DS ∧
    ds ∩ cs = ∅ ∧
    linkedC  :  cdlinks  →  cs ∧
    linkedD  :  cdlinks  →  ds ∧
    att₁  :  cdlinks  →  T₁ ∧ ...
END
```

Again, this specification could be partitioned into three machines, one defining the attributes of existing instances of C, another those of existing instances of D, and another the attributes of the association, and which imports the other two machines via an `INCLUDES` or `USES` clause.

Aggregations are modelled via class composition in Z^{++}. If we have an OMT class C which has aggregation associations r, s to (single instances of) classes D, E, then we simply define:

```
CLASS C
OWNS
    r : D;
    s : E;
    ... other attributes of C ...
END CLASS
```

An alternative would be to inherit D and E in C, if full access to the state of D and E were required. This combination of classes is termed a *co-product* if no attributes of the same name are used in D and E. Only the first technique can be applied if there are sets of D or E instances aggregated into one instance of C or if recursive aggregation is used.

Similarly, in B AMN, we can use the `INCLUDES` facility to inherit or delegate to another class or class instance:

```
MACHINE C
SETS
    CS
INCLUDES
    D, E
VARIABLES
    cd, d, e
INVARIANT
    cs ⊆ CS ∧ d : ds ∧ e : es ...
END
```

in the first case.

Class attributes (that is, attributes which belong to the class rather than to individual objects) require that a variable representing all existing instances of a class be defined, in either Z^{++} or B. They can be directly represented, however, in OOZE via the meta-class concept and the variable *objs* holding the current existing set of instances of a class.

Constraints are modelled by predicates constraining the formal items corresponding to the OMT object model items upon which the constraint is placed. If there are constraints on the relation between two associations then these associations need in general to be represented as attributes of a single class, and similarly for more complex examples. Constraints involving time can often be translated into temporal constraints of a class. For instance, the statement that 'if M occurs, then N can never occur again' is directly expressed by the temporal logic formula

$$\Box(M \Rightarrow \Box(\neg N))$$

Inheritance is modelled by inheritance in Z^{++}. Subtleties concerning name clashes need to be explicitly considered: both renaming and explicit merging of same-named attributes from distinct inherited classes can be expressed in Z^{++}. We suggest extending the OMT notation by the use of exclamation marks ! on lines representing inheritance relationships when the analyst is not sure that the inheritance is conformant. If a conformant inheritance is indicated between OMT classes C and D, then we add the assertion

$$C \sqsubseteq_{true} D$$

to the resulting specification, which states that D is a refinement of C via the *true* data refinement and the identity mapping of methods of C to methods of D. In OOZE, the identity view between C and D would be asserted.

In B, forms of inheritance which do not introduce new operations which directly update the variables of the inherited class can be modelled by means of the machine inclusion facilities INCLUDES, SEES, USES, EXTENDS and IMPORTS. In general, we must include all subtypes of a given class type in a machine representing their common supertype. If D is a subtype of C, and C has no further supertypes, then C is represented by a machine C of the following form:

MACHINE C
SETS CS
VARIABLES cs, ds, ...
INVARIANT
$\qquad ds \subseteq cs \wedge$ ...
END

Any attribute $att : cs \rightarrow T$ of C is then automatically inherited by D. Moreover, any operation creating an instance of D (element of ds) must then create an instance of C (element of cs). Distinctions between purely abstract and non-purely abstract supertypes of a set of class types can be formally expressed.

3.4.2   Animation and Rapid Prototyping

One significant means by which a formalised requirements specification can be validated against a user's expectations is by animation. Support for animation of specifications is provided by the B Toolkit, and the languages OOZE, MooZ and Z^{++} also provide prototype tools for animation of specifications. We would view an animation stage during or after formalisation of requirements as a highly desirable component of a life cycle using formal object-oriented specifications. Our experience with the B and Z^{++} toolkits has been that many mistakes in expression of requirements can be caught through animation, and that this can save considerable effort at later stages such as formal proof of refinements or internal consistency of specifications.

3.5   Specification

3.5.1   Specification Techniques

Some of the specification techniques of Z are supported or enhanced by the included languages based upon Z, and we list these below.

Specification Disjunction
A common style of operation specification in Z is to separate error cases from the normal cases by means of the disjunction operation ∨ on schemas. This is very important for increasing the clarity of specifications, and has been retained, albeit in different forms, in the included languages. In Z^{++}, it is possible to divide an operation into two different cases of a 'normal' behaviour and an 'error' behaviour, provided the pre-conditions of these schemas are disjoint:

```
CLASS  C
OWNS
  ....
OPERATIONS
  Op_Ok  :  X  →  Y ;
  Op_Error  :  X  →  Y ;
  Op  :  X  →  Y
ACTIONS
  Op_Ok x? y!  ==>  Pre_Ok  ∧  Def_Ok ;
  Op_Error x? y!  ==>  Pre_Error  ∧  Def_Error ;
  Op x? y!  ==>  Op_Ok  ∨  Op_Error
END CLASS
```

The effect is the same as the explicit definition

$$Op \; x? \; y! \;\; ==> \;\; Pre\_Ok \; \wedge \; Def\_Ok \; \vee$$
$$Pre\_Error \; \wedge \; Def\_Error$$

An equivalent process is supported by the use of the *choice* operator [] in Object-Z. The disjoint disjunction construct is 'refinement preserving' in a precise sense [113]. Since the operations Op_Ok and Op_Error are internal to the class, a new class should be defined which hides them from external users (including inheriting classes):

$$D \triangleq C \setminus (Op\_Ok, Op\_Error)$$

Similarly, in Object-Z or MooZ, these operations could be made private to the defining class. This distinction could not be formally made in a Z specification.

Promotion of Specifications

Another well-developed technique is called *promotion* in Z [202]. This is simply a special case of the process of lifting an operation from a supplier class to one of its client classes, and again, is supported by the included languages, with different syntax forms. In Z^{++}, for instance, if we have in class D an attribute $v : \mathbf{P}\,C$, where C is a class with operation m, then m can be used with a framing method

$$Frame\ a\ a' \ ==> \quad a \in v \ \wedge$$
$$v' \ = \ (v \ \backslash \ \{a\}) \ \cup \ \{a'\}$$

defined in D to provide an operation which applies m to a selected element of the set:

$$M \ ==> \quad \exists \ a, a' : C \ \bullet \ Frame \ \wedge$$
$$a' \ = \ m \ a$$

Such framing schemas can be re-used to lift any operation of the supplier class to the client. Object-Z uses a reference semantics for objects which simplifies the promotion of an operation on a selected object within an aggregation – see Chapter 5, Section 5.1.3.

An example of promotion from the MooZ specification of Chapter 4 is the following. *Take* is a method of a generic *Table*[*ID, VALUE*] class:

```
┌─ Take ──────────────────────────────────────────────
│ Δ(store)
│ id? : ID
│ value, value' : VALUE
├─────────────────────────────────────────────────────
│ id? ∈ store dom
│ value = store(id?)
│ store' = store ⊕ {id? ↦ value'}
└─────────────────────────────────────────────────────
```

This method is used as a frame to promote operations from one of the instantiating classes of an instantiation of *Table* to the instantiation. For example, in the instantiation

$$StorageSystem \ \hat{=} \ Table(ID \ \backslash \ FID, VALUE \ \backslash \ File)$$

of *Table* to represent an association between files and file identities we can lift the *Read* method of *File* to a method which takes a particular file id, and applies the *Read* operation to the associated file, updating it in the table and leaving other table elements unchanged:

```
┌─ Read ──────────────────────────────────────────────
│ Take(id? \ fid?, value \ file)
│ file Read
└─────────────────────────────────────────────────────
```

3.5.2 Concurrency

An important area of concern for object-oriented languages is the need to specify the dynamic behaviour of objects or object collections, including synchronisation constraints [50, 112]. Such specification capabilities would enable these languages to be used for some applications involving realtime constraints: process control, communication protocols, and so forth, in areas involving safety- or mission-critical systems. At present, the languages Object-Z and Z^{++} which include temporal logic history constraints require that, for constraints to be placed on the interaction of two classes, the relevant parts of the state and features of these two classes must be visible to the class imposing the constraint. For example, if class *Belt* has an attribute *positioned*, which must be in state 1 for the operation *Pick_up* of class *Selector* to execute, we can either form the co-product of the two classes:

CLASS *Belt_Selector*
  EXTENDS *Belt*, *Selector*
HISTORY
    $\Box(Pick\_up \Rightarrow positioned = 1)$
END CLASS

or we can create a class which contains instances of the two classes and that promotes the *Pick_up* operation:

CLASS *BS_System*
OWNS
    selector : *Selector*;
    belt : *Belt*
OPERATIONS
    System_Pick_up : →
ACTIONS
    System_Pick_up ==> *selector.Pick_up*
HISTORY
    $\Box(System\_Pick\_up \Rightarrow belt.positioned = 1)$
END CLASS

The second approach is more verbose, but is conceptually more natural, and is more extendable (for instance, such global operations will usually involve a combination of operations on the subcomponents, such as to set the *positioned* attribute of the belt to 0 after a pick-up). It is also possible to make the execution of an operation conditional upon the state of a subordinate *Clock* object (so that waiting and time-outs can be modelled), or a superordinate clock (with a system being specified as a class containing instances of the subsystems controlled by the clock, together with the clock instance itself), and upon the state of a subordinate or superordinate sensor. If the subordinate choice is made:

```
CLASS  BS_System
OWNS
    . . . .
    clock  :  Clock
OPERATIONS
    . . . .
    Action1  :  →
ACTIONS
    . . . .
    Action1  ==>  ....
HISTORY
    □(Action1  ⇒  clock.Finished)
END CLASS
```

the implication is that the clock or sensor instance is local to the controlled system, and its state does not need to be seen by any other object instance (but derived information, involving the state of the controlled system, may still be passed upwards). Inheritance provides a natural way of expressing such locally controlled systems as extensions of systems with no such constraints over their action executions (i.e. passive versions of the system).

3.6   Design

3.6.1   Architectural Design: Top-down and Bottom-up Techniques

In building up a system we can choose some combination of *top-down* and *bottom-up* design techniques. Top-down design proceeds from the external services required of the application to be developed, and builds a hierarchy of classes which can provide objects to implement these services, in a layered manner. Bottom-up design proceeds from the 'lowest'-level classes, those concerned with the physical machine and operating system on which the application will run, upwards to the classes which directly implement the services required by the users. In either case, we must have an idea of the overall architecture of the system before we start the detailed architectural design, to avoid 'dead-ends' and waste of resources.

One notation form which is useful to support architectural design is the *configuration diagram*. In the object-oriented systems analysis of Shlaer and Mellor these are termed *Object Communication Models*. The version of these defined in [34] uses boxes to denote objects or object classes (in the case of B AMN, machines) and named solid lines connected to these boxes to denote services that the class provides, and dashed lines denoting services required by the class. For example, the specification part

IMPLEMENTATION *Ref2*

```
REFINES Ref1
IMPORTS Scalar
INVARIANT t = z
OPERATIONS
    enter(n) ≙
        VAR b IN
            b ← compare(n);
            IF b = TRUE THEN modify(n) END
        END;

    m ← maximum ≙
        BEGIN m ← value END
END
```

in B AMN has the configuration diagram shown in Figure 3.3. This helps us to
check that our intended system architecture is actually able to provide the services
that we require, and that its decomposition is internally consistent. Commonalities
between classes in different parts of a specification may also be recognised, allowing
the elimination of redundancy in the design.

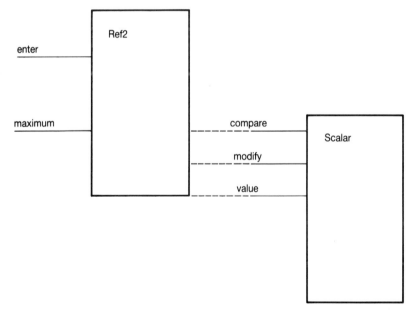

Figure 3.3: Configuration Diagram for Maximum Specification

A related form of documentation is the *usage* diagram, which indicates the various ways in which one class can refer to or use another class. The MooZ Unix
File System specification uses one such notation, with thin lines representing subclassing and thick lines the client/supplier relationships. For B, similar notations

have been proposed, with arrows pointing from the used to the using machines, with the arrow annotated with the name of the usage form. For Z^{++} the following notation is used:

$$C \longrightarrow \texttt{refined\_by} \longrightarrow D$$

for a refinement relation $C \sqsubseteq D$,

$$C \longrightarrow \texttt{inherited\_by} \longrightarrow D$$

for a general, possibly non-conformant, inheritance of C in D,

$$C \longrightarrow \texttt{supplier\_of} \longrightarrow D$$

for the use of C as a type in D, and

$$C \longrightarrow \texttt{instantiates} \longrightarrow D$$

for the use of C as a generic class which is instantiated to produce D.

Such notations, in graphical forms, can help to provide an overview of a specification and the internal dependencies between its parts. In particular, these diagrams can be checked against configuration diagrams to ensure consistency in a specification: if class D is required to utilise services from class C on the configuration diagram of a system, a suitable form of usage should exist from C to D in the usage diagram. It can also be checked if these usage relationships are the correct ones – for instance, if inheritance is being used in place of composition. Outline specifications could be generated from usage and configuration diagrams.

3.6.2   Top-down Design

Top-down design is a technique for developing designs whereby the designer starts at the highest level of the system and specifies in outline form the classes that provide the services required from the system. The implementation of these services (identified with methods of the classes) is, however, not detailed, as this will depend on classes lower in the design hierarchy. These classes may initially be specified as 'given sets' in Z terminology: no internal structure of the corresponding data types is assumed.

The result of this initial specification is a list of supplier classes and methods that are required of these classes by their clients, in addition to design specifications describing the form and general properties of the top-level methods. Such general properties could include algebraic constraints on the possible interactions between the methods (for instance, that $Pop\,(Push\,x)\,s = s$ for all stacks s), or constraints on the possible order in which these methods can occur (for instance, in a telephone specification, that $(\mathbf{op} = ConnectRequest \Rightarrow \bigcirc(\mathbf{op} = Ring))$).

The process is then recursively repeated for lower-level classes, until the level of basic types, integers and symbols, etc. or classes which can be re-used from existing developments or libraries are reached. In this book the Z^{++} specification of a learning system (Chapter 7) exemplifies this approach: the specification starts from a very general model of learning, and refines and specialises this specification by defining a hierarchy of classes below the top-level system.

For the Z-based languages, it is possible also to refine a given set to a schema type, whose attributes can be modified and accessed directly by classes which use a variable of this type, and then to replace this schema type by a class type with the components of the schema as its attributes and the required operations on this type (expressed previously as direct modification of attributes of instances of the schema) encapsulated as methods of the class. For example, one schema type used in an Object-Z specification of the sliding-window protocol [24] is as follows:

$$
\begin{array}{|l|}
\hline
\quad FwdSU \\
\hline
\quad msg : MSG \\
\quad sn : SeqNum \\
\hline
\end{array}
$$

An instance *fsu!* of this schema is then used as the output of an operation *AcceptAndTrans* of a class *SafeTransmitter* with the update:

$$
\begin{array}{|l|}
\hline
\quad AcceptAndTrans \\
\hline
\quad \Delta(msbuf, lastsn, retrans) \\
\quad msg? : MSG \\
\quad fsu! : FwdSU \\
\hline
\quad \ldots \\
\quad fsu!.msg = msg? \\
\quad fsu!.sn = lastsn' \\
\hline
\end{array}
$$

Other uses of instances of the schema have the same form, so it could be replaced by a class

$$
\begin{array}{|l|}
\hline
\quad FwdSU \\
\hline
\quad\quad
\begin{array}{|l|}
\hline
\quad msg : MSG \\
\quad sn : SeqNum \\
\hline
\end{array} \\
\\
\quad\quad
\begin{array}{|l|}
\hline
\quad Set \\
\hline
\quad \Delta(msg, sn) \\
\quad msg? : MSG \\
\quad sn? : SeqNum \\
\hline
\quad msg' = msg? \\
\quad sn' = sn? \\
\hline
\end{array} \\
\hline
\end{array}
$$

with *Set* being used in place of the above direct attribute assignments.

One possible negative consequence of the top-down approach is the production of system specifications which are unduly specialised: each supplier class may have only the features required of it by its clients in the specification. This limits the re-usability of such intermediate classes in future versions of the same system or in different ones. However, the specifier could endevour to generalise these classes where reasonable. If a domain analysis phase had been undertaken, classes related to domain concepts would already exist, and would be likely to be in a more general form than their specialisations in a particular specification.

3.6.3   Bottom-up Approaches

These techniques involve the specifier recognising the features of the low-level data components involved in a system, rather than the high-level features required of it. These low-level data components are then specified in a quite general way as classes, which are then extended or used to build higher levels of the specification until the global features required can be implemented.

The Object-Z specification of a mobile phone system in Chapter 5 exemplifies this approach: the subcomponents of the overall system are specified first and are composed into the entire system as a final step. A similar approach is used in the MooZ specification of the Unix file system, with the additional feature that commonalities between the several forms of table used in the specification have been made explicit and captured in a generic class.

A potential difficulty with this approach is that premature design decisions can be taken on supplier classes which limit the choices available for specification of their clients, thus leading to distorted and unclear system specifications. Revisions may be needed to restructure and rationalise the class hierarchy. As with top-down approaches, a clearer system and domain analysis could prevent these situations.

In practice, a combination of these two approaches would probably be the most effective, with rigid adherence to one or other leading to problems.

3.6.4   Design Partitioning

Inheritance gives a specifier the capability of partitioning the design of a system into many partial fragments, each of which fulfils some function on its own, but which needs to be extended with other 'deltas' in the terminology of Fresco [196] in order to meet the requirements of the entire system. Such partitioning can clearly be taken to excess: one could incrementally add one method at a time to a class, or incrementally add one conjunct to a method, by means of the forms of inheritance supported in the languages covered by this book.

Instead, a design should be partitioned in such a way that the design or specification fragments can be used and re-used in their own right, or such that these fragments represent a coherent concept which is important for understanding of

the system. Excessive partitioning simply adds to the burden of searching a specification library for re-usable components and to searching through the specification
to determine the definition of a descendant class from its ancestors [160, 195].

3.6.5 Recognition of Common Components

A further potential advantage of the object-oriented design style is the capability to
express common aspects of different parts of a system in an explicit form. There
are two principal mechanisms for this capability: inheritance and instantiation
of generic classes. These mechanisms have different roles. Inheritance allows a
designer to specify a class A which involves a set of features u which are a subset
of the sets v, w of features of other classes B, C, say (and for possibly more than
two 'using' classes, in addition). This means that A is by itself a coherent system
description, but that B and C can elaborate the definitions of the methods of A
to specify extra behaviour on the parts of their states which are not included in A.
They can, in addition, define new types, attributes, functions, and methods. The B
notation, whilst not fully object-oriented, does define several forms of inheritance
via the clauses *SEES*, *USES* and *INCLUDES* of abstract machines [1], which allow
variables from inherited machines to be accessed in the invariant and operations
of the inheriting machine.

Parameterisation is, however, a means by which commonalities concerning the
use of supplier classes within two or more classes can be expressed. The designer
recognises that some classes, A, B, say, perform essentially identical operations
upon respective client classes C and D. This means that this commonality can
be expressed as a generic class G with a parameter X in place of C and D. If a
mechanism for constrained genericity is available, it should also be specified that
X provides at least the services which A and B require of their clients. Then we
can simply write $A = G[C]$, $B = G[D]$, and maintainability has been enhanced: a
change request involving both A and B can be translated into one involving only
G. In many cases, the details of the generic parameter are almost irrelevant to the
operation of the parameterised class. For instance, a class encapsulating a list of
natural numbers is very similar to one encapsulating lists of strings, if the internal
details of the list elements are not used. Both of these classes can be generalised
to a generic *List*[X] class, and individually defined as *List*[$\mathbb{N}$] or *List*[*String*].

In the MooZ specification of the Unix Filing System there are several classes
defined by means of instantiation of a generic class *Table*[*ID, VALUE*] with various parameters. This produces a conceptual simplicity, in that once we have
understood the basic mechanisms of *Table* we will understand the common features of the four instantiations *StorageSystem*, *ChannelSystem*, *AccessSystem* and
NamingSystem of this class.

3.7   Refinement

Refinement, or reification, is the process of moving from an abstract specification language (which will use abstract data types, or set-theoretic operations on sets and sequences) into a conventional procedural language, via a sequence of transformations which increase in some sense the 'concreteness' of the specification. Refinement for object-oriented languages has a particularly close relationship with type compatibility: if class D is a refinement of class C, it should be possible to use an instance of D in place of an instance of C – that is, all the facilities provided by C are also provided by D, possibly via some syntactic translation, and with some 'improvement' in terms of determinism. Given a formal semantics for a specification language, laws relating inheritance, refinement and compositionality (use of classes as parameters or as types within another class) can be derived. These will allow a designer to rewrite a class into an equivalent form, to, for example, make it conceptually clearer, or to put it into strict command/query form [142], or to replace computed functions of the state by new attributes. Critical to system adaptability will be laws concerning the situations under which refinements of supplier classes result in refinements of client classes: enabling a refining modification to be made to a supplier class without requiring changes to its clients. Z^{++}, for example, provides laws which state that standard forms of promotion preserve refinement, and that *strict* inheritance preserves refinement [115]. More complex forms of refinement have been defined for the concurrent systems specifiable by Object-Z [48].

Another process required during refinement, in the Z-based languages, is that of moving invariant properties into methods. It may be the case that invariant properties of a class are specified only in the invariant of that class, which is used (implicitly) to require the methods of the class to preserve it. This is a common mechanism in Z, where a state schema

```
┌─ State ────────────────────────────────────────
│  v : V
│ ─────────────────
│  θ(v)
└────────────────────────────────────────────────
```

can include an invariant $\theta(v)$ which is automatically conjoined to the pre-condition of any operation which acts on the state, and which leads to $\theta(v')$ being conjoined to the post-condition (as with Eiffel class invariants [142]). For procedural implementation, such predicates must be replaced or supplemented by explicit functionality within the methods which ensures the preservation of the invariant condition. The B method, for instance, requires the operation specifications of an abstract machine to already explicitly preserve the invariant of that machine at the initial specification stage.

There are usually conditions of internal consistency upon a class which require that the actual pre-condition of an operation (the set of states and inputs over which its behaviour is well defined) is implied by the explicit pre-condition of the

,operation – so that the method can never be applied in a invalid state if users of the class adhere to this pre-condition. Z^{++}, OOZE and B allow such explicit pre-conditions to be declared, although in the other Z-based languages these are part of the schemas defining methods and it is up to the specifier to make these explicit by a notational convention. In refinement, pre-conditions can be replaced by a conditional statement which performs some exception action and returns an error message in the case that the pre-condition is violated. In a language such as Eiffel, pre-conditions could be retained in the actual code.

3.8 Conclusion

We have illustrated some of the rich variety of object-oriented design facilities which it is possible to use in the languages described in this book. These appear to be much more expressive than those available for Z or VDM, and indeed, attempts at design in Z and VDM, even for applications such as security systems [27], often seem, in retrospect, to be attempts at object-oriented or object-based design. Once we are able to successfully integrate informal notations and design techniques with the formal specification notations, we obtain a twofold benefit in allowing precise semantics to be added to informal notations, and in allowing user-validatable and comprehensible notations to be used to support design and explanation of the formal specifications.

Chapter 4

The Unix Filing System: A MooZ Specification

Silvio Lemos Meira[1], Ana Lúcia C. Cavalcanti and Cássio Souza Santos

We present an object-oriented specification of the Unix Filing System using MooZ, an object-oriented extension to Z. A MooZ specification is a set of hierarchically related classes with objects as values whose types are classes. A powerful message-passing mechanism allows communication between objects. MooZ is aimed at the specification of large software systems and constitutes an effective framework for module definition and management.

We emphasise the benefits of using object-oriented concepts and MooZ, more specifically, in a brief comparison between MooZ, plain Z and other object-oriented extensions, using the filing system specification as an illustration.

4.1 Introduction

Z is now recognised as a specification language that offers a powerful modularisation mechanism, using schemas and the schema calculus. However, it is now felt that those features alone are not enough to structure very large specifications.

A number of proposals have been put forward in the last few years to overcome this problem. That is the case of **Zc** [175], which introduces chapters and documents, along with import and export mechanisms, as a way to allow the modularisation of large specifications. An example of its use can be seen in [10].

More recently, Z extensions have centred on the object-oriented paradigm, which is deemed to be more suitable for the construction of fairly large software systems.

---

[1]Research reported in this paper was supported by The British Council, IBM Brasil, CNPq and The Pernambuco State Science Foundation (FACEPE) and was partly conducted when this author was a Visiting Research Fellow at The Computing Laboratory, University of Kent at Canterbury, UK. Author's e-mail address: `srlm@di.ufpe.br`.

Proposals are based on the lessons learned from software design and implementation and consist of the introduction of object-oriented mechanisms, in particular those of inheritance, encapsulation and polymorphism, which together allow the building of well-structured specifications with a good degree of modularisation, re-usability, extensibility and, last but not least, readability.

Simple as it seems, the idea of combining object-orientation with Z led to a group of different proposals [24, 104, 135, 183] which differ somewhat in the semantics of the object-oriented frame wrapping the Z kernel. Such languages look similar from the syntactic point of view, but there are significant differences in their semantics.

Features common to most extensions include:

- Z is extended to allow the definition of classes as these are conceived in object-oriented languages. Classes allow the definition of the structure and behaviour of similar objects. In particular, classes can be parameterised.
- Classes can be extended using inheritance.
- Operations can be polymorphically defined.
- Objects communicate through message-passing.

The way in which such features are added to Z varies from one extension to another but they are all present to some extent. Object orientation supports, in a number of ways, the use of formal specification in the development of large software systems. Specifications, as well as programs, can be naturally extended and re-used. In addition, the object-oriented structure given to a specification makes it easier to maintain and to be used as a reference for an object-oriented implementation.

In what follows, we give an overview of MooZ (for Modular Object-oriented Z) and an informal presentation of the Unix Filing System, followed by its MooZ specification, where characteristics of the language and related issues are discussed in more detail. Finally, in the light of the specification, we discuss the benefits obtained by using MooZ when compared to other approaches, including plain Z.

4.2   MooZ

This brief description of MooZ has an emphasis on the form of a MooZ specification and its object-oriented features. Further details are given in Section 4.3, when describing the Unix Filing System. A full account of the language is given in [136][2]. The presentation assumes some knowledge of Z [182].

As mentioned earlier, the object-oriented paradigm was chosen for MooZ because it incorporates important mechanisms of modularisation and abstraction. These include the concepts of object, class and inheritance:

- Objects are collections of operations which define a behaviour and have an internal state.

---

[2] Available via anonymous FTP from `gctc.itep.br`, `pub/MooZ/MooZ.ps.Z`

- A class specifies a set of objects with the same structure.
- Inheritance allows the re-use of the behaviour of one or more classes (superclasses) in the definition of new ones (subclasses). Moreover, inheritance provides second-order sharing, management and manipulation of behaviour, complementing first-order management of objects by classes.

These concepts allow for powerful methods of defining and managing modules. They have a high conceptual modelling power and applications can be viewed as objects which communicate by means of messages, allowing systems to be specified in a modular and incremental fashion.

To achieve the benefits of object orientation, it is important to use the same paradigm for specification, design and implementation of applications. The process of transforming a MooZ specification into an object-oriented program is more natural than doing the same for a Z specification.

A MooZ specification consists of a set of class definitions related by some hierarchy. One of these classes is named after the system being defined. The state and behaviour of the objects of this class specify the system under analysis. A MooZ class also specifies an abstract data type. The general form of a class is

Class $\langle Class - Name \rangle$
    givensets $\langle type - name - list \rangle$
    superclasses
          $\langle class - reference - list \rangle$
          $\langle auxiliary - definitions \rangle$
    private $\langle definition - name - list \rangle$
      or
    public $\langle definition - name - list \rangle$
    constants
          $\langle axiomatic - description - list \rangle$
          $\langle auxiliary - definitions \rangle$
    state
          $\langle anonymous - schema \rangle$ or $\langle constraint \rangle$
          $\langle auxiliary - definitions \rangle$
    initialstates
          $\langle schema \rangle$
          $\langle auxiliary - definitions \rangle$
    operations
          $\langle definition - list \rangle$
EndClass $\langle ClassName \rangle$.

The **superclasses** clause introduces the names of inherited classes allowing the renaming of inherited definitions and the association of given sets (in the inherited classes) to other types, thus instantiating generic classes.

The **givensets** clause introduces names of given sets in the class, which may serve the purpose of abstraction or generality. New classes can be defined by associating types to such parameters.

The **private** clause allows definitions to be hidden from the interface of the objects or of the class whereas the **public** clause puts definitions into the interface. Such clauses are also available when declaring superclasses in a **superclasses** clause.

The **constants** clause introduces global constants by means of axiomatic descriptions and it is the proper place to define the constants necessary for the definition of state and operations.

The state components in a class definition (the state of its instances) are the state components of each of its superclasses and the components introduced in the class itself, if any. Such components are introduced in an anonymous (nameless) schema defined in the **state** clause. For instance, a state with components a, b of type A, B, respectively, and invariant p can be defined by

$$
\begin{array}{|l}
\hline
a \; : \; A \\
b \; : \; B \\
\hline
p \\
\hline
\end{array}
$$

As the state as a whole does not have a name, we cannot use Δ and Ξ as in traditional Z style. Therefore schemas like

$$
\begin{array}{|l}
\underline{\quad \Delta(a, b) \qquad\qquad\qquad\qquad\qquad\qquad} \\
a, a' \; : \; A \\
b, b' \; : \; B \\
\hline
p \\
p' \\
\hline
\end{array}
$$

and

$$
\begin{array}{|l}
\underline{\quad \Xi(a, b) \qquad\qquad\qquad\qquad\qquad\qquad} \\
\Delta(a, b) \\
\hline
a = a' \\
b = b' \\
\hline
\end{array}
$$

that represent Δ- and Ξ-lists, respectively, are implicitly defined. Thus, the state components modified are separately declared from those only referenced in the definition of the operations. State components not mentioned in either a Δ- or a Ξ-list are not modified and cannot be referred to.

A subclass may also introduce new constraints on the state components of its superclasses.

The **initialstates** clause introduces one or more schemas defining the possible initial values of the state components. Schemas defined in such a clause are logically related to those with the same name defined in the same clause in the superclasses by an **and** logical operator. In other words, initial states may be incrementally defined.

The operations of a class are those of each superclass plus the operations defined in its **operations** clause. Operations defined in superclasses can be redefined. An operation O of a superclass SC can be referred to as $O.SC$ to avoid ambiguities, whenever necessary.

An operation overrides any other previously defined operation with the same name in a superclass or even in the same class where it was defined. Incremental definition of an operation must be explicitly stated using schema inclusion.

Auxiliary operations, functions and types can be defined in the **state**, **initialstates**, **operations**, **superclasses** or **constants** clauses. In addition, a definition can be made private, in which case it is not visible to clients of the class, although it can be seen by its heirs and used in definitions therein.

An object is represented by an identifier whose type is the class from which it is an instance. Objects communicate by means of messages. The notation $o\ m$ means that message m is being sent to object o.

The messages an object can answer are specified in its class. These are the state components, the schemas defining operations (schemas including Δ- or Ξ-lists) and semantic operations. The answer to a state component message is its value and to a schema message the schema definition itself.

Semantic operations are defined upon instances of the class where they are specified. When applied to an object, they return a possibly modified instance of it, in contrast to the expected response from a schema message.

Given sets, free and schema types, abbreviations and axiomatic descriptions correspond to class messages because they are state independent. The notation used for a class message is the same as that for objects. The answer to a given set, free type, schema or abbreviation message is the type specified by the corresponding definition. The answer to a constant message is its value.

4.3   The Unix Filing System

Here we give an informal description of the Unix Filing System as specified in [86] using plain Z.

Files are sequences of bytes which are basic objects in the system. They can be accessed using their names, which are defined when they are created. Different names can be associated to a given file after it has been created, and files can be renamed and grouped in directories. The names of all files in a given directory can be listed. Files are also accessed through channels for certain operations.

The following operations are available:

- Create – creates a new file with the given name and inserts the file in the filing system.
- Destroy – Removes the file associated with the provided name if there is not another name or a channel associated with it.
- Open – associates a new channel to a file. Files must be opened before being read or written to.
- Close – removes from the system a channel associated to a file.
- Read – reads a file from a given position for a number of bytes.

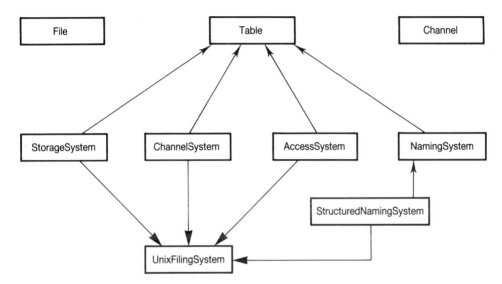

Figure 4.1: Class Hierarchy

- Write – writes to a file from a given position.
- Link – associates a new name to a file. The name is given along with another one already associated to the file. Thereafter the file can be referred to by also using the new name.
- Unlink – removes the association of a name to a file in the system.
- Seek – sets the position of a channel associated to a file to an absolute value. The channel identifier must be provided.
- Size – Returns the size of the file associated to the given name.
- Ls – lists the names of all files which belong to a given directory.
- Move – changes the name of a file and it may also imply changing the directory in which the file is located.

These operations will be incrementally defined in the classes specified in the next section and are listed in class *UnixFilingSystem*, where their final definition can be found.

4.4   The Formal Specification

The presentation in this section assumes no previous knowledge of either MooZ or of the Unix Filing System. However, it assumes some familiarity with the Z notation [182].

This is not what we consider a large software specification. However, it will give some grasp of MooZ pragmatics and the advantages of using an object-oriented approach in specifying a system. Figure 4.1 shows the hierarchical class structure of the specification. Thin lines represent subclassing (if class A points to B then A is a subclass of B) whereas thick ones represent the client relationship (B's state has a component of type A).

The classes *File* and *Channel* specify the structure and behaviour of files and channels, respectively, the basic objects with which the system deals.

Table is an abstract class that groups the definition of common characteristics of the four subsystems of the Unix Filing System, namely, the Storage, Channel, Access and Naming Systems. The classes *StorageSystem*, *ChannelSystem*, *AccessSystem* and *NamingSystem* define these systems, respectively, and are subclasses of *Table*.

The Access System defined by *AccessSystem* relates the Storage and Channel Systems to provide sequential access to files.

NamingSystem specifies a linear name space for the files which is then extended by *StructuredNamingSystem* to specify the directory structure of the Unix Filing System.

Finally, *UnixFilingSystem* is a combination of the four subsystems mentioned above and defines the Unix Filing System as a whole. Most of the operations of the system are already defined at this point and need only to be promoted to the system level.

In what follows, we give the specification of each class in detail with comments and explanations using a literate specification style.

4.4.1   Class *File*

Files are modelled as sequences of bytes, which in turn are elements of the given set $BYTE$.

Class *File*

givensets $BYTE$

The state of a file has a sole component which is an instance of a class obtained from the primitive generic class Seq^3 by associating its parameter to the given set $BYTE$. This type is given the abbreviated name *Bytes* and represents $BYTE$ sequences.

---

[3] An alias for *FiniteSequence*, see Appendix.

state

$$\boxed{\text{file} \; : \; \text{Bytes}}$$

$Bytes == Seq\ BYTE$

The initial state of a file is given in terms of the schema defining the initial state of sequences, which is accessed by sending the *Init* message to *file*.

initialstates

```
┌─── CreateFile ────────────────────
│ Δ(file)
├────────────────────────────────────
│ file Init
└────────────────────────────────────
```

Initial state schemas can be given input values so as to properly initialise the contents of receiver objects. This is not needed for objects of class *Seq* and the *Init* schema has no parameters, neither does the schema *CreateFile* in the current class.

operations

In the *Read* operation we specify that no changes are performed on the state of a file, by including *file* in a Ξ-list. Explicit inclusion of all the components referenced in an operation in Ξ- and Δ-lists improves readability, leaving no doubt on the way the operation is intended to affect the state. State components not mentioned in the predicate of the schema need not be included in any list and are not modified.

Reading a number of bytes (*length?*) starting at a given position (*offset?*) is specified by sending *Seq*'s subsequencing message $((\_,\_))$ to *file*, resulting in a subsequence of the receiver from the position specified by the first parameter, *offset?*, and of size given by the second parameter, *length?*, if that does not exceed the length of the sequence receiving the message; otherwise, the sequence returned is smaller than the one requested. Whatever the case, *data!* is the sequence of bytes actually read.

```
┌─── Read ──────────────────────────
│ Ξ(file)
│ offset?, length?  : N
│ data!  : Bytes
├────────────────────────────────────
│ data! = file (offset?, length?)
└────────────────────────────────────
```

Write includes the state component *file*, which is changed by the operation, in a Δ-list in the declarative part of the schema. A sequence of bytes (*data?*) is written in the file starting at *offset?*.

```
┌─ Write ─────────────────────────────────────────────
│ Δ(file)
│ offset?  : N
│ data?  : Bytes
├─────────────────────────────────────────────────────
│ file' = file(1, offset? − 1) ⌢
│         (data? ⌢ file(offset? + data? len, file len))
└─────────────────────────────────────────────────────
```

The specification of *Seq*'s $(\_,\_)$ operation, given in the Appendix, guarantees that if the value of the first parameter exceeds the length of the receiver, an empty sequence is returned. Finally, *Size* returns the size of a file and has the trivial specification

```
┌─ Size ──────────────────────────────────────────────
│ Ξ(file)
│ size! :  N
├─────────────────────────────────────────────────────
│ size! = file  len
└─────────────────────────────────────────────────────
```

EndClass *File*.

4.4.2   Class *Channel*

Channels are used to retain the current position of an open file and, together with files, are basic objects the system deals with.

Class *Channel*

Instances of *Channel* have as state the current position in which the file associated to the channel was left after initialisation, reading or writing. A channel is initialised by *CreateChannel*, defined in the **initialstates** clause below.

state

```
┌─────────────────────────────────────────────────────
│ posn  : N
└─────────────────────────────────────────────────────
```

initialstates

```
┌─ CreateChannel ─────────────────────────────────────
│ Δ(posn)
├─────────────────────────────────────────────────────
│ posn' = 0
└─────────────────────────────────────────────────────
```

operations

Advance is a generic operation used later by *UnixFilingSystem* to specify reading and writing operations on files. It adds the length of *data?*, a *Bytes* object, to *posn*. The type of *data?* is the result of a message to a class, *File*, which, in this case, returns a type.

```
┌─ Advance ──────────────────────────────────────────────
│ data? : File Bytes
│ Δ(posn)
├────────────────────────────────────────────────────────
│ posn' = posn + (data? len)
└────────────────────────────────────────────────────────
```

Type definitions such as *Bytes* in class *File* are public and can be accessed from other classes by sending a message to the class where they are defined. The decision to define a type in a given class must be based on how closely related it is to the definitions in that class. Alternatively, an abstract class can be defined to group public type definitions as well as constants and other definitions (like auxiliary functions) which one wants to be public. This is a common practice in object-oriented programming languages and is based on the idea that classes are not only data type abstractions but also modularisation units that can be used to partition the set of public definitions regardless of any data abstraction [17].

The *Seek* operation equates the value of the state component *posn* to that of its input *newposn?*.

```
┌─ Seek ─────────────────────────────────────────────────
│ Δ(posn)
│ newposn? : N
├────────────────────────────────────────────────────────
│ posn' = newposn?
└────────────────────────────────────────────────────────
```

EndClass *Channel.*

4.4.3   Class *Table*

Table is an abstract class which is further refined in the definition of the Storage, Channel, Access and Naming Systems, which are specified as tables associating keys to values. Definitions common to these systems are grouped in this class. Its only state component is an instance of class *Map*, a primitive class specified in the Appendix.

Class *Table*

The values in the domain and co-domain of the state component *store* are taken from the given sets *ID* and *VALUE* respectively.

givensets *ID, VALUE*

The *Take* operation is made private; therefore, the *Take* message cannot be sent to an instance of either *Table* or its subclasses. *Take* could, however, be made public in a subclass, using the **public** subclause of the **superclasses** clause.

private *Take*

state

$$store \: : Map \ ID \ VALUE$$

The *store*, an instance of *Map* (see Appendix), is initially empty, and this is guaranteed by the specification below:

initialstates

```
___ Init _____
Δ(store)
store' Init
```

There is no conflict in using *store*'s *Init* to define *Table*'s *Init* because the former is clearly one of *Map*'s messages.

operations

The operations defined here and re-used in the definition of the four subsystems allow the inclusion and removal of values, as well as table look-up.

```
___ Insert _____
Δ(store)
id? : ID
value? : VALUE
_____
id? ∉ store dom
store' = store ⊕ {id? ↦ value?}
```

```
___ Remove _____
Δ(store)
id? : ID
_____
id? ∈ store dom
store' = store ◁ {id?}
```

```
___ LookUp _____
Ξ(store)
id? : ID
value! : VALUE
_____
id? ∈ store dom
value! = store(id?)
```

An additional definition is provided to be used as a framing schema in the definition of operations in the subclasses.

```
___ Take _____
Δ(store)
id? : ID
value, value' : VALUE
_____
id? ∈ store dom
value = store(id?)
store' = store ⊕ {id? ↦ value'}
```

The following auxiliary definition is used in the subclasses. It says that there is no key associated to the value given as an input.

```
__NoKeyToValue_____
  Ξ(store)
  value?  : VALUE
_____
  value? ∉ store ran
```

EndClass *Table*.

4.4.4 Class *StorageSystem*

This class refines its superclass, *Table*, by instantiating its type parameters to *FID* (another given set from which file identifiers are taken) and *File*, defined earlier.

A Storage System describes the aggregation of files in the system as it associates a unique identifier to each of them.

Class *StorageSystem*

givensets *FID*

Some operations defined in the superclass are not to be available in the public interface of an instance of this class. Such is said in the **private** part of the **superclasses** clause below.

superclasses *Table(ID\FID, VALUE\File)*

private *LookUp, NoKeyToValue*

Listing public and private definitions serves to emphasise those which describe the behaviour of an object with respect to the external world and the ones used as auxiliary (private) definitions.

operations

The insertion of a new file in the table is specified by *Insert*, re-using the operation *Insert* defined in class *Table* with properly renamed components.

```
__Insert_____
  Insert(id?\fid!, value?\file)
_____
  ∃ file' :  File • file CreateFile ∧ file = file'
```

We then hide *file* in the final definition of the operation, because it should not be seen from the outside:

$Insert \mathrel{\hat=} Insert \setminus (file)$

Remove simply removes a file from the storage system, and is trivially defined as

$Remove \triangleq Remove(id?\backslash fid?)$

Reading a file is specified by renaming *Take*'s *id?* to *fid?* and introducing the receiver *file* for *Read*:

$$\begin{array}{l}\text{\_\_\_\_}Read\text{_____}\\ Take(id?\backslash fid?, value\backslash file)\\ file\ Read \end{array}$$

Both *file* and *file'* are hidden in *Read*'s final definition: they are accessed through *fid?* and need not, or rather must not, be visible from the outside.

$Read \triangleq Read\backslash(file, file')$

In a similar way, *Write* is defined as:

$$\begin{array}{l}\text{\_\_\_\_}Write\text{_____}\\ Take(id?\backslash fid?, value\backslash file)\\ file\ Write \end{array}$$

$Write \triangleq Write\backslash(file, file')$

and *Size* returns the size of the file associated to the identifier provided as input.

$$\begin{array}{l}\text{\_\_\_\_}Size\text{_____}\\ Take(id?\backslash fid?, value\backslash file)\\ file\ Size \end{array}$$

$Size \triangleq Size\backslash(file, file')$

EndClass *StorageSystem.*

4.4.5   Class *ChannelSystem*

Again, this class is defined in terms of *Table*, with *ID* and *VALUE* associated to the given set *CID* and *Channel*. A Channel System aggregates channels in the system by associating a unique channel identifier taken from *CID* to each channel.

Class *ChannelSystem*

givensets *CID*

superclasses $Table(ID\backslash CID, VALUE\backslash Channel)$

   private $LookUp, NoKeyToValue$

operations

To open a channel a properly initialised channel is inserted in the channel table.

$$
\begin{array}{l}
\underline{\quad Insert\quad\quad\quad\quad\quad\quad\quad\quad\quad\quad\quad\quad\quad\quad\quad\quad\quad\quad\quad\quad\quad} \\
Insert(id?\backslash cid!, value?\backslash channel) \\
\hline
\exists\, channel' : Channel \bullet channel\ CreateChannel \wedge channel' = channel \\
\end{array}
$$

$Insert \triangleq Insert\backslash(channel)$

Remove simply removes a channel from the table and is defined straightforwardly in terms of the superclass operation.

$Remove \triangleq Remove(id?\backslash cid?)$

The following definitions promote operations defined in class *Channel* to the *ChannelSystem* level.

$$
\begin{array}{l}
\underline{\quad Seek\quad\quad\quad\quad\quad\quad\quad\quad\quad\quad\quad\quad\quad\quad\quad\quad\quad\quad\quad\quad\quad\quad\quad} \\
Take(id?\backslash cid?, value\backslash channel) \\
channel\ Seek \\
\end{array}
$$

$Seek \triangleq Seek\backslash(channel, channel')$

$$
\begin{array}{l}
\underline{\quad Advance\quad\quad\quad\quad\quad\quad\quad\quad\quad\quad\quad\quad\quad\quad\quad\quad\quad\quad\quad\quad\quad} \\
Take(id?\backslash cid?, value\backslash channel) \\
channel\ Advance \\
\end{array}
$$

$Advance \triangleq Advance\backslash(channel, channel')$

EndClass *ChannelSystem*.

4.4.6   Class *AccessSystem*

AccessSystem is also defined as a subclass of *Table* and appears thus:

Class *AccessSystem*

givensets CID, FID

We must hide *NoKeyToValue* from the public interface, but *LookUp* is public, for it will be sent as a message to an instance of the current class in the definition of the read and write operations in class *UnixFilingSystem*. The instantiation in

superclasses $Table(ID\backslash CID, VALUE\backslash FID)$

$\qquad\qquad$ **private** $NoKeyToValue$

gives us a state which is a table relating channel to file identifiers. *Insert*, *Remove* and *LookUp* are inherited and we just do some renaming:

operations

$Insert \triangleq Insert(id?\backslash cid?, value?\backslash fid?)$

$Remove \triangleq Remove(id?\backslash cid?)$

$LookUp \triangleq LookUp(id?\backslash cid?, value!\backslash fid!)$

The auxiliary definition given below will be used as a pre-condition when defining *Destroy* in class *UnixFilingSystem*. It could have been defined there but, as it has no dependencies with respect to definitions in a class other than this one, it is natural to define it here.

$FileHasNoChannel \triangleq NoKeyToValue(value?\backslash fid?)$

EndClass *AccessSystem*.

4.4.7   Class *NamingSystem*

A Naming System allows the association of names to file identifiers. File names are selected from the given set *NAME*. A given identifier can be associated to different names, thus allowing the creation of links to files.

Class *NamingSystem*

givensets *NAME*, *FID*

superclasses $Table(ID\backslash NAME, VALUE\backslash FID)$

$\qquad\qquad$ **private** $NoKeyToValue$

operations

In addition to the inherited operations for creating, removing and accessing files,

$Insert \triangleq Insert(id?\backslash name?, value?\backslash fid?)$

$Remove \triangleq Remove(id?\backslash name?)$

$LookUp \triangleq LookUp(id?\backslash name?, value!\backslash fid!)$

we have operations for linking a new name to the file identifier already associated to a name:

$Link \triangleq LookUp(name?\backslash oldname?); \; Insert(name?\backslash newname?, fid?\backslash fid!)$

Link is specified using schema composition, where the final state of the first schema becomes the initial state of the second one:

$Link \triangleq Link\backslash(fid!)$

and for changing the name to which an identifier is associated within the system:

$Move \triangleq Link; \; Remove(name?\backslash oldname?)$

The definition below is similar to *AccessSystem*'s *FileHasNoChannel* and will be used to define the *Destroy* operation in *UnixFilingSystem*.

$FileHasNoName \triangleq NoKeyToValue(value?\backslash fid?)$

EndClass *NamingSystem*.

4.4.8 Class *StructuredNamingSystem*

This class extends its sole superclass to allow names to be structured and to give the system the ability to manipulate directory names.

Class *StructuredNamingSystem*

Structured names are sequences of single names selected from the given set *SINGLENAME*.

givensets *SINGLENAME*

superclasses *NamingSystem*($NAME\backslash STRUCTUREDNAME$)

$STRUCTUREDNAME == Seq \; SINGLENAME$

FromDirectory is just an auxiliary definition used in the *LS* operation definition and is made private.

private *FromDirectory*

The state schema introduces one more state component, *dnames*, which is a derived component obtained from *store*, the table associating structured names to file identifiers (because the inherited given set *NAME* is now associated to

STRUCTUREDNAME). *dnames* is a subset of *store*'s domain and includes the 'front' of every structured name in the system.

The front of a structured name (the front of a sequence) is obtained by removing its last element, with the empty sequence having no front. This behaviour is specified in *Seq* (see Appendix). Therefore, *dnames* is the set of all directory names.

The predicate part of the anonymous schema defining the state says that every file or directory, except root, whose name is the empty sequence, must appear in some directory.

state

$$
\begin{array}{l}
\textit{dnames } : \mathbb{P} \, \textit{STRUCTUREDNAME} \\
\hline
\{s \; : (\textit{dnames} \cup \textit{store dom}) \bullet s \; \textit{front}\} \subseteq \textit{dnames} \\
\textit{dnames} \subseteq \textit{store dom}
\end{array}
$$

operations

The *LS* operation shows the contents of a directory, given its name. *last* returns the last element of a sequence. The auxiliary definition *FromDirectory* returns all structured names whose front is equal to the directory name given to *LS*.

$$
\begin{array}{l}
\underline{\quad LS\underline{\quad\quad\quad\quad\quad\quad\quad\quad\quad\quad\quad\quad\quad\quad}} \\
\Xi(\textit{store}, \textit{dnames}) \\
\textit{dir?} \; : \textit{STRUCTUREDNAME} \\
\textit{contents!} \; : \mathbb{P} \, \textit{SINGLENAME} \\
\hline
\textit{dir?} \in \textit{dnames} \\
\textit{contents!} = \{n \; : \textit{FromDirectory}(\textit{dir?}, \textit{store}) \bullet n \; \textit{last}\}
\end{array}
$$

$$
\begin{array}{l}
\textit{FromDirectory} : \quad \textit{STRUCTUREDNAME} \times \textit{Map STRUCTUREDNAME FID} \\
\qquad\qquad\qquad\qquad \to \mathbb{P} \, \textit{STRUCTUREDNAME} \\
\hline
\forall \, \textit{dir} : \textit{STRUCTUREDNAME}; \; \textit{store} : \; \textit{Map STRUCTUREDNAME FID} \bullet \\
\quad \textit{FromDirectory}(\textit{dir}, \textit{store}) = \{n \; : \textit{store dom} \bullet n \; \textit{front} = \textit{dir}\}
\end{array}
$$

EndClass *StructuredNamingSystem*.

4.4.9 Class *UnixFilingSystem*

The complete filing system is now specified as a composition of the four previously described subsystems.

Class *UnixFilingSystem*

This class has no superclasses and its state has four components, one for each of the subsystems described so far. The predicate relating the components is the state invariant, saying that every channel identifier stored in the Access System must have an entry in the Channel System and that every file identifier referenced in the Access and Naming Systems must also have an entry in the Storage System.

state

ss : *StorageSystem*
cs : *ChannelSystem*
as : *AccessSystem*
ns : *StructuredNamingSystem*
$\forall\, cid \in as\ store\ dom \bullet cid \in cs\ store\ dom$
$\forall\, fid \in (as\ store\ ran \cup ns\ store\ ran) \bullet fid \in ss\ store\ dom$

The meaning of, for example, *as store dom* is the same as (*as store*) *dom*, which is the set of all channel identifiers stored in the Access System.

initialstates

Init
$\Delta(ss, cs, as, ns)$
$ss\ Init$
$cs\ Init$
$as\ Init$
$ns\ Init$

operations

Insert creates a new file and associates a name and a newly created channel to it. The operation expects a file name as input and the internally created channel identifier is returned as output.

$$Insert \;\hat{=}\; \Delta(ss, cs, as, ns) \wedge ss\ Insert \wedge cs\ Insert \wedge$$
$$as\ Insert(cid?\backslash cid!, fid?\backslash fid!) \wedge ns\ Insert(fid?\backslash fid!)$$

The output value *fid!* is hidden in the final definition of *Insert*. Thus, this operation has *name?* as input and *cid!* as output.

$$Insert \;\hat{=}\; Insert\backslash(fid!)$$

The expansion of *Insert* is given below, to clarify the meaning of message-sending.

```
┌─ Insert ─────────────────────────────────────────────────────
│ Δ(ss, cs, as, ns)
│ cid! : ChannelSystem CID
│ name? : StructuredNamingSystem STRUCTUREDNAME
├──────────────────────────────────────────────────────────────
│ ∃ fid! : StorageSystem FID •
│    fid! ∉ ss store dom ∧
│    cid! ∉ cs store dom ∧
│    cid! ∉ as store dom ∧
│    name? ∉ ns store dom ∧
│    (∃ file : File •
│       (∃ file' : File • file' fileseq = {} ∧ file = file') ∧
│       ss' store = ss store ⊕ {fid! ↦ file}) ∧
│    (∃ channel : Channel •
│       (∃ channel' : Channel • channel' posn = 0 ∧ channel = channel') ∧
│       cs' store = cs store ⊕ {cid! ↦ channel}) ∧
│    as' store = as store ⊕ {cid! ↦ fid!} ∧
│    ns' store = ns store ⊕ {name? ↦ fid!}
└──────────────────────────────────────────────────────────────
```

Open defines how the file associated to *name?* is opened. The file identifier is found using *LookUp* and a channel identifier associated to a newly created channel is associated to it through *Insert* in class *AccessSystem*. The channel identifier is given as output.

$$Open \; \hat{=} \; \Delta(ns, cs, as) \wedge ns \; LookUp \wedge cs \; Insert \wedge as \; Insert(cid?\backslash cid!, fid?\backslash fid!)$$

$$Open \; \hat{=} \; Open\backslash(fid!)$$

Destroy removes a file from the system if there is no name or channel associated to it.

$$Destroy \; \hat{=} \; \Delta(ns, cs, ss) \wedge ns \; FileHasNoName \wedge cs \; FileHasNoChannel \wedge ss \; Remove$$

Operations for reading from and writing to a file are built on top of those defined in the subsystems.

$$Read \; \hat{=} \; \Delta(as, ss, cs) \wedge as \; LookUp \wedge ss \; Read(fid?\backslash fid!) \wedge cs \; Advance(data?\backslash data!)$$

$$Read \; \hat{=} \; Read\backslash(fid!)$$

and the expanded version of *Read* appears as follows:

_____ *Read*_____
| $\Xi(as)$
| $\Delta(ss, cs)$
| $cid? : AccessSystem\ CID$
| $offset?, length? : \mathbb{N}$
| $data! : File\ Bytes$
| _____
| $\exists fid! : AccessSystem\ FID \bullet$
| $cid? \in as\ store\ dom \wedge$
| $fid! = (as\ store)(cid?) \wedge$
| $(\exists file, file' : File \bullet$
| $fid! \in ss\ store\ dom \wedge$
| $file = (ss\ store)(fid!) \wedge$
| $ss'\ store = ss\ store \oplus \{fid! \mapsto file'\} \wedge$
| $file\ file = file'\ file \wedge$
| $data! = (file\ file)(offset?, length)) \wedge$
| $(\exists channel, channel' : Channel \bullet$
| $cid? \in cs\ store\ dom \wedge$
| $channel = (cs\ store)(cid?) \wedge$
| $cs'\ store = cs\ store \oplus \{cid? \mapsto channel'\} \wedge$
| $channel'\ posn = channel\ posn + (data!\ len))$

$Write \,\hat{=}\, \Delta(as, ss, cs) \wedge as\ LookUp \wedge ss\ Write(fid?\backslash fid!) \wedge cs\ Advance$

$Write \,\hat{=}\, Write\backslash(fid!)$

$Size \,\hat{=}\, \Delta(ns, ss) \wedge ns\ LookUp \wedge ss\ Size(fid?\backslash fid!)$

$Size \,\hat{=}\, Size\backslash(fid!)$

The following definitions are built from those previously described and need no further explanation. They simply promote a definition to the filing system level.

$Close \,\hat{=}\, \Delta(cs) \wedge cs\ Remove$

$Link \,\hat{=}\, \Delta(ns) \wedge ns\ Link$

$Unlink \,\hat{=}\, \Delta(ns) \wedge ns\ Remove$

$Seek \,\hat{=}\, \Delta(cs) \wedge cs\ Seek$

$LS \,\hat{=}\, \Delta(ns) \wedge ns\ LS$

$Move \,\hat{=}\, \Delta(ns) \wedge ns\ Move$

EndClass *UnixFilingSystem.*

4.5   Discussion

In spite of being small, the Unix Filing System specification given here is significant as it brings to light the advantages of using MooZ instead of plain Z. The Z specification given in [86] is a landmark and, in fact, introduced a number of ideas on style and organisation of specifications which are still of importance. However, in spite of its bottom-up presentation, it lacks a proper structure.

The original specification is built as a number of schemas whose relationship must be inferred from their text alone, a task not very straightforward to accomplish, especially if the specification were larger. It is sometimes redundant and redefines similar operations each time they are needed.

In the MooZ specification, definitions common to a number of classes are grouped in the abstract superclass *Table* and re-used in its subclasses. The bottom-up structure comes into play naturally via the classification and inheritance mechanisms, whereas in Z it must be imposed as a style rather than a rule for constructing the specification.

Of course, one could write a MooZ specification of the Unix Filing System as only one class with all definitions in it. But that would be like not using schemas and the schema calculus in plain Z.

Extensibility is a natural property of our specification as one can easily extend the system to meet new requirements. Each subsystem is properly encapsulated and the behaviour of the whole system can be understood as the interaction of its parts as specified in class *UnixFilingSystem*.

Another object-oriented specification for this system is given in [47], using Object-Z, another object-oriented extension of Z. At first, the Object-Z specification and its MooZ counterpart seem very similar, as would be expected, since such a small system does not offer many different interesting possibilities of modularisation. Some significant differences must be noticed, however:

- Object-Z allows definitions to be put outside classes. In a MooZ specification, every definition must be part of a class. Further constructs to group classes in modules are under analysis for MooZ. Nevertheless, for the time being, definitions intended to be global to a set of classes can be put into a stateless class and inherited by all classes to which access to such definitions is to be given. An example of this can be found in the Appendix, where a class with mathematical definitions is given as an implicit superclass of every other class.

   The classification and multiple inheritance mechanisms are very flexible and when used together with hiding they constitute a powerful way to structure specifications. Of course, they can also lead to many undesired results if misused. Decisions on how to structure a given system must be well founded so as to avoid awkward configurations.

- In [47], classes are presented as boxes similar to those used to define schemas, with informal comments usually presented outside the boxes. Exceptionally, comments are inserted between definitions in some classes, for readability purposes.

  MooZ takes a different approach, as it does not enclose definitions in boxes but instead introduces groups of related definitions by well-defined clauses. Interspersed informal text is considered as part of the specification, as with Z. This style is enforced by ForMooZ [138, 176], an environment that supports the construction of MooZ specifications. The environment is hypertext-based and pieces of definitions, as well as pieces of informal text, compose nodes interconnected by compiler-inferred and user-defined links.

- The Object-Z specification of the Unix Filing System given in [47] discusses the existence of similarities between classes but does not define common generic classes to aggregate them. It is known that genericity is a key to achieve re-usability. Classes that have been committed to the intrinsics of a given system specification are hardly ever re-used. Here again the influence of an environment in the way specifications are built must be emphasised. ForMooZ promotes genericity as it prompts the user to define classes to be stored in a public repository. Users must be aware of the genericity implicit in their specifications so as to provide generic classes to the public class library.

- Object-Z borrows basic constructors like those for sequences and finite functions from Z. The Mathematical Toolkit, as defined in [182], is taken for granted.

  MooZ, instead, keeps to the object-oriented paradigm and provides a library of basic primitive classes, which eliminate the Z Mathematical Toolkit and provide a uniform notation. In addition, they are a good example of the advantages of being true to object orientation from the very beginning, since they are incrementally defined through inheritance. A complete specification of the basic primitive classes can be found in [136] and a partial specification is given in the Appendix.

In addition to the differences listed above, the semantics given to Object-Z is quite different from that of MooZ. In short, while in Object-Z the semantics of objects is given in terms of their histories, in MooZ it is given in terms of abstract data types. For more details see [136].

4.6 Conclusions

A MooZ specification of the Unix Filing System has been presented in detail and then contrasted with its plain Z and Object-Z counterparts.

At present, efforts are centred on building a set of significant MooZ case studies so as to define the pragmatics of the language. A specification of a distributed object-oriented language, for example, is given in [137]. A formal semantics for MooZ is under development and an informal description of its semantics is available along with some case studies.

A prototype of ForMooZ [138, 176], an environment for the construction and management of MooZ specifications, is available and a formal specification of its kernel (its hypertext-based data model) is also being written in MooZ. This environment supports cooperative work within a distributed specification (class) library. It includes a MooZ compiler and allows fast access to interrelated definitions.

In the Appendix we give a partial specification of MooZ primitive classes, not only for the sake of completeness, since the specification of the Unix Filing System makes use of some of them, but also as another example of MooZ usage.

4.7   Appendix

4.7.1   MooZ Type Constructors

Type constructors, in MooZ, are defined by generic classes. These classes are primitive and, like any other MooZ class, are assumed to have *MathematicalDefinitions* as superclass. This, in turn, is yet another primitive class also presented in this Appendix.

The use of classes in defining the type constructors illustrates the benefits of using object-orientation in the definition of data types in a specification. There is a strong hierarchical relation among the classes (see Figure 4.2) and the high degree of re-usability makes the specification more concise and structured than its equivalent in plain Z.

In what follows, each section defines one of the type constructors. The definitions are mostly MooZ versions of those presented in [182] and need no further explanation. The presentation is somewhat restricted to the classes used in the specification of the Unix Filing System. A complete specification of all primitive classes is given in [136].

Relation

Class *Relation*

givensets X, Y

private $\rightarrow$

state

$$rel : \mathbf{P}(X \times Y)$$

initialstates

_Init_____
$\Delta(rel)$
_____
$rel' = \varnothing$

operations

Domain and range of a relation.

$dom :\quad rel : \mathbf{P}(X \times Y) \rightarrow \mathbf{P}\,X$
$ran :\quad rel : \mathbf{P}(X \times Y) \rightarrow \mathbf{P}\,Y$
_____
$dom(rel) = \{x : \ X;\ y : \ Y \mid (x,y) \in rel \bullet x\}$
$ran(rel) = \{x : \ X;\ y : \ Y \mid (x,y) \in rel \bullet y\}$

Inverse and composition of relations.

$\sim :\quad rel : \mathbf{P}(X \times Y) \rightarrow (Y \leftrightarrow X)$
_____
$\sim (rel)\ rel = \{x : \ X;\ y : \ Y \mid (x,y) \in R \bullet (y,x)\}$

___$[Z]$_____
$;\ :\quad rel : \mathbf{P}(X \times Y) \times (Y \leftrightarrow Z) \rightarrow (X \leftrightarrow Z)$
_____
$\forall S : \ Y \leftrightarrow Z \bullet$
$\quad (;\ S)(rel)\ rel = \{x : \ X;\ y : \ Y;\ z : \ Z \mid (x,y) \in rel \wedge z \in S(\!|\ \{y\}\ |\!) \bullet (x,z)\}$

___$[Z]$_____
$\circ :\quad rel : \mathbf{P}(X \times Y) \times (Z \leftrightarrow X) \rightarrow (Z \leftrightarrow Y)$
_____
$\exists\, self : \ X \leftrightarrow Y \bullet$
$\quad self\ rel = rel \wedge$
$\quad\quad \forall S : \ Z \leftrightarrow X \bullet (\circ S)(rel) = S;\ self$

Domain and range restriction.

$\vartriangleleft :\quad rel : \mathbf{P}(X \times Y) \times \mathbf{P}\,X \rightarrow rel : \mathbf{P}(X \times Y)$
$\vartriangleright :\quad rel : \mathbf{P}(X \times Y) \times \mathbf{P}\,Y \rightarrow rel : \mathbf{P}(X \times Y)$
_____
$\forall S : \mathbf{P}\,X \bullet$
$\quad (\vartriangleleft S)(rel) = \{x : \ X;\ y : \ Y \mid x \in S \wedge (x,y) \in rel \bullet (x,y)\}$
$\forall T : \mathbf{P}\,Y \bullet$
$\quad (\vartriangleright T)(rel) = \{x : \ X;\ y : \ Y \mid y \in T \wedge (x,y) \in rel \bullet (x,y)\}$

Domain and range anti-restriction.

$$\lhd : \quad rel : \mathbf{P}(X \times Y) \times \mathbf{P}\,X \to rel : \mathbf{P}(X \times Y)$$
$$\rhd : \quad rel : \mathbf{P}(X \times Y) \times \mathbf{P}\,Y \to rel : \mathbf{P}(X \times Y)$$

$$\forall S : \mathbf{P}\,X \bullet$$
$$(\lhd S)(rel) = \{x : X; \; y : Y \mid x \notin S \wedge (x,y) \in rel \bullet (x,y)\}$$
$$\forall T : \mathbf{P}\,Y \bullet$$
$$(\rhd T)(rel) = \{x : X; \; y : Y \mid y \notin T \wedge (x,y) \in rel \bullet (x,y)\}$$

It must be noted that the order of the arguments of $\lhd$ and $\lhd$ is reversed. This is because these are messages that may be sent to relations. Therefore, for a relation r and a set s, the Z expressions $s \lhd r$ and $s \lhd r$ correspond to the MooZ expressions $r \lhd s$ and $r \lhd s$ respectively.

Relational image.

$$\_(\!\|\,\_\,\|\!) : \quad rel : \mathbf{P}(X \times Y) \times \mathbf{P}\,X \to \mathbf{P}\,Y$$

$$\forall S : \mathbf{P}\,X \bullet$$
$$(\!\| S \|\!)(rel) = \{x : X; \; y : Y \mid x \in S \wedge (x,y) \in R \bullet y\}$$

Relational correspondence.

$$(\_,\_) : \quad rel : \mathbf{P}(X \times Y) \times X \times Y \to \mathbf{B}$$
$$\forall x : X; \; y : Y \bullet (x,y)(rel) = (x,y) \in rel$$

This operation determines if two elements x and y of the sets X and Y, respectively, are related. In Z, the notation xRy is used for a relation R.

EndClass *Relation.*

Partial Function

Class *PartialFunction*

superclasses *Relation*

state
$$\vdash \forall x : X; \; y \bullet 1, y \bullet 2 : Y \bullet (x, y \bullet 1) \in rel \wedge (x, y \bullet 2) \in rel \Rightarrow y \bullet 1 = y \bullet 2$$

operations

Functional overriding and application.

$$\oplus : \quad rel : \mathbf{P}(X \times Y) \times X \twoheadrightarrow Y \to rel : \mathbf{P}(X \times Y)$$
$$\forall g : X \twoheadrightarrow Y \bullet (\oplus g)(rel) = (\lhd g \; dom)(rel) \cup (g \; rel)$$

$$(\_) : \quad rel : \mathbf{P}(X \times Y) \times X \to Y$$
$$\forall x : X \bullet (x, (x)(rel)) \in rel$$

EndClass *PartialFunction*.

Finite Partial Function

Class *FinitePartialFunction*

superclasses *PartialFunction*

state

$\vdash dom(rel) \in F\ X$

EndClass *FinitePartialFunction*.

Finite Sequence

This class has a unique state component that represents the sequence elements. This is a mapping (finite partial function) from natural numbers to the set to which the sequence elements belong.

This class could have been defined as a subclass of *FinitePartialFunction*. However, in this case, every operation that could be applied to (finite) partial function would also be applicable to sequences and the representation of sequences would not be completely hidden.

For instance, it would be possible to ask for the domain of a sequence. However, the domain operation does not make sense for sequences and would be applicable only in consequence of the particular representation chosen for defining sequences.

Alternatively, *FiniteSequence* could also have been defined as a subclass of *FinitePartialFunction* with all operations of the latter not applicable to the former made private. This is mainly a matter of style and, as most definitions would have to be hidden, there is no advantage in using inheritance in this case.

Class *FiniteSequence*

givensets X

state

$seq : Map\ \mathbb{N}\ X$
$\exists n : \mathbb{N} \bullet seq\ dom = 1..n$

initialstates

Init
$\Delta(seq)$
$seq = \{\}$

operations

Length of sequence.

$$\frac{len:\quad seq:\ Map\ \mathsf{N}\ X \to \mathsf{N}}{len(seq) = \#(seq\ dom)}$$

Sequence indexing.

$$\frac{(\_):\quad seq:\ Map\ \mathsf{N}\ X \times \mathsf{N} \to X}{\forall\, n:\ 1..len(seq)\ \bullet\ (n)(seq) = seq(n)}$$

Subsequence: this operation returns the subsequence that starts at the ith element and has length n.

$$\frac{(\_,\_):\quad seq:\ Map\ \mathsf{N}\ X \times \mathsf{N} \times \mathsf{N} \to seq:\ Map\ \mathsf{N}\ X}{\begin{array}{l}\forall\, i, n:\ \mathsf{N}\ \bullet \\ \quad 0 \le i \land i \le len(seq) \Rightarrow \\ \qquad (i, n)(seq) = \lambda\, j:\ 1..min(\{i + n - 1, len(seq)\})\ \bullet\ seq(i + (j - 1))\ \land \\ \quad i > len(seq) \Rightarrow (i, n)(seq) = \{\}\end{array}}$$

Elements.

$$\frac{elems:\quad seq:\ Map\ \mathsf{N}\ X \to \mathsf{P}\ X}{elems(seq) = seq\ ran}$$

In plain Z, the representation of a sequence is directly accessible and the four operations above are not defined in the Mathematical Toolkit.
Concatenation.

$$\frac{\frown:\quad seq:\ Map\ \mathsf{N}\ X \times Seq \to seq:\ Map\ \mathsf{N}\ X}{\forall\, t:\ Seq\ \bullet\ (\frown t)(seq) = \lambda\, n:\ len(seq) + 1..len(seq) + t\ len\ \bullet\ seq \oplus t(n - len(seq))}$$

The encapsulation of the representation makes the definition of some sequence operations different from those presented in the Z Mathematical Toolkit. Here, the union operation cannot be applied to a (finite partial) function directly and so the definition of $\frown$ is given using functional overriding.

Sequence decomposition and reversal.

$$\frac{\begin{array}{l} head, last:\quad seq:\ Map\ \mathsf{N}\ X \to X \\ tail, front:\quad seq:\ Map\ \mathsf{N}\ X \to seq:\ Map(X\backslash\mathsf{N},\ Y\backslash X) \end{array}}{\begin{array}{l} len(seq) > 0 \Rightarrow \\ \quad head(seq) = seq(1)\ \land \\ \quad last(seq) = seq(len(seq))\ \land \\ \quad tail(seq) = (2, len(seq))(seq)\ \land \\ \quad front(seq) = (1, len(seq) - 1)(seq) \end{array}}$$

$$\frac{rev: \quad seq: \; Map \; \mathbb{N} \; X \rightarrow seq: \; Map \; \mathbb{N} \; X}{rev(seq) = \lambda \, n: \; seq \; dom \bullet seq(len(seq) - n + 1)}$$

EndClass *FiniteSequence*.

MooZ Mathematical Definitions

The primitive class *MathematicalDefinitions* introduces useful definitions and abbreviations for making specifications more concise and readable. It is assumed to be a superclass of every MooZ class, excluding itself. It is implicitly included, so it is not necessary to mention it in the **superclasses** clause. A partial specification of this class including the definitions used in the specification of the Unix Filing System is given below and the complete specification is part of [136].

Class *MathematicalDefinitions*

operations

The following abbreviations allow the use of the traditional symbols to represent the classes *Relation*, *PartialFunction*, etc.

$A \leftrightarrow B == Relation(X \backslash A, \; Y \backslash B)$
$A \nrightarrow B == PartialFunction(X \backslash A, \; Y \backslash B)$
$A \rightarrow B == TotalFuncion(X \backslash A, \; Y \backslash B)$
$A \nrightarrow\!\!\!\!\rightarrow B == FinitePartialFunction(X \backslash A, \; Y \backslash B)$
$Map \; A \; B == FinitePartialFunction$
$Seq \; A == FiniteSequence$

The following definitions are generic and can be applied to values of any type.

Inequality.

$$\frac{[X]}{\begin{array}{l} \_ \neq \_ : \quad X \times X \rightarrow \mathbb{B} \\ \hline \forall \, x, y: \; X \bullet x \neq y = \neg(x = y) \end{array}}$$

Maplet.

$$\frac{[X, Y]}{\begin{array}{l} \_ \mapsto \_ : \quad X \times Y \rightarrow X \times Y \\ \hline \forall \, x: \; X; \; y: \; Y \bullet x \mapsto y = (x, y) \end{array}}$$

Non-membership.

$$\frac{[X]}{\begin{array}{l} \_ \notin \_ : \quad X \times \mathbb{P} \, X \rightarrow \mathbb{B} \\ \hline \forall \, x: \; X; \; S: \; \mathbb{P} \, X \bullet x \notin X = \neg(x \in S) \end{array}}$$

Subsets.

$$\underline{\quad[X]\quad}$$
$$\_\subseteq\_, \_\subset\_ : \quad \mathsf{P}\,X \times \mathsf{P}\,X \to \mathsf{B}$$
$$\forall\, S, T : \mathsf{P}\,X \bullet$$
$$\quad (S \subseteq T \Leftrightarrow \forall\, x : X \bullet x \in S \Rightarrow x \in T)\, \wedge$$
$$\quad (S \subset T \Leftrightarrow S \subseteq T \wedge S \neq T)$$

Set algebra.

$$\underline{\quad[X]\quad}$$
$$\_\cup\_, \_\cap\_, \_\backslash\_ : \quad \mathsf{P}\,X \times \mathsf{P}\,X \to \mathsf{P}\,X$$
$$\forall\, S, T : \mathsf{P}\,X \bullet$$
$$\quad S \cup T = \{x : X \mid x \in S \vee x \in T\}\, \wedge$$
$$\quad S \cap T = \{x : X \mid x \in S \wedge x \in T\}\, \wedge$$
$$\quad S\backslash T = \{x : X \mid x \in S \wedge x \notin T\}$$

Generalised union and intersection.

$$\underline{\quad[X]\quad}$$
$$\bigcup, \bigcap : \quad \mathsf{P}(\mathsf{P}\,X) \to \mathsf{P}\,X$$
$$\forall\, A : \mathsf{P}(\mathsf{P}\,X) \bullet$$
$$\quad \bigcup A = \{x : X \mid \exists\, S : A \bullet x \in S\}\, \wedge$$
$$\quad \bigcap A = \{x : X \mid \forall\, S : A \bullet x \in S\}$$

Number range.

$$\_..\_ : \quad \mathsf{Z} \times \mathsf{Z} \to \mathsf{P}\,\mathsf{Z}$$
$$\forall\, a, b : \mathsf{Z} \to a..b = \{k : \mathsf{Z} \mid a \leq k \wedge k \leq b\}$$

Special sets.

Empty set.
$$\phi X == \{x : X \mid \mathsf{false}\}$$
Non-empty and finite sets and strictly positive integers.
$$\mathsf{P}_1\,X == \{S : \mathsf{P}\,X \mid S \neq \varnothing\}$$
$$\mathsf{F}\,X == \{S : \mathsf{P}\,X \mid \exists\, n : \mathsf{N} \bullet \exists\, f : 1..n \to S \bullet f\ ran = S\}$$
$$\mathsf{F}_1\,X == \mathsf{F}\,X\backslash\{\varnothing\}$$
$$\mathsf{N}_1 == \mathsf{N}\backslash\{0\}$$

Cardinality of a set.

$$\underline{\quad[X]\quad}$$
$$\# : \quad \mathsf{F}\,X \to \mathsf{N}$$
$$\forall\, S : \mathsf{F}\,X \bullet \exists\, n : \mathsf{N} \bullet \exists\, f : 1..n \to S \bullet f\ ran = S \wedge \#S = n$$

Minimum and maximum of a set of numbers.

$$
\begin{array}{|l}
\hline
min, max : \quad \mathsf{P}\,\mathsf{Z} \rightarrow \mathsf{Z} \\
\hline
\forall S : \mathsf{P}\,\mathsf{Z} \mid S \neq \varnothing \bullet \\
\quad min(S) \in S \wedge \forall n : \ S \bullet min(S) \leq n \wedge \\
\quad max(S) \in S \wedge \forall n : \ S \bullet min(S) \geq n \\
\hline
\end{array}
$$

Projection functions for ordered pairs.

$$
\begin{array}{|l}
\underline{\quad [X, Y]} \\
\hline
first, second : \quad X \times Y \rightarrow Y \\
\hline
\forall x : \ X; \ y : \ Y \bullet first(x, y) = x \wedge second(x, y) = y \\
\hline
\end{array}
$$

Identity relation.

$$
\begin{array}{|l}
\underline{\quad [X]} \\
\hline
id : \quad \mathsf{P}\,X \rightarrow X \leftrightarrow X \\
\hline
\forall A : \mathsf{P}\,X \rightarrow (id(A))rel = \{x : \ X \bullet (x, x)\} \\
\hline
\end{array}
$$

Empty map.

$$
\begin{array}{|l}
\underline{\quad [X, Y]} \\
\hline
\{\} : \quad Map \ X \ Y \\
\hline
\{\} \ rel = \varnothing \\
\hline
\end{array}
$$

Map construction.

$$
\begin{array}{|l}
\underline{\quad [X, Y]} \\
\hline
\{\_\} : \quad X \times Y \rightarrow Map \\
\hline
\forall x : \ X; \ y : \ Y \bullet \{x \mapsto y\} \ rel = \{x \mapsto y\} \\
\hline
\end{array}
$$

Empty sequence.

$$
\begin{array}{|l}
\underline{\quad [X]} \\
\hline
\langle\rangle : \quad Seq \ X \\
\hline
\langle\rangle \ seq = \{\} \\
\hline
\end{array}
$$

Sequence construction.

$$
\begin{array}{|l}
\underline{\quad [X, Y]} \\
\hline
\langle\_\rangle : \quad X \rightarrow Seq \\
\hline
\forall x : \ X \bullet \langle x \rangle seq = \{1 \mapsto x\} \\
\hline
\end{array}
$$

EndClass *MathematicalDefinitions.*

Chapter 5

An Object-Z Specification of a Mobile Phone System

Gordon Rose and Roger Duke

After a brief introduction to the syntax and semantics of the specification language Object-Z, this chapter uses Object-Z to develop a formal specification of a mobile telephone system. In addition to the usual object-oriented constructs such as encapsulation into classes and inheritance, this specification illustrates some of the distinct features of Object-Z: instantiation, aggregation and message passing. Instantiation involves the declaration of references to objects of class type, with this reference capturing the concept of persistent identity. Aggregation enables the specification of classes composed of an arbitrary number of similar objects (e.g. an aggregate of mobile telephones). Message passing involves specifying the protocol by which objects in a system synchronise and communicate.

5.1   Object-Z Overview

5.1.1   Introduction

Object-Z [24, 46, 47] is an extension of the formal specification language Z [86, 182, 204] to accommodate object orientation [17, 142]. The main reason for this extension is to improve the clarity of large specifications through enhanced structuring.

A Z specification typically defines a number of state and operation schemas. A state schema groups together variables and defines the relationship that holds between their values. At any instant, these variables define the state of that part of the system which they model. An operation schema defines the relationship between the 'before' and 'after' states corresponding to one or more state schemas. Therefore, inferring which operation schemas may affect a particular state schema requires examining the signatures of all operation schemas. In large specifications

110

this is impracticable. Conventions, such as chapters, group states and operations informally, but cannot enforce structure.

Object-Z overcomes this problem by confining individual operations to refer to one state schema. The definition of a state schema with the definitions of its associated operations (and those of other components to be detailed later) constitute a *class*.

A class is a template for *objects* of that class: for each such object, its states are instances of the class' state schema and its individual state transitions conform to individual operations of the class. An object is said to be an instance of a class and to evolve according to the definitions of its class.

A class may specify part of a system, so that the potential behaviour of that part may be considered and understood in isolation. Complex classes can be specified to inherit other classes, or to include references to objects. These structuring mechanisms are called *inheritance* and *instantiation* respectively.

An Object-Z specification of a system typically includes a number of class definitions related by inheritance and instantiation which build towards a class representing the entire system.

Section 5.1.2 introduces the syntax of classes, Section 5.1.3 outlines some semantic issues. Section 5.1.4 demonstrates instantiation and Section 5.1.5 inheritance. Section 5.2 illustrates the application of Object-Z to a mobile phone system.

5.1.2   Classes

Class Definition
Syntactically, a class definition is a named box, optionally with generic parameters. In this box the constituents of the class are defined and related. Possible constituents are: a visibility list, inherited classes, type and constant definitions, a state schema, an initial state schema, operation schemas, and a history invariant.

```
┌─ ClassName[generic parameters] ──────────────────────────
│  visibility list
│  inherited classes
│  type definitions
│  constant definitions
│  state schema
│  initial state schema
│  operation schemas
│  history invariant
│
└──────────────────────────────────────────────────────────
```

The visibility list, if included, restricts access to the listed features (feature is defined below) of objects of the class. If omitted, all features are visible. Visibility is not inherited so that a derived class may nominate any inherited feature as visible.

Inheritance is described in Section 5.1.5, and type and constant definitions are as in Z.

The state schema is nameless and comprises declarations of state variables and a state predicate. Constants and state variables are collectively called *attributes*. The conjunction of any predicate imposed on the constants and the state predicate is called the *class invariant*.

The attributes and class invariant are implicitly included in the initial state schema and each operation schema. In addition, the state variables and predicate in primed form are implicitly included in the operation schemas. Hence the class invariant holds at all times: in each possible initial state and before and after each operation.

The initial state schema is distinguished by the keyword I_{NIT}: in conjunction with the implicit class invariant, it defines the possible initial states (i.e. initialisation is not restricted to a unique state).

Operation schemas differ from Z operation schemas in that they have a Δ-list of those individual state variables whose values may change when the operation is applied to an object of the class (this is in contrast to the granularity of the Δ convention in Z which applies to entire schemas).

Attributes and operations are collectively called *features*.

The *history invariant* is a predicate over histories of objects of the class (typically in temporal logic) which further constrains the possible behaviours of such objects.

A Generic Stack Example

Consider the following specification of the generic class *Stack*. We adopt the Z style of writing explanatory text on detail after the formal specification.

$$
\begin{array}{|l}
\underline{Stack[T]} \\
\hline
\quad
\begin{array}{|l}
max : \mathbb{N} \\
\hline
max \leqslant 100
\end{array} \\[2ex]
\quad
\begin{array}{|l}
items : \text{seq } T \\
\hline
\#items \leqslant max
\end{array} \\[2ex]
\quad
\begin{array}{|l}
\underline{I_{NIT}} \\
\hline
items = \langle \rangle
\end{array}
\end{array}
$$

$$
\begin{array}{|ll}
\hline
\text{\_\_Push}\rule{4cm}{0.4pt} \\
\Delta(items) \\
item? : T \\
\hline
\#items < max \\
items' = \langle item? \rangle \frown items \\
\hline
\end{array}
\qquad
\begin{array}{|ll}
\hline
\text{\_\_Pop}\rule{4cm}{0.4pt} \\
\Delta(items) \\
item! : T \\
\hline
items \neq \langle\,\rangle \\
items = \langle item! \rangle \frown items' \\
\hline
\end{array}
$$

The class has a constant *max* which does not exceed 100. Distinct *Stack* objects may have different values of *max*, each remaining constant throughout the evolution of the particular stack.

The state schema has one state variable *items* denoting a sequence of elements of the generic type T. The state invariant stipulates that the size of the sequence cannot exceed *max*. An initialised stack has no items.

Operation *Push* prepends a given input *item?* to the existing sequence of items provided the stack has not already reached its maximum size.

The understanding of a Δ-list is that state variables not listed are unchanged. In *Push* then, *items* is subject to change, and the second conjunct of *Push* specifies the change (without that conjunct, *items* would become unspecified).

Operation *Push* implicitly expands to:

$$
\begin{array}{|l}
\hline
\text{\_\_Push}\rule{6cm}{0.4pt} \\
max : \mathbb{N} \\
items, items' : \mathrm{seq}\ T \\
item? : T \\
\hline
max \leqslant 100 \\
\#items \leqslant max \\
\#items' \leqslant max \\
\#items < max \\
items' = \langle item? \rangle \frown items \\
\hline
\end{array}
$$

By convention, no Δ-list is equivalent to an empty Δ-list. When operations are compounded to define new operations, the Δ-list of the result is the merge of the individual Δ-lists. In the expansion of a compound operation, only state variables not in the resultant Δ-list are implicitly unchanged.

Operation *Pop* outputs a value *item!* defined as the head of sequence *items* and reduces *items* to the tail of its original value.

When a class is applied, actual types replace generic types, and features and operation parameters may be renamed as, for example, in the following class descriptor:

$$
Stack[\mathbb{N}][nats/items, nat?/item?, nat!/item!]
$$

The scope of renaming is the whole class, except that variables of a particular operation may be renamed by qualifying the substitution by the operation's name, e.g. *Push*[*nat?*/*item?*]. Simultaneous substitution is indicated by list pairs as in '$(x, y/y, x)$'. Care must be taken when renaming to avoid conflicts with existing bound variables.

5.1.3   Outline of Semantics

The following is an informal description of some aspects of Object-Z semantics.

Declaration $c : C$ declares c to be a reference to an object of the class described by C. There is no implication that an object reference declaration introduces a distinct object reference and by implication a distinct object, nor does the declaration imply that the introduced object is initialised. Thus, declaration $c, d : C$ need not mean that c and d reference distinct objects. If the intention is that they do so at all times, then the predicate $c \neq d$ would be included in the class invariant. If c and d are to refer to distinct objects initially, but subsequently synonymously to the same object, then $c \neq d$ would be a predicate of *INIT* but an operation would, for example, specify $c' = d$ (with c in the operation's Δ-list).

The term $c.att$ denotes the value of attribute *att* of the object referenced by c, the term $c.Op$ denotes the evolution of the object according to the definition of C's Op, and $c.INIT$ denotes the predicate based on the object according to C's initial state schema.

The semantics of an Object-Z class is similar to that of a Z system with one state schema: it comprises a set of attribute bindings consistent with the attribute signatures and class invariant, a set of initial bindings, and a set of relations on attribute bindings, each relation corresponding to an operation with specific parameters. A history or trace semantic model includes the sequences of possible bindings and corresponding relations, further constrained by any history invariant.

The advantage of adopting object references is that the object referenced by c may evolve without changing the value of c. This is particularly significant in modelling aggregates as it effectively eliminates the need for 'framing' which is often used when modelling aggregates in Z. For example, the declaration $sc : \mathsf{F}\, C$ can model an aggregate of objects which may evolve without changing the value of sc, as the object references do not change. Evolution of a constituent object is effected by defining a selection environment such as:

$$
\begin{array}{|l}
\underline{\;Select\;} \\
\quad c? : C \\
\hline
\quad c? \in sc \\
\end{array}
$$

and applying it as in:

$$Op \mathrel{\widehat{=}} Select \bullet c?.Op$$

This effectively 'promotes' the operation Op on the selected object to be an operation on the aggregate, which in this example happens to be also named Op.

(The notation $schema_1 \bullet schema_2$ means that variables declared in the signature of $schema_1$ are accessible when interpreting $schema_2$. That is, the scope of $schema_1$ is extended to the end of $schema_2$'s text. The resulting schema is semantically identical to the conjunction of $schema_1$ and $schema_2$.)

Several objects of the aggregate may undergo an evolutionary step concurrently using a multiple selection environment such as:

$$
\begin{array}{|l}
\hline
\text{\_\_} SelectTwo \text{\_\_} \\
c_1?, c_2? : C \\
\hline
c_1? \neq c_2? \\
\{c_1?, c_2?\} \subseteq sc \\
\hline
\end{array}
$$

and applying it as in:

$$TwoStep \triangleq SelectTwo \bullet (c_1?.Op_1 \wedge c_2?.Op_2)$$

Distributed operation conjunction may be used to specify an operation in which all aggregated objects are subject to the same operation Op concurrently, e.g.

$$AllStep \triangleq \wedge c : cs \bullet c.Op$$

With reference semantics, an object reference, such as c or d above, is only Δ-listed if the reference may change value and refer to another object. A set variable, such as sc above, is only Δ-listed if the set may change value, i.e. if references are added, removed or substituted.

5.1.4   Instantiation

Objects may have object references as attributes, i.e. conceptually, an object may have constituent objects. Such references may either be individually named or occur in aggregates: the two cases are illustrated in this section.

Two Stacks Example
Consider the class *StackPair* which contains two individually named references to stacks of natural numbers.

$$NatStack \; == \; Stack[\mathbb{N}][nats/items, \, nat?/item?, \, nat!/item!]$$

```
┌─ StackPair ──────────────────────────────────────────────────┐
│  ┌──────────────────────────────────────────                 │
│  │ $s_1, s_2$ : NatStack                                      │
│  ├──────────────────────────────────────────                 │
│  │ $s_1 \neq s_2$                                             │
│  └──────────────────────────────────────────                 │
│  $\#s_1.nats \leqslant \#s_2.nats$                            │
│                                                                │
│  ┌─ INIT ─────────────────────────────────                    │
│  │ $s_1.INIT \wedge s_2.INIT$                                 │
│  └────────────────────────────────────────                    │
│  $Push_1 \;\widehat{=}\; s_1.Push$                            │
│  $Push_2 \;\widehat{=}\; s_2.Push$                            │
│  $PushBoth \;\widehat{=}\; Push_1 \wedge Push_2$              │
│  $PushOne \;\widehat{=}\; Push_1 \;[]\; Push_2$               │
│  $[other\ operations]$                                        │
└────────────────────────────────────────────────────────────────┘
```

It is intended that the references s_1 and s_2 do not change, so they are declared as constants. Moreover, it is intended that the referenced stacks be distinct, hence the references are explicitly distinguished. The state invariant requires that the size of the first stack does not exceed that of the second. It is also intended that initially each stack be initialised, hence the explicit initialisation provision. Object-Z does not imply initialisation because some applications do not require initialisation or have class invariants which could not be satisfied if all constituent objects were initialised.

Operation $Push_1$ promotes s_1's *Push* operation to be an operation of *StackPair*. Its implied expansion is:

```
┌─ Push₁ ──────────────────────────────────────────────────────┐
│  $s_1, s_2$ : NatStack                                        │
│  $s_1.max$ : $\mathbb{N}$                                     │
│  $s_1.nats, s_1.nats'$ : $\text{seq}\,\mathbb{N}$             │
│  $nat?$ : $\mathbb{N}$                                        │
│  ├──────────────────────────────────────────                 │
│  $s_1 \neq s_2$                                               │
│  $\#s_1.nats \leqslant \#s_2.nats$                            │
│  $\#s_1.nats' \leqslant \#s_2.nats'$                          │
│  $s_1.max \leqslant 100$                                      │
│  $\#s_1.nats \leqslant s_1.max$                               │
│  $\#s_1.nats' \leqslant s_1.max$                              │
│  $\#s_1.nats < s_1.max$                                       │
│  $s_1.nats' = \langle nat? \rangle \frown s_1.nats$           │
└────────────────────────────────────────────────────────────────┘
```

As s_1 and s_2 are declared to be constants, neither s_1' nor s_2' appear in the expansion, i.e. s_1 and s_2 continue to refer to their respective objects. The primed form of the state invariant follows from the interpretation that $(s_1.nats)'$ is $s_1'.nats'$ which is $s_1.nats'$ as s_1 is constant. The interpretation of $s_1.nats'$ is the value of the *nats* attribute of the object referenced by s_1 after $Push_1$.

Operation *PushBoth* is the conjunction of the above expansion with a similar expansion with qualification by 's_2.' instead of 's_1.' The individual push operations proceed independently except that the same value $nat?$ applies to both stacks.

Operation *PushOne* is a compound operation involving choice. The choice operator '[]' indicates non-deterministic choice of one operation from those constituent operations with satisfied pre-conditions. Thus, the choice is deterministic if exactly one pre-condition is satisfied and the construct fails if no pre-condition is satisfied. The interfaces of the several operations must be identical.

Stack Aggregation Example
As a second example of instantiation, consider an aggregation of a fixed but arbitrary number of stacks. We wish to push an item onto, or pop an item from, any stack in the aggregation, and also to transfer an item from one stack to another.

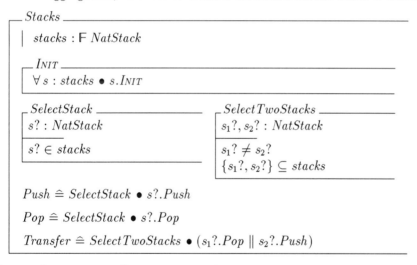

The parallel operator, '‖', used in the definition of *Transfer* above, achieves inter-object communication. The operator conjoins operation schemas but also identifies (equates) and hides inputs and outputs having the same type and basename (i.e. apart from '?' or '!'). The parallel operator is not associative – input/output equating and hiding apply to the conjunction (which is associative).

5.1.5 Inheritance

Inheritance is a mechanism for incremental specification, whereby new classes may be derived from one or more existing classes. Inheritance therefore is particularly significant in the effective re-use of existing specifications.

The type and constant definitions of the inherited classes and those declared explicitly in the derived class are merged. Similarly, the schemas of the inherited classes and those declared explicitly in the derived class are merged. Any schemas with the same name (or in the case of state schemas, without a name) are conjoined. The history invariants of the inherited classes and that of the derived class are also conjoined.

Name clashes, which lead to unintentional merging, can be resolved by renaming when nominating inherited classes.

Indexed Stack Example
We can derive an indexed stack from *Stack* by adding a distinguished stack position.

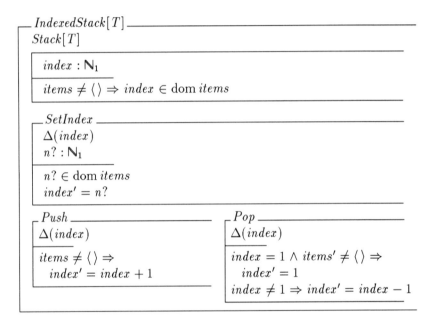

The index continues to relate to the same item except that if the top item is indexed and the stack popped, the index then relates to the new top item. The index is unspecified if the stack is empty.

5.1.6   History Invariants

Consider again the *Stack* class. Suppose we wish to specify that the *Pop* operation is (weakly) fair, i.e. whenever *Pop* is continuously enabled then it must eventually occur. Such a fairness condition can be specified using a history invariant:

$$\begin{array}{|l}
\hline
\;\textit{FairStack}[T] \underline{}\\
\;\;\;\textit{Stack}[T]\\
\;\;\underline{}\\
\;\;\;\Box(\textit{items} \neq \langle\,\rangle \;\Rightarrow\; \Diamond((\bigcirc\#\textit{items}) < \#\textit{items}))\\
\hline
\end{array}$$

Syntactically, the history invariant is placed at the bottom of the class box and separated from the body of the class by a short horizontal bar. In this case, the history invariant is expressed using the temporal logic operators

$\Box$	(always)
$\Diamond$	(eventually)
$\bigcirc$	(next)

(For an introduction to temporal logic and a semantic description of these operators see Moszkowski [152].)

Informally, the history invariant for *FairStack* determines that for any complete history of a *FairStack* object, if in some state the stack is not empty (*items* $\neq \langle\,\rangle$) then at some future stage the size of the stack will be reduced (($\bigcirc\#\textit{items}$) < #*items*), i.e. *Pop* must occur, as this is the only operation that reduces the size of the stack.

For a more detailed treatment of history invariants in Object-Z see [46].

5.2   A Mobile Phone System

5.2.1   Introduction

The specification is based upon particular aspects of an extensive informal (natural language) description of a mobile phone system by Chadha *et al.* [28], Fluhr and Porter [62] and MacDonald [127]. To focus on the application of Object-Z rather than on the technicalities of mobile phones, we have deliberately simplified some aspects of the system.

The specification has evolved from a previous mobile phone specification by the authors [49] but has significant differences: it eliminates explicit cell and mobile identifiers by using object reference semantics and has improved modularity through the introduction of intermediate classes. Cam and Vuong [23] have also described a mobile phone system but used LOTOS as the specification language and identified some difficulties with aggregation, contention and timeouts.

A mobile phone system services a number of mobiles situated within a designated region. For the purposes of this specification we shall assume that mobiles stay within the region. The region is partitioned into cells which transmit signals to, and receive them from, the mobiles. We do not consider the physical disposition of cells or how this can improve reception. In practice, the cells are controlled by a mobile telecommunications switching office (MTSO). To maintain our focus on Object-Z, however, we omit the specification of the MTSO but invest its intelligence, such as the allocation of voice channels to mobiles, in the cells. Information passes between cells and mobiles in different ways: each cell has control channels (for paging and access) as well as predetermined voice channels.

When there is a call for a mobile, all cells page the mobile. The mobile responds by seizing (accessing) the cell with the strongest signal. The seized cell then allocates a voice channel frequency, instructs the mobile to tune to that frequency and rings its phone. Answering the phone completes the establishment of the call.

When a mobile wishes to request a call it begins by seizing a cell. The cell allocates a frequency and instructs the mobile to tune to it, thereby completing call establishment.

As a mobile moves throughout the designated region, the cell responsible for communication with the mobile may need to be changed. The process of changing cells is known as 'hand-over'. The current cell releases the associated frequency ('hand-off'), while the new cell allocates a new frequency and instructs the mobile to tune to it ('hand-on').

Any mobile that has seized a cell or has a frequency allocated by the cell can be disconnected by that cell – the specification models disconnection but omits the detail of events which lead to disconnection.

The mobile phone system is specified as a cooperation between the collection of mobiles and the collection of cells. A mobile is specified using two previously defined classes, and similarly for a cell. The specification is presented 'bottom-up' commencing with the component classes of a mobile, through the mobile class to the aggregation of mobiles. Then the aggregation of cells is progressively built from the component classes of a cell. Finally the mobile phone system is assembled.

We now commence the specification.

5.2.2   The Mobiles

The class *MobileState* is concerned only with state definition and transition. The enumeration of states (*State*) is an example of a local type definition: more states would be needed in a fully detailed mobile phone system, but as stated previously, we wish to focus on Object-Z rather than technical completeness.

Initially, a mobile is in the idle state (*INIT*). An idle mobile may be paged (*BePaged*) and subsequently may respond (*Respond*). Next, the mobile is tuned and receives a ringing tone remotely from the controlling cell (*BeRinging*). On answering, the incoming call is established (*Answer*). Schema *Talking* is simply a convenient identification of the state being *talking*.

```
┌─ MobileState ─────────────────────────────────────────────────────────
│
│   State ::= idle | paged | responded | ringing | talking | requested
│
│  ┌────────────────────────────────────────────────────────────────
│  │ state : State
│  └────────────────────────────────────────────────────────────────
│
│  ┌─ INIT ──────────────────────────────────────────────────────────
│  │ state = idle
│  └────────────────────────────────────────────────────────────────
│
│  ┌─ BePaged ──────────────────────     ┌─ Respond ───────────────────
│  │ Δ(state)                            │ Δ(state)
│  ├──────────────────────────────      ├──────────────────────────────
│  │ state = idle                        │ state = paged
│  │ state' = paged                      │ state' = responded
│  └──────────────────────────────      └──────────────────────────────
│
│  ┌─ BeRinging ────────────────────     ┌─ Answer ────────────────────
│  │ Δ(state)                            │ Δ(state)
│  ├──────────────────────────────      ├──────────────────────────────
│  │ state = responded                   │ state = ringing
│  │ state' = ringing                    │ state' = talking
│  └──────────────────────────────      └──────────────────────────────
│
│  ┌─ Request ──────────────────────     ┌─ BeConnected ───────────────
│  │ Δ(state)                            │ Δ(state)
│  ├──────────────────────────────      ├──────────────────────────────
│  │ state = idle                        │ state = requested
│  │ state' = requested                  │ state' = talking
│  └──────────────────────────────      └──────────────────────────────
│
│  ┌─ Talking ──────────────────────     ┌─ BeIdle ────────────────────
│  │ state = talking                     │ Δ(state)
│  └──────────────────────────────      ├──────────────────────────────
│                                        │ state' = idle
│                                        └──────────────────────────────
└───────────────────────────────────────────────────────────────────────
```

For an outgoing call from the mobile, the mobile requests a connection by seizing a cell (*Request*), and is subsequently connected to the callee thereby establishing the call (*BeConnected*).

On disconnection for reasons not detailed, the mobile reverts to the idle state (*BeIdle*).

Operations of a class are named to reflect causality, e.g. *BePaged* reflects the mobile's passive role, whereas *Respond* reflects an active role. Causality, however, is not included in Object-Z semantics.

Given type *Frequency* denotes the set of allocatable voice channel frequencies to which mobiles may be tuned.

[*Frequency*]

A separate class, *Tuner*, is concerned with a mobile's view of its voice channel. State variable *tuned* is binary: if true, state variable *frequency* represents the mobile's current voice-channel frequency; if false, the mobile is not currently tuned to any voice channel, i.e. *frequency* is unspecified.

┌─ *Tuner* ──
│
│ ┌──
│ │ *tuned* : *Boolean*
│ │ *frequency* : *Frequency*
│ └──
│
│ ┌─ INIT ──
│ │ ┌────────
│ │ │ ¬ *tuned*
│
│ ┌─ *BeTuned* ────────   ┌─ *BeRetuned* ────────   ┌─ *BeUntuned* ──────
│ │ $\Delta(tuned, frequency)$ │ $\Delta(frequency)$ │ $\Delta(tuned)$
│ │ *freq?* : *Frequency*   │ *freq?* : *Frequency*   │ ────────────
│ │ ────────────────   │ ────────────────   │ ¬ *tuned'*
│ │ ¬ *tuned* ∧ *tuned'*   │ *tuned*
│ │ *frequency'* = *freq?*   │ *freq?* ≠ *frequency*
│ │   │ *frequency'* = *freq?*
│
└──

┌─ *Mobile* ───
│ *MobileState*
│ │ *tuner* : *Tuner*
│
│ ┌──
│ │ *tuner.tuned* ⇒ *state* ∈ {*ringing*, *talking*}
│
│ ┌─ INIT ──
│ │ *tuner.INIT*
│
│ ┌─ *SelectCell* ──────────────────────────────────────
│ │ *cell!* : *Cell*
│ │ ──
│ │ *state* ∈ {*idle*, *paged*}
│
│ *SeizeAsResponder* ≙ *SelectCell* ∧ *Respond*
│
│ *BeTunedAsResponder* ≙ *tuner.BeTuned* ∧ *BeRinging*
│
│ *SeizeAsRequester* ≙ *SelectCell* ∧ *Request*
│
│ *BeTunedAsRequester* ≙ *tuner.BeTuned* ∧ *BeConnected*
│
│ *BeHandedOver* ≙ *tuner.BeRetuned* ∧ *Talking*
│
│ *BeDisconnected* ≙ *tuner.BeUntuned* ∧ *BeIdle*
│
└──

The tuner, initially untuned, may be instructed by a cell to tune to a given frequency (*BeTuned*), to change to a different frequency (*BeRetuned*) or revert to untuned (*BeUntuned*).

Class *Mobile* is derived from class *MobileState* by inheritance, and includes an instance (object) of class *Tuner*. The class invariant of *Mobile* requires that a tuned mobile is in either the ringing or talking state. As the tuner is instantiated, tuner features are qualified by the prefix '*tuner.*'; in contrast, mobile state features, being inherited, are used directly. *Mobile* inherits *MobileState*'s *INIT*, but explicit initialisation of instantiation *tuner* is required.

The operations within *Mobile* define a mobile's participation in the mobile phone system. Again, names are chosen to reflect causality.

SeizeAsResponder and *SeizeAsRequester* involve the mobile selecting a cell (*SelectCell*) and changing state (*Respond* and *Request* respectively). Both operations output the selected cell (*cell!*), which will be used as seen later to identify the seized cell. The tuner is not involved.

BeTunedAsResponder is the conjunction of the tuner being tuned and the state becoming ringing. The remaining mobile operations follow in a similar way.

It is asserted that separating the concerns of mobile state and mobile tuning clarifies the mobile specification (and defines two classes which may be re-used elsewhere). That *tuner* is defined as a constant means that we are not changing the identification of the tuner object even though we are changing its internal state.

The specification is further structured by considering the collection of all mobiles as a meaningful entity in the mobile phone system. Class *Mobiles* defines this collection.

The class illustrates aggregation using a set (*mobiles*) which necessarily identifies distinct mobile objects. In this particular class, *mobiles* is a constant set which is consistent with a fixed collection of mobiles with persistent identity regardless of their internal evolution. (A complete specification would model mobiles entering or leaving the system's region; in that case, *mobiles* would be a state variable and add and remove operations would be included.)

Mobiles

$mobiles : \mathbb{F}\ Mobile$

INIT

$\forall\, m : mobiles \bullet m.INIT$

SelectedMobile

$mob? : Mobile$

$mob? \in mobiles$

SelectMobile

$mob! : Mobile$

$mob! \in mobiles$

$BePaged \mathrel{\widehat{=}} SelectedMobile \bullet mob?.BePaged$

$SeizeAsResponder \mathrel{\widehat{=}} SelectMobile \bullet mob!.SeizeAsResponder$

$BeTunedAsResponder \mathrel{\widehat{=}} SelectedMobile \bullet mob?.BeTunedAsResponder$

$Answer \mathrel{\widehat{=}} SelectMobile \bullet mob!.Answer$

$SeizeAsRequester \mathrel{\widehat{=}} SelectMobile \bullet mob!.SeizeAsRequester$

$BeTunedAsRequester \mathrel{\widehat{=}} SelectedMobile \bullet mob?.BeTunedAsRequester$

$BeHandedOver \mathrel{\widehat{=}} SelectedMobile \bullet mob?.BeHandedOver$

$BeDisconnected \mathrel{\widehat{=}} SelectedMobile \bullet mob?.BeDisconnected$

INIT specifies that an initialised instance of *Mobiles* would have each of its constituent mobiles initialised according to *INIT* within *Mobile*.

The two similar schemas *SelectedMobile* and *SelectMobile* reflect the causality of selection from outside and from within *Mobiles* respectively. They are used as local environments to promote individual mobile operations. For example, *Mobiles*'s *BePaged* promotes the paging of the externally nominated mobile (*mob?*) to become an operation of *Mobiles*. As will be seen, the nomination comes from the cells. *Mobiles*'s *SeizeAsResponder*, on the other hand, illustrates the use of *SelectMobile* which communicates the seizing mobile's identity (*mob!*) to the selected cell (*cell!*) output by *mob!*'s *SeizeAsResponder*. The structure of *Mobiles* is straightforward: it simply defines a collection of mobiles and promotes their individual operations.

5.2.3   The Cells

A cell is modelled as having a frequency allocator unit and a seize unit thereby separating the concerns of voice channel (frequency) allocation and seizure. *FreqAllocator* models a cell's set of predetermined allocatable frequencies (*freqs*) and its associated tuned mobiles and their allocated frequencies.

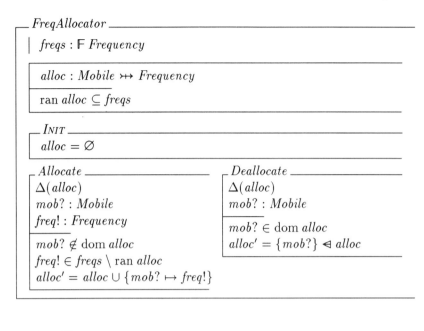

Function symbol '$\rightarrowtail$' defines *alloc* to be partial (not all mobiles are associated with one cell) and one-to-one (an injection – mobiles associated with the same cell must be tuned to distinct frequencies). The class invariant requires that the allocated frequencies are allocatable frequencies. Initially, no frequencies are allocated. *Allocate* models the allocator causing a frequency *freq*! to be allocated to the given mobile *mob*?. (Its second conjunct, which requires *freq*! to be an allocatable frequency not currently allocated, is redundant as it is ensured by the signature of *alloc*, the class invariant and the first conjunct.) *Deallocate* removes the given mobile *mob*? from the domain of *alloc* (using the Z domain subtract symbol '◁') – this also removes the associated frequency from the range because *alloc* is one-to-one.

SeizeUnit has structural similarities to *Tuner* although they represent quite different physical aspects.

If *seized*, *mobile* denotes the seizing mobile. *BeSeized* models seizure by an externally nominated mobile. *ReleaseSeizer* is designed to transfer the seized mobile's identification to the frequency allocator as will be seen, and variant *ReleaseIfSeizer* is designed as a conditional reversion to unseized if the externally nominated *mob?* is the seizing mobile. Variable *seized*, as well as indicating whether or not *mobile* has a specified value, controls the sequencing of operations, e.g. an unspecified mobile identification cannot be transferred to the allocator as *BeSeized* must precede *ReleaseSeizer* and *ReleaseSeizer* can only release the seizing mobile once.

Class *Cell* comprises a frequency allocator and a seize unit represented by the two objects *freq_allocator* and *seize_unit* respectively. The invariant requires that the seizing mobile, if any, cannot have an allocated frequency.

$$
\begin{array}{l}
\underline{Cell} \\[4pt]
\quad\begin{array}{|l}
freq\_allocator : FreqAllocator \\
seize\_unit : SeizeUnit \\
\hline
seize\_unit.seized \Rightarrow seize\_unit.mobile \notin \mathrm{dom}\, freq\_allocator.alloc \\
\hline
\\
\quad\begin{array}{|l}
\underline{Page} \\
mob! : Mobile \\
\hline
mob! \notin \mathrm{dom}\, freq\_allocator.alloc \\
seize\_unit.seized \Rightarrow mob! \neq seize\_unit.mobile \\
\end{array} \\
\\
BeSeized \;\widehat{=}\; seize\_unit.BeSeized \\
Tune \;\widehat{=}\; (freq\_allocator.Allocate \wedge seize\_unit.ReleaseSeizer \wedge \\
\qquad\qquad\quad [\,mob?, mob! : Mobile \mid mob? = mob!\,]) \setminus mob? \\
HandOff \;\widehat{=}\; freq\_allocator.Deallocate \\
HandOn \;\widehat{=}\; freq\_allocator.Allocate \wedge seize\_unit.NotSeized \\
Disconnect \;\widehat{=}\; freq\_allocator.Deallocate \;[\!]\; seize\_unit.ReleaseIfSeizer \\
\end{array}
\end{array}
$$

Page nominates a mobile to be paged (in reality, the cell, along with the other cells, would be instructed to page the mobile by the MTSO). A pre-condition is that the mobile to be paged is neither tuned nor seizing.

Operation *Tune* is cooperative between the frequency allocator and the seize unit: the seize unit releases the seizing mobile's identity to the allocator for frequency allocation. The second line of *Tune*'s definition equates the two versions of mobile identification and hides *mob?* – this leaves *mob!* visible so that the seizing mobile can be instructed to tune, as will be seen later.

HandOff simply involves deallocation of a frequency (from the cell's point of view) and *HandOn* involves frequency allocation by a cell which is unseized (i.e. a mobile which has seized a cell has allocation priority over a mobile to be handed on to it).

Disconnect applies the choice operator [] to distinguish the two cases of disconnection; one involving frequency deallocation, the other involving clearing the seize unit. The cases are disjoint because a mobile cannot be both tuned and seizing. Note that the interfaces of *freq_allocator.Deallocate* and *seize_unit.ReleaseIfSeizer* are identical, namely *mob?*, which becomes the interface for *Disconnect*.

Class *Cells* aggregates the individual cells.

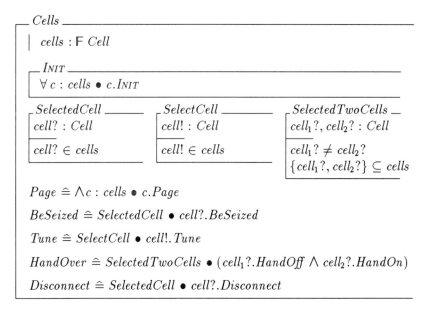

Cell selection may be external (*SelectedCell*) or internal (*SelectCell*). *Page* is defined as the distributed conjunction of every cell paging. The output parameter *mob!* is merged and therefore necessarily identical for every cell.

SelectedTwoCells provides for external nomination of the hand-off and hand-on cells: it is applied as a local environment for hand-off, hand-on synchronisation as specified by *HandOver*.

5.2.4   The Mobile Phone System

MobilePhoneSystem brings cell and mobile aggregations together: most system operations have the form of a parallel composition of an operation on each aggregate.

$\qquad$ *MobilePhoneSystem* $\qquad$

$\quad$ *cells : Cells*
$\quad$ *mobiles : Mobiles*

$\qquad$ *INIT* $\qquad$

$\quad$ *cells.INIT* $\wedge$ *mobiles.INIT*

Page $\hat{=}$ *cells.Page* $\parallel$ *mobiles.BePaged*

RespondSeize $\hat{=}$ *cells.BeSeized* $\parallel$ *mobiles.SeizeAsResponder*

TuneResponder $\hat{=}$ *cells.Tune* $\parallel$ *mobiles.BeTunedAsResponder*

Answer $\hat{=}$ *mobiles.Answer*

RequestSeize $\hat{=}$ *cells.BeSeized* $\parallel$ *mobiles.SeizeAsRequester*

TuneRequester $\hat{=}$ *cells.Tune* $\parallel$ *mobiles.BeTunedAsRequester*

HandOver $\hat{=}$ *cells.HandOver* $\parallel$ *mobiles.BeHandedOver*

Disconnect $\hat{=}$ *cells.Disconnect* $\wedge$ *mobiles.BeDisconnected*

The parallel operator '$\parallel$' is similar to conjunction, but input and output variables with a common base name and of the same type are equated and hidden (internalised). For example, the system operation *Page* involves all cells paging *mob*! which controls selection of the paged mobile *mob*? within *mobiles*'s *BePaged* operation.

Answer involves the mobiles only. *Disconnect* does not require parallel composition as its constituent operations are independent.

The specification could include requirements such as:

1. The mobile sets allocated frequencies by individual cells are disjoint.
2. A mobile can seize, at most, one cell at any time.
3. The mobiles' view of being tuned must agree with the cells' view of tuned mobiles.

Alternatively and preferably, the above predicates could be candidates for theorems derivable from the specification as presented.

Proofs proceed by induction; i.e. by showing that the predicate is true initially and, for each operation, showing that if the predicate holds in the operation's pre states, it holds in the corresponding post states.

5.2.5   Ensuring Progress

In order to ensure that the mobile phone system makes satisfactory progress, we may wish to insist that a seized cell is eventually released, i.e. that either the

Tune or *Disconnect* cell operation must eventually occur. We can specify this requirement using a history invariant to modify the *Cell* class to give the class *CellProgress*

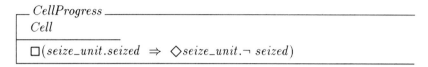

and then instantiating *cells* : F *CellProgress* in the *Cells* class. It now becomes the responsibility of the implementor of the mobile phone system to ensure this condition is met, i.e. that a cell cannot remain seized indefinitely.

In practice, it may happen that progress conditions such as this will depend upon the willingness of the environment and so cannot be guaranteed in an implementation. In the case of a cell seized by a mobile, for example, if the mobile then malfunctions and refuses to be tuned, the system as specified will fail to satisfy the history invariant of *CellProgress*. A possible solution at implementation is to add a *Timeout* operation to the *Cell* class which throws off a seizing mobile if it does not tune within a specified time. Such lower-level detail is often not specifically included in a top-level specification such as we have presented here. Including history invariants at the top level, however, can signal to the implementor the overall progress constraints that would be desirable.

Acknowledgements

The financial support of AOTC (Australia) and contributions to the development of Object-Z by Cecily Bailes, David Carrington, David Duke, Ian Hayes, Paul King, Anthony Lee and Graeme Smith are gratefully acknowledged.

Chapter 6

Object-oriented Specification in VDM++

Swapan Mitra

This chapter discusses some of the important features of VDM++, a VDM-based object-oriented specification language. A brief example, a specification of various forms of quadrilaterals and of a system for manipulating sets of these graphical objects, is developed to facilitate this discussion.

6.1 Introduction

VDM++ is a formal specification language for object-oriented systems. It is based on VDM [96] and it is an extension of VDM. A description of VDM++ is available in draft form [51]. At present it supports several novel features, such as:

- multiple inheritance;
- behavioural inheritance;
- concurrency and synchronisation;
- trace expressions.

The objectives of this chapter are:

- to analyse the basic features (i.e. excluding the realtime features) of VDM++;
- to suggest some improvements to the language to facilitate its expressiveness.

A brief example, a specification of various forms of quadrilaterals and a system for manipulating sets of quadrilaterals, is used for this purpose. A similar example is used by the case studies of [183] to describe other object-oriented extensions to Z and VDM.

The class hierarchy of quadrilaterals comprises:

Quadrilateral a basic class, a general four-sided figure;

Parallelogram a subclass of Quadrilateral, with opposite sides parallel;
Rhombus a subclass of Parallelogram, with all sides equal;
Rectangle a subclass of Parallelogram, with perpendicular sides;
Square a subclass of Rectangle and Rhombus.

Vectors are used to specify the sides of a quadrilateral. We assume that types *Vector*, *Scalar* and *Angle* are already defined. We also assume that definitions of vector addition, dot-product, modulus, scalar division and angle between two adjacent sides are given.

$$\_ + \_ : Vector \times\ Vector \to Vector$$

$$\_ \bullet\ \_ : Vector \times\ Vector \to Scalar$$

$$|\_| : Vector \to Scalar$$

$$\_/\_ : Scalar \times\ Scalar \to Scalar$$

$$\cos^{-1} : Scalar \to Angle$$

We shall use these functions in the specifications of the *methods* of the quadrilateral classes. We also acknowledge the existence of the null vector, O.

6.2 Quadrilaterals

In VDM++, a class definition starts with the key-word **Class** followed by the class name, and ends with the key-word **end** followed by the class name. Instance variables, if any, are declared after the key-word **Instance Variables**. The state invariants, constraints on the instance variables, if any, are specified next. These invariants are VDM-SL logical expressions. The key-word **Methodlist** heralds the definitions of the methods. The methods can be specified in either functional style or VDM-SL operation style.

The instance variables of *Quadrilateral* are:

edges: a sequence of vectors representing four sides of the figure, and
position: a vector representing the position of the figure with respect to some origin.

This is followed by the specifications of the invariants on the instance variables. Each invariant is labelled with the name(s) of the variable(s).

The *Quadrilateral* class has only one method, *move*. Its input parameter, x, is a vector. In VDM++, output specification of a method is optional. The default output is the class instance itself. The effect of *move* is expressed by the postcondition of the method. It specifies the change in the state variable, *position*.

The formal specification of the Quadrilateral class is presented below.

> **Class** *Quadrilateral*
>> **Instance Variables**
>>> *edges*: **seq of** *Vector* ;
>>> *position*: *Vector* ;
>> **Invar-** *edges*1: **len** *edges* = 4 ;
>> **Invar-** *edges*2: *edges*(1) + *edges*(2) + *edges*(3) +
>>> *edges*(4) = *O* ;
>> **Methodlist**
>>> *move*(*x*: *Vector*)
>>>> **ext wr** *position* ;
>>> **pre:**   *true*
>>> **post++:** $position = \overleftarrow{position} + x$;
> **End** *Quadrilateral* ;

6.2.1   Parallelogram

The *Parallelogram* class is a subclass of *Quadrilateral* with an additional invariant on *edges*[1].

The only additional method associated with this class is *angleQuad*. It does not need any argument and returns the value of the parameter, *angle*. The output declaration of the method follows the key-word **Value**. This method does not change the state of (an instance of) *Parallelogram*.

> **Class** *Parallelogram*
>> **Is subclass of** *Quadrilateral* ;
>> **Invar-** *edges*3: *edges*(1) + *edges*(2) = *O* ;
>> **Methodlist**
>>> *angleQuad*() **Value** *angle*: *Angle*
>>>> **ext rd** *edges* ;
>>>> **pre:**   *true*
>>>> **post++:** $angle = \cos^{-1} \frac{(edges(1) \bullet edges(2))}{|edges(1)||edges(2)|}$;
> **End** *Parallelogram* ;

---

[1]VDM++ syntax [51] does not allow specification of invariants without explicit declaration of instance variables. If the invariants are on the state variables of the superclass, re-declaration of instance variables creates further ambiguity. Therefore here we have omitted the re-declaration of instance variables.

6.2.2 Rhombus

Rhombus is a subclass of *Quadrilateral* with an added invariant on *edges* stating that all of its sides are equal.

> **Class** *Rhombus*
>   **Is subclass of** *Parallelogram* ;
>   **Invar-** $edges4$: $edges(1) = edges(2)$;
> **End** *Rhombus* ;

6.2.3 Rectangle

The class *Rectangle* is a subclass of *Rhombus* with an added invariant. The adjacent sides of a rectangle are perpendicular to each other (i.e. the dot product of any two adjacent sides is the null vector, O).

> **Class** *Rectangle*
>   **Is subclass of** *Parallelogram* ;
>   **Invar-** $edges5$: $edges(1) \bullet edges(2) = O$;
> **End** *Rectangle* ;

6.2.4 Square

The class *Square* is a subclass of both *Rhombus* and *Rectangle*. That is, its sides are equal and perpendicular to each other. Therefore it can be naturally defined by using the multiple inheritance feature of VDM++.

> **Class** *Square*
>   **Is subclass of** *Rhombus, Rectangle* ;
> **End** *Square* ;

6.3 Workspace

The drawing system, consisting of various instances of quadrilaterals displayed at various positions on the screen, can be regarded as the VDM++ *Workspace*. Each quadrilateral in the *Workspace* is uniquely identified by its identifier. We assume that *QID* is a given set of quadrilateral identifiers (that is, they can be considered to belong to the VDM 'token' type). The state of the *Workspace* is defined by the set of instances of quadrilaterals and their identifiers.

This class has six methods:

lookUpQuad: returns the instance of the quadrilateral associated with the given
identifier;
angle: returns the angle between the two adjacent sides of the quadrilateral associated with the given identifier;
addQuad: adds a quadrilateral to the *Workspace*;
deleteQuad: deletes a quadrilateral from the *Workspace*;
updateQuad: overwrites a quadrilateral;
move: repositions a quadrilateral; it is achieved by invoking two methods, *move*
of *Quadrilateral* and *updateQuad* of *Workspace*.

> **Class** *Workspace* ;
> > **Instance Variables**
> > > *screen*: $QID \rightarrow @Quadrilateral$;
> > **Methodlist**
> > > *lookUpQuad*(qd: QID) **Value** *quad*: $@Quadrilateral$
> > > > **ext rd** quad ;
> > > > **pre:** $qd \in$ **dom** *screen*
> > > > **post++:** $quad = screen(qd)$;
> > >
> > > *angle*(qd: QID) **Value** *ang*: *Angle*
> > > > **pre:** $qd \in$ **dom** *screen*
> > > > **post++:** $ang = screen(qd) \ ! \ angleQuad$;
> > >
> > > *addQuad*(quad: @Quadrilateral) **Value** qd: QID
> > > > **ext wr** screen ;
> > > > **pre:** $qd \notin$ **dom** *screen*
> > > > **post++:** $screen = \overleftarrow{screen} \cup \{qd \mapsto quad\}$;
> > >
> > > *deleteQuad*(qd: QID)
> > > > **ext wr** screen ;
> > > > **pre:** $qd \in$ **dom** *screen*
> > > > **post++:** $screen = \{qd\} \triangleleft \overleftarrow{screen}$;
> > >
> > > *updateQuad*(qd: QID, *quad*: $@Quadrilateral$)
> > > > **ext wr** *screen* ;
> > > > **pre:** $qd \in$ **dom** *screen*
> > > > **post++:** $screen = \overleftarrow{screen} \dagger \{qd \mapsto quad\}$;

$$move(qd:\ QID, vec:\ Vector)$$

> **ext wr** *screen* ;
> **internal** *quad*: @*Quadrilateral* ;
> **pre:** *qd* ∈ **dom** *screen*
> **post++:** *quad* = *screen*(*qd*)!*move*(*vec*)
> ∧ *updateQuad*(*qd*, *quad*) ;

End *Workspace* ;

6.4 Suggestions for Improvement

The syntax of VDM++, as proposed in [51], contains all the major features necessary for specifying an object-oriented system. It is quite comprehensive and easy
to use. However, the current syntax does not fully address some issues. These are
discussed below with suggestions for improvement:

1. The formal syntax could be extended to include text items and VDM-SL
   specifications. Thus, a complete specification comprises a set of 'Paragraphs',
   where a 'Paragraph' can be a descriptive text, a VDM-SL or VDM++ specification. A rigorous style would insist on having informal description for
   every formal paragraph.

System-Specification	::=	{ Informal-Spec, Formal-Spec }*
Informal-Spec	::=	Word, Informal-Spec
		| Word
Formal-Spec	::=	VDM-SL-Spec
		| VDM++-Spec
VDM++-Spec	::=	Class-Description
		| Workspace_Description

   ...

2. The class definition could allow state variables of anonymous class and anonymous type. For instance, the present syntax cannot be used to specify a class
   representing generic *Tree*.
3. The specification of a invariant requires explicit declaration of all instance
   variables that it uses. This could be relaxed if the invariants are on the state
   variables of the superclass. The invariant specification could be liberalised
   by modifying the 'Instance-variable' declaration in the following manner.

   Instance-variable-part ::= "**Instance Variables**", one-declaration,
   { ";" , one-declaration }, ";",

[Invariants] , [Initialisations]
| [Invariants] , [Initialisations]

...

4. The syntax for specifying the method output restricts this output to be a single parameter. A more liberal syntax would allow a method to have multiple output parameters.

method-header   ::= identifier, par-typelist, [value-part] ;

...

...

value-part   ::= "**Value**", id-type-pair;
id-type-pair   ::= par-name-list, ":", type-indication.

6.5   Conclusion

We have demonstrated the way in which object-oriented concepts are represented in VDM++, and have given a simple example illustrating inheritance and class composition. It is important to note here that the present study does not include the realtime features of the language, due to the lack of a developed semantics for these features.

Chapter 7

Specifying a Concept-recognition System in Z++

K. Lano and H. Haughton

This chapter gives a formal specification of a machine-learning system in the language Z++ [104]. We give an overview of the language, and describe the process of specifying and refining the system to code. The result is a machine-learning tool which has been used for practical diagnostic tasks [105]. We also discuss the advantages for maintenance and adaptability of adopting the formal object-oriented approach.

Research and development of systems in artificial intelligence has been characterised by the approach of rapid prototyping, of testing ideas by implementation rather than by proof. Implementations are often described by means of outline algorithms, and this makes comparison and adaptation of these systems difficult. We concentrate on the area of machine-learning, which typifies these problems, from a software engineering perspective, and describe techniques that have been used to design and implement a learning system in accordance with the use of formally based specification methods.

7.1 Z++: Syntax and Semantics

7.1.1 Background

Z++ arose from the Esprit II project REDO, and the need within this project to provide an abstract representation for large data–processing systems. The UNIFORM procedural language adopted by the project was a key influence, as was the B abstract machine notation of Abrial. The aim from the outset was to produce a language which could naturally express designs, in addition to providing a means for structuring and incremental correct development of large systems. While seeking to provide alternative means of specification, such as algebraic and

temporal, it is also a strong aim to minimise the size of the language, so reducing the burden of learning. Z^{++} is intended for practical use in an industrial
environment, and hence, can be considered a compromise between generality and
implementability: in terms of the standard life cycle, it seeks to support expression
of requirements, designs and specifications.

7.1.2   Syntax

The surface syntax of the language appears to be quite different from that of Z,
and from that of other object-oriented extensions to Z, such as OOZE [3], Object-Z
[47], and ZEST [37]. This syntax was chosen in order to stress the commonalities of
the concepts of the language with those of object-oriented languages such as Eiffel
[142], and in addition, to enable simpler extension of the notation by the addition of
new clauses to a class definition, rather than subordinate schema boxes. However,
tools for translating (a subset of) the language into a Z style 'object-oriented Z' do
exist. The syntax was also inspired by an early version of the B abstract machine
notation [1].

7.1.3   Using Methods

A class method m declared as

$$m : \ X \ \rightarrow \ Y$$
$$m \ x \ y \ ==> \ \phi(x, u, y, u')$$

in a class C, with state $v : V$, where u is the list of state variables explicitly
mentioned in the predicate, can be used in one of three ways:

1. As an operation on elements of C (objects). If m is deterministic, $a, a' \in C$,
    $x : X$; $y : Y$, then $(m \ x) \ a = (y, a')$ implies that a' is the unique object
    whose state v' satisfies $Inv_C(v) \land Inv_C(v') \land \phi(x, u, y, u') \land w' = w$, where
    Inv_C is the invariant of C, v is the tuple of attributes of a, and where w
    is the list of variables from v not occurring in u. Any component of v' not
    mentioned in the list u' will be unchanged from its value in v;
2. As a schema

$$
\begin{array}{|l}
\hline
\ m \ \\
\hline
\ v, v' : V; \\
\ x : X; \\
\ y : Y \\
\hline
\ Inv_C(v) \land Inv_C(v') \land \\
\ \phi(x, u, y, u') \land \\
\ w' = w \\
\hline
\end{array}
$$

on the state of C. Such applications are written as

$$m[ap/fp]$$

for specific actual parameters ap substituted for formal parameters fp. If the actual parameters are variables with identical names ap to the formal parameters, the notation

$$m(ap)$$

can be used;

3. As a schema

$$
\begin{array}{|l|}
\hline
\;a.m_{full} \makebox[3cm]{\hrulefill} \\
\;a, a' : V; \\
\;\Delta State_C; \\
\;x : X; \\
\;y : Y \\
\hline
\;\theta State_C = a\;\wedge \\
\;\theta State'_C = a'\;\wedge \\
\;Inv_C(v) \wedge Inv_C(v')\;\wedge \\
\;\phi(x, u, y, u')\;\wedge \\
\;w' = w \\
\hline
\end{array}
$$

$State_C$ is the state schema of the class in which a is an instance. $\Delta State_C$ is then hidden to produce the schema $a.m$. Applications of such a schema are written as

$$a.m[ap/fp]$$

for a specific object a and actual parameters ap substituted for formal parameters fp. Again the abbreviation

$$a.m(ap)$$

can be used if the actual parameter names are the same as the formal parameter names. This is the general case of 1. The notation is similar to that of Object-Z.

In order to be able to use a method in mode two m must be defined in an ancestor class of the using class D (i.e. D inherits C directly or indirectly, or D is C, and the state of C is fully visible in D), and m can be disambiguated if necessary by using the notation $C.m$ to refer to the version of m defined in C. In order to use m in mode one or three C must be a supplier class of D (i.e. D contains the attribute definition $a : C$).

7.1.4   Philosophy

An attempt has been made at conceptual simplicity in the language in making refinement the central concept of the semantics and in providing a strong mathematical structure for this concept, so yielding the operations for composing classes as described in [115]. We have the equations:

$$class == type$$
$$instance == object == element$$

The existence of a refinement relation between two classes implies that the more refined class is type-compatible with the less refined class, in the usual sense of object-oriented specification [142]. Moreover, refinement means increasing the implementation focus of a specification.

Restrictions have been made, however: recursively refined classes are not possible (i.e. a strict definition before use requirement is made on class expressions), and assignment is by value rather than reference, to avoid the difficulties of reasoning about aliasing which the latter would bring. We also attempt to remain consistent with the style of Z, so that, for instance, we do not support the idea of 'the set of objects from a class that currently exist', which is written as $\overline{C} \bullet objs$ in OOZE [3]. Object identity is only modelled implicitly, via the idea of a local naming system (that is, an object only has an identity in a specification part to the degree to which it can be accessed at that point as an individual entity). Extension of the semantics to include modules and multi-methods is currently an area of research, as is the specification of many properties of concurrent systems.

7.2   Formal Methods Applied to Software Maintenance

The problem of software maintenance has been recognised as one of the most significant contributors to the 'software crisis' [208]. Work within the REDO [109] project has identified methodologies and techniques which seem to offer significant potential improvements in the maintenance of future applications. These techniques are based on a combination of formal methods, particularly high-level specification languages such as Z, and on object-oriented design. The management of *change* is central to maintenance, since systems must, in general, either retain a capacity for evolution and adaptation under changing requirements or become severely degraded in usefulness [121]. In artificial intelligence especially, the need for systems to be easily modifiable and extendable, both before and after 'delivery', is an essential property.

Much research has been done in the area of providing machine assistance for maintenance and development [79, 168]. A unifying feature of these approaches is the use of links between specifications and implementations, and the preservation of a record of the development history. This allows the user to identify the parts of the specification which need to change given a request for change at the requirements level or at the code level. Parts of an old development can be replayed or adapted, thus saving work in redevelopment.

The approach to maintenance identified within REDO emphasises that effective maintenance of an application can best be achieved through maintenance of a specification, and propagation of the changes to this specification to the code, via the development history, in a machine-supportable manner [109].

In the following sections we give a brief overview of the representation of machine-learning in this formalism, and provide examples of the refinement of this general model to specifications of existing systems.

7.3   Machine Learning

We can consider learning to be the reformulation of knowledge under new experiences. An abstract specification of learning which encompasses most existing examples of such systems is as follows:

Definition 1   A *learning system* is a tuple $(\|\ \|, \mathcal{L}, DB, L)$ where $\mathcal{L}$ is a logical formal language, DB is a set of databases or theories, which we will usually wish to identify with sets of sentences from *Fmla*, the well-formed formulae of $\mathcal{L}$. L is a value space for the formulae of $\mathcal{L}$.

The *update function*

$$\|\ \| : Fmla \rightarrow (DB \rightarrow \mathbb{P}(L \times DB))$$

expresses the update of a theory by a new example (a formula), giving rise to a possible set of new theories and measures of how far that event is in 'agreement' with the original theory. In the following we will refer to $\mathcal{L}$ as the *language* of the learning system $\ell = (\|\ \|, \mathcal{L}, DB, L)$, L as the *value space*, and DB as the set of *databases* or *theories*.

Definition 2   A learning system is *deterministic* if $\|\theta\|\sigma$ is always a singleton set.

A general learning system can be regarded as an instance of the following generic *object class*:

```
CLASS Learning_System[Fmla, DB, L]
OWNS
    σ  :  DB;
    ‖ ‖  :  Fmla  →  (DB  →  ℙ (L  ×  DB))
OPERATIONS
    Learn  :  Fmla  →  L
ACTIONS
    Learn θ ε   ==>   (ε, σ') ∈ ‖ θ ‖ σ
END CLASS
```

Learn is a *method* or operation of this class. By convention, a method has the state of the class as both an input and an output, and if no next state version w' of a component w of this state is mentioned in the predicate of the method, w is assumed to not be changed by the method. Here, for instance, an application of *Learn* will not change the definition of ∥ ∥.

During refinement, methods such as *Learn* can be divided into submethods, for positive and negative revision of the theory, and there will be additional methods which (for instance) reorganise and simplify the knowledge base using special examples, as in explanation-based learning [155].

Typically, the result ϵ of assimilation of an example θ by a learning system represents the degree to which θ is derivable from or explainable by T, the existing database or theory. As in [61], we can make very weak or general assumptions about the nature of this derivability: for the result $\epsilon = 1$ we might only require that $T \cup \{\theta\}$ is consistent, for instance. If the example is inconsistent, in some sense, with T, we will usually trigger a revision of T to T', so that $T' \cup \{\theta\}$ is consistent. Otherwise, θ will be used to further generalise the theory.

7.4   Applications of the Model

This model can be refined, in a precise sense given by the formal semantics of Z^{++} [116], to represent existing machine-learning systems such as ITOU [172] and many others. This uniform formalism should facilitate the comparison and comprehension of these systems, which use a wide variety of techniques and terminologies. We will give an example development of a system within our framework. Comparison with other approaches to using formal methods in AI [188] will be given, as well as suggestions for its applicability within other areas of AI.

7.5   A Specification-based Development and Maintenance Method

In [109] we have described how development and maintenance can be carried out using Z^{++} as a specification language, and by using a methodology that implements changes to software at the *highest useful level of abstraction* possible, i.e. at some stage in the refinement history of the specification of the system, rather than at the code level. Z is an excellent language for high-level specification, since it allows very general descriptions of systems to be made, with outline properties and restrictions, and for these descriptions to be successively refined and constrained, until the details of an actual system can be given. However, its lack of structuring methods beyond the schema calculus means that the production of imperative code from specifications is very much a matter of the skills of the developer, and few guidelines are available in the syntax to assist this process. Z^{++} is intended to provide these necessary structuring facilities, and it also provides a high-level semantics in terms of inheritance and refinement of specifications, so enabling reasoning about transformations of classes and systems of classes.

The steps in the specification-based development process are as follows:

- provide a general formal framework for the domain, e.g. of learning systems, or inference processes [188];
- use Z or a similar high-level specification language to create an initial specification within this framework, from the system requirements;
- use laws of refinement [150, 110] where possible to derive refinements of this specification;
- encode the system from the specification using automatic code-generation tools [7, 43, 101];
- wherever possible, maintain the application by modifying the specification, and regenerating the code [109].

Tools have been developed to support this process, and additional processes, such as reverse-engineering old code into a formal specification language, to aid re-use [102].

In the following section we illustrate the method by representing and developing a classification system based on fuzzy sets in the above formalism for learning systems.

7.5.1 Proximity-based Classification Systems

An interesting approach to classification problems, and one that is in agreement with psychological findings about the classification methods adopted by humans, is to use conceptual prototypes or 'examplers' as the basis of a conceptual category. The view of some cognitive scientists that all conceptual categories can be defined in the crisp way that we define mathematical concepts is not plausible for many real-world examples, and the idea of categories as formed from a clustering of data around a conceptual prototype, with an associated nearness measure, was substituted in its place [171]. By using object classes which can possess 'prototypes', and 'metrics' which measure distance from these prototypes, the classification system that we describe below [105] reconciles the object-class classification approach with the fuzzy set approach needed to represent real concepts.

The system described in this chapter therefore falls within the proximity-based classification group of algorithms. A basic method of learning associated with these systems is outlined in [161]. It involves an interactive process whereby the learning system attempts a categorisation, and produces explanations which are then criticised by an expert. The system learns from this criticism more effective ways of classifying. This can be represented in our formalism as follows:

$$\forall\, e : Fmla;\ \sigma : DB \bullet$$
$$\|e\|\sigma\ =\ (c, \sigma')$$
where
$$\|e\|_1 \sigma\ =\ (explanation, \sigma)$$

is the initial classification produced by the matching and explanation part of the system. This is then referred to an expert, who provides a correct classification and new information relating to the classification process:

$$(c, \sigma') = expert\_criticism(e, \sigma, explanation)$$

In our system the process of expert criticism leads to a modification of the metrics used in the category representations contained in the database.

7.5.2   Learning System Specification, Version 1

In the initial specification, we have the following types and classes. A set (at present without internal details) of explanations:

$$[Explain]$$

and a parameterised class of learning systems:

```
CLASS  Learning_System[Fmla, DB, L]
OWNS
    σ  :  DB
RETURNS
    AttemptAllocate  :  Fmla   →  Explain
OPERATIONS
    InitiateLS  :  Fmla L  → ;
    Allocate  :  Fmla Explain  →  L  ;
    Learn  :  Fmla  →  L
ACTIONS
    Learn θ ε'   ==>
                  ∃ exp! :  Explain •
                        AttemptAllocate(θ, exp!)  ∧
                        Allocate(θ, exp!, ε')
END CLASS
```

Only definitions of the typing of the other methods are provided, so that the default, completely non-deterministic definition is taken for these.

The distinction between a method listed in the RETURNS list and one listed in the OPERATIONS sequence is that the latter is allowed to change the state of the class, in addition to potentially returning a property of the class instance. The general format for writing a call of a deterministic method Op to a class instance a, with input parameters x and output parameters y, will be:

$$(Op\ x)\ a = (y, a')$$

where a' represents the modified instance. In the case of a returnable property Op, a' can be omitted, since $a' = a$. Likewise, if the operation has no outputs, then y can be omitted. If the method being called in the class belongs to the class, then the method can be used as a schema, with parameters being supplied via schema renaming, or optionally if no renaming is required.

There are alternative notations for object classes, in particular the Object-Z [47] notation, which is closer to that of Z, so it may be preferred.

The databases $\sigma \in DB$ will be hierarchies or trees of conceptual categories, represented as fuzzy sets with additional information, such as membership thresholds, in addition to a basic metric of membership. In order to facilitate further refinement we separate out the three levels of the learning system:

- user interaction and top-level operations;
- the category hierarchy and operations on the hierarchy: restructuring, inclusion of new categories;
- individual categories and operations on individual categories: creation, addition of a new example, etc.

By doing this we will increase the genericity of the specification, as well as the independence of the levels. The top level is represented by the *Learning_System* specification above, the type of databases will be the class DB representing trees of categories, and individual categories will also be represented by a class, of *Concepts*.

We need a type of *Trees*:

```
CLASS  Tree[X]
TYPES
   tree X   ::=   node ⟪ X  ×  seq (tree X) ⟫
OWNS
   value :  tree X
RETURNS
   Nodes  ·  →   ℙ  X
OPERATIONS
   Initiate T  :   X   → ;
   Replace Node  :   X  X   →
ACTIONS
   Initiate T  x   ==>    value'  =  node (x, ⟨ ⟩)
END CLASS
```

with *Nodes* being an operation that returns all the data items contained in a tree. All internal details of implementation have been omitted for other operations.

At the level of the category hierarchy, we define the class:

```
CLASS DB
OWNS
 concepts  :  Tree[Concepts]
RETURNS
 FindHighestMembership  :  Fmla  →  Concepts L L
OPERATIONS
 InitiateH  :  Concepts  →
END CLASS
```

Globally, there is a type of *Metrics*:

$$Metric == Fmla \rightarrow L$$

At the level of individual concepts we have:

```
CLASS Concepts
OWNS
 concept_name  :  Ident;
 prototype  :  Data;
 metric  :  Metric;
 proximity_metric  :  Metric;
 examples_covered  :  N ;
 threshold  :  L
RETURNS
 MembershipValue  :  Fmla  →  L L
OPERATIONS
 InitiateC  :  Fmla L  →  ;
 AddToConcept  :  Fmla  →
END CLASS
```

The membership value function returns two measures of membership of the example in the concept: the first is some 'absolute' value of membership, obtained via an oracle such as the user's or expert's intuition, and the second is a value of membership based on learning some proximity function.

Finally, we will need a *user*, globally defined:

$$user : User$$

where

```
CLASS User
RETURNS
 AskUserForMetric  :  →  Metric;
 AskUserForName  :  →  Ident
END CLASS
```

This structure will allow us to make changes to each level independently of changes to other levels. For example, we may want to change the way the metric of a concept is modified under the assimilation of new examples, which is a change that should not affect higher levels of the specification. In our specification, we would only need to change the class of *Concepts*, not the classes that use this class.

We shall refine this version by refining each level of the specification. An important feature of Z^{++} is *compositionality*: if we refine specification A to specification B, and specification C uses A, then replacing A by B in C leads to a refinement D of C, under certain conditions [113]. The *AttemptAllocate* operation will be implemented in terms of the operation *FindHighestMembership* at the *DB* level, which in turn will use the *MembershipValue* operation at the *Concepts* level.

7.5.3   Learning System Specification, Version 2

We will carry out several refinements simultaneously, to make the presentation more concise. We make the design decision to define explicitly the low-level types we are using:

$L == [0, 1]$
$Fmla == (Ident \nrightarrow Values)$
$Explain == Concepts \times L \times L$
$Metric == Fmla \rightarrow L$

where a formula $f \in Fmla$ represents the assignation of values to named attributes. An explanation is a concept together with associated degrees of membership.

CLASS *Learning_System*$[Fmla, DB, L]$
OWNS
  σ : *DB*
RETURNS
  AttemptAllocate : *Fmla* $\rightarrow$ *Explain*
OPERATIONS
  InitiateLS : *Fmla L* $\rightarrow$;
  Allocate : *Fmla Explain* $\rightarrow$ *L* ;
  Learn : *Fmla* $\rightarrow$ *L*
ACTIONS
  Learn θ ϵ' ==>
           $\exists$ *exp* : *Explain* •
                AttemptAllocate(θ, exp) $\wedge$
                Allocate(θ, exp, ϵ');
  InitiateLS θ ϵ ==>
           $\exists$ *c, c'* : *Concepts* •
                (*InitiateC* θ ϵ) c = c' $\wedge$
                σ' = (*InitiateH* c) σ;

$$AttemptAllocate\ \theta\ exp\ \ ==>$$
$$(FindHighestMembership\ \theta)\ \sigma\ =\ exp;$$
$$Allocate\ \theta\ (c,\epsilon,\eta)\ \epsilon'\ ==>$$
$$\exists\ c'\ :\ Concepts\ \bullet$$
$$(\epsilon\ <\ (Threshold\ c)\ \wedge$$
$$(CreateNewConcept\ c\ \theta)\ \sigma\ =\ (c',\sigma'))\ \vee$$
$$(\epsilon\ \geq\ (Threshold\ c)\ \wedge$$
$$\eta\ <\ \epsilon\ /\ 2\ \wedge$$
$$(CreateNewConcept\ c\ \theta)\ \sigma\ =\ (c',\sigma'))\ \vee$$
$$(\epsilon\ \geq\ (Threshold\ c)\ \wedge$$
$$\eta\ \geq\ \epsilon\ /\ 2\ \wedge$$
$$(AddToConcept\ \theta)\ c\ =\ c'\ \wedge$$
$$(ReplaceConcept\ c\ c')\ \sigma\ =\ \sigma')\ \wedge$$
$$\exists\ x\ :\ L\ \bullet\ (MembershipValue\ \theta)\ c'\ =\ (\epsilon',x)$$

END CLASS

Here we have applied the refinement operation of refining a previously undefined method (for *Allocate*, *InitiateLS* and *AttemptAllocate*). The explanation records the selected category, and the value of the user-supplied metric of membership in the selected category, in addition to the proximity-based metric. The *Allocate* operation uses properties of the explanation to determine what action to take: whether to create a new concept for the example, or to add it to the selected example. Methods can be decomposed into subparts and constructed via the operations of schema disjunction or conjunction. For instance, the *Allocate* operation could be written using:

$$DefineNewConcept\ \theta\ (c,\epsilon,\eta)\ c'\ ==>$$
$$(\epsilon\ <\ (Threshold\ c)\ \vee$$
$$(\epsilon\ \geq\ (Threshold\ c)\ \wedge$$
$$\eta\ <\ \epsilon\ /\ 2)\ )\ \wedge$$
$$(CreateNewConcept\ c\ \theta)\ \sigma\ =\ (c',\sigma');$$

to define the addition of a new concept to the concept hierarchy in the cases that the 'absolute' metric ϵ of membership of the example in the selected (optimal) concept is less than the pre-set threshold for meaningful membership (so that no existing concept can account for the example, and a new concept needs to be created with this example as its prototype), or in the case that the proximity measure of the example in the selected concept is less than half of the absolute measure of membership (so that a new subdivision of the concept needs to be created).
    Similarly, we define

$$AddToExistingConcept\ \theta\ (c,\epsilon,\eta)\ c'\ ==>$$
$$\epsilon\ \geq\ (Threshold\ c)\ \wedge$$

$$\eta \geq \epsilon / 2 \wedge$$
$$(AddToConcept \ \theta) \ c \ = \ c' \ \wedge$$
$$(ReplaceConcept \ c \ c') \ \sigma \ = \ \sigma';$$

in the case that the example satisfies both 'nearness' criteria, and can be added directly to the concept in which it has the highest membership grade. These separate definitions are combined to produce the definition

$$Allocate \ \theta \ (c, \epsilon, \eta) \ \eta' \ ==>$$
$$\exists \ c' \ : \ Concepts \ \bullet$$
$$(\ DefineNewConcept(\theta, (c, \epsilon, \eta), c') \quad \vee$$
$$AddToExistingConcept(\theta, (c, \epsilon, \eta), c') \ ) \quad \wedge$$
$$\exists \ x \ : \ L \ \bullet \ (Membership\,Value \ \theta) \ c' \ = \ (\epsilon', x)$$

Note that the explicit parameters in the subordinate methods are actually redundant: we could have simply written

$$Allocate \ \theta \ (c, \epsilon, \eta) \ \eta' \ ==>$$
$$\exists \ c' \ : \ Concepts \ \bullet$$
$$(\ DefineNewConcept \ \vee$$
$$AddToExistingConcept \ ) \ \wedge$$
$$\exists \ x \ : \ L \ \bullet \ (Membership\,Value \ \theta) \ c' \ = \ (\epsilon', x)$$

to obtain the same effect, although less clearly.

In this version of the specification we will not detail how the proximity metric of a concept will be updated as a result of *AddToConcept*: it could be maintained either as the average distance to previously encountered examples or by a more sophisticated process involving machine learning.

```
CLASS DB
OWNS
  concepts  :  Tree[Concepts]
RETURNS
  FindHighestMembership  :  Fmla  →  Explain
OPERATIONS
  InitiateH  :  Concepts  →  ;
  ReplaceConcept  :  Concepts Concepts  →  ;
  CreateNewConcept  :  Concepts Fmla  →  Concepts
ACTIONS
  InitiateH concept   ==>   concepts' = (InitiateT concept) concepts ;
  FindHighestMembership θ (c, ε, η)  ==>
          c ∈ (Nodes concepts) ∧
          (ε, η) = (MembershipValue θ) c ∧
          ∀ c': Concepts; ε', η': L | c' ∈ (Nodes concepts) ∧
                  (ε', η') = (MembershipValue θ) c' • ε' ≤ ε
END CLASS
```

The definition of *FindHighestMembership* is a (non-procedural) specification of a 'find maximal member' operation. As such, it is potentially non-deterministic, but it avoids needless overspecification of the operation, unlike a procedural definition of a search. Overspecification is harmful both because it constrains refinement and because it can make proofs about a system more complex.

```
CLASS Concepts
OWNS
  concept_name  :  Ident;
  prototype  :  Fmla;
  metric  :  Metric;
  proximity_metric  :  Metric;
  examples_covered  :  N ;
  threshold  :  L
RETURNS
  MembershipValue  :  Fmla  →  L L;
  Threshold  :  →  L;
  Prototype  :  →  Fmla
OPERATIONS
  InitiateC  :  Fmla L  →  ;
  AddToConcept  :  Fmla  →
ACTIONS
  InitiateC   θ  thd   ==>
```

$$prototype' \ = \ \theta \ \land$$
$$examples\_covered' \ = \ 1 \ \land$$
$$threshold' \ = \ thd \ \land$$
$$concept\_name' \ = \ (AskUserForName \ user) \ \land$$
$$metric' \ = \ (AskUserForMetric \ user);$$

```
  MembershipValue θ ϵ η    ==>
```

$$\epsilon \ = \ metric(\theta) \ \land$$
$$\eta \ = \ proximity\_metric(\theta) \ ;$$

```
  Threshold ϵ  ==>  ϵ = threshold;
  Prototype φ   ==>  φ = prototype
END CLASS
```

dom *prototype* gives the list of attributes considered relevant to a particular concept. This list may change (the above specification, since it omits a definition of *AddToConcept*, cannot be proved to preserve this list).

7.5.4   Learning System Specification, Version 3

In this version, we give more complete details, and illustrate how modifications to the specification can be simply performed. The *Learning_System* class is unchanged, but we add more detail to the other classes, and we need a global function that gives the range of possible values for each attribute:

$$\begin{array}{|l}
type\_of : Ident \rightarrow \mathbb{P}\,\Re \\
extent : Ident \rightarrow \Re \\
\hline
\forall\, v : Ident \bullet \\
\quad extent(v) = \bigvee\{a, b : \Re \mid a, b \in type\_of(v) \bullet a - b\}
\end{array}$$

where $\Re$ is the set of real numbers.

```
CLASS DB
OWNS
  concepts  :  Tree[Concepts]
RETURNS
  FindHighestMembership  :  Fmla  →  Explain
OPERATIONS
  InitiateH   :  Concepts  → ;
  ReplaceConcept   :  Concepts Concepts  → ;
  CreateNewConcept   :  Concepts Fmla  →  Concepts
ACTIONS
  InitiateH  concept   ==>    concepts′ = (InitiateT concept) concepts;
  FindHighestMembership θ (c, ϵ, η)  ==>
        c ∈ (Nodes concepts) ∧
        (ϵ, η) = (MembershipValue θ) c ∧
        ∀ c′ : Concepts;  ϵ′, η′ : L | c′ ∈ (Nodes concepts) ∧
              (ϵ′, η′) = (MembershipValue θ) c′ • ϵ′ ≤ ϵ
  ReplaceConcept c c′  ==>  (ReplaceNode c c′) concepts = concepts′;
  CreateNewConcept c θ c′ ==>
              (∃ c″ : Concepts • c′ = (InitiateC θ 0.3) c″ ) ∧
              (dom (Prototype c) ⊆ dom θ  ∧
               concepts′ = (AddDescendant c c′) concepts )   ∨
              (¬ (dom (Prototype c) ⊆ dom θ) ∧
               concepts′ = (AddSibling c c′) concepts )
END CLASS
```

The *CreateNewConcept* operation generates a new concept c' with the prototype θ, and with a threshold of 0.3. If the set of attributes of the concept c are a subset of those of θ then c' is made a descendant of c in the concept hierarchy, otherwise c' is made a 'sibling' of c in the concept hierarchy.

We have extended the *Tree* class by operations of *AddDescendant* and *AddSibling*.

```
CLASS Concepts
OWNS
  concept_name  :  Ident;
  prototype  :  Fmla;
  metric  :  Metric;
```

$proximity\_metric$: $Metric$;
$examples\_covered$: N ;
$threshold$: L

RETURNS
$Membership\,Value$: $Fmla$ $\rightarrow$ $L\ L$;
$Threshold$: $\rightarrow$ L;
$Prototype$: $\rightarrow$ $Fmla$

OPERATIONS
$InitiateC$: $Fmla\ L$ $\rightarrow$;
$AddToConcept$: $Fmla$ $\rightarrow$

INVARIANT

$\forall\, x : Fmla \bullet$
   $proximity\_metric(x) = 1 - (\sum \{v : \text{dom}\, x \cap \text{dom}\, prototype \bullet$
$$(\frac{x(v) - prototype(v)}{extent(v)})^2\})^{\frac{1}{2}} / (\# \,\text{dom}\, x \cap \text{dom}\, prototype)^{\frac{1}{2}}$$

ACTIONS
$InitiateC$ θ thd $==>$

$prototype'$ $=$ θ $\wedge$
$examples\_covered'$ $=$ 1 $\wedge$
$threshold'$ $=$ thd $\wedge$
$concept\_name'$ $=$ $(AskUserForName\ user)$ $\wedge$
$metric'$ $=$ $(AskUserForMetric\ user)$;

$Membership\,Value$ θ ϵ η $==>$

ϵ $=$ $metric(\theta)$ $\wedge$
η $=$ $proximity\_metric(\theta)$;

$Threshold$ ϵ $==>$ ϵ $=$ $threshold$;
$Prototype$ ϕ $==>$ ϕ $=$ $prototype$;

$AddToConcept$ θ $==>$
   $(\forall$ $v :$ dom $prototype$ $\bullet$
      v $\in$ dom θ $\wedge$
         $prototype'(v)$ $=$
            $(examples\_covered$ $*$ $prototype(v)$ $+$ $\theta(v))$
                      $/$ $examples\_covered')$
         $\vee$ v $\notin$ dom θ $\wedge$
            $prototype'(v)$ $=$ $prototype(v))$ $\wedge$
   $examples\_covered'$ $=$ $examples\_covered$ $+$ 1 $\wedge$
   $metric'$ $=$ $metric$

END CLASS

The proximity metric here is maintained as the distance to the average of previous examples. A more sophisticated alternative is to use some learning system such as GOLEM [156] to learn the correct metric, assuming that an explicit definition of the user-provided metric is not available (and may not even be known to the user).

This requires only a small change in the *Concepts* class, and the introduction of another learning system:

$$Fmla2 == Fmla \times L$$

CLASS $LS2[Fmla2, DB2, L]$
OWNS
  σ : $DB2$
RETURNS
  $Apply$: $\rightarrow$ $Metric$
OPERATIONS
  $Learn2$: $Fmla2 \rightarrow L$
END CLASS

CLASS *Concepts*
OWNS
  $concept\_name$: $Ident$;
  $metric\_rules$: $LS2$;
  $prototype$: $Fmla$;
  $proximity\_metric$: $Metric$;
  $examples\_covered$: N ;
  $threshold$: L
RETURNS
  $Membership Value$: $Fmla \rightarrow L \ L$;
  $Threshold$: $\rightarrow L$;
  $Prototype$: $\rightarrow Fmla$
OPERATIONS
  $InitiateC$: $Fmla \ L \rightarrow$;
  $AddToConcept$: $Fmla \rightarrow$
INVARIANT
  $\forall \ \phi$: $Fmla$ •
      $proximity\_metric(\phi) = (Apply \ metric\_rules)(\phi)$
ACTIONS
  $InitiateC \quad \theta \ thd \ ==>$
$$prototype' = \theta \ \wedge$$
$$examples\_covered' = 1 \ \wedge$$
$$threshold' = thd \ \wedge$$
$$concept\_name' = (AskUserForName \ user);$$
  $Membership Value \ \theta \ \epsilon \ \eta \quad ==>$
$$\epsilon = (AskUserForMetric \ user) \ \theta \quad \wedge$$
$$\eta = proximity\_metric(\theta) \ ;$$
  $Threshold \ \epsilon \ ==> \ \epsilon = threshold$;
  $Prototype \ \phi \ ==> \ \phi = prototype$;

AddToConcept θ ==>

           $(\exists \ \epsilon \ : \ L \ \bullet \ (AskUserForMetric \ user) \ \theta \ = \ \epsilon \ \wedge$

               $metric\_rules' \ = \ (Learn2 \ \theta \ \epsilon) \ metric\_rules) \ \wedge$

            $examples\_covered' \ = \ examples\_covered \ + \ 1$

END CLASS

Each concept given by this specification updates its metric by learning a new association of a value to a formula, the value being provided by the judgement of the user (this judgement might involve automatic experimentation, rather than human intervention), and using the derived metric (*Apply* ℓ) of the changed learning system instance ℓ after assimilation of the new fact. The interface with higher levels of the specification remains unchanged: only the internal details of the definitions have changed, but these details are hidden from the classes that use the *Concepts* class.

7.5.5   Refinement and Implementation

A set of tools to assist in the refinement of Z^{++} specifications to procedural code has been developed [101] and their target language is a high-level PASCAL-like language called UNIFORM, but other destination languages are possible. A considerable amount of work has taken place in producing Prolog programs from Z specifications, and refinement of these programs into efficient forms [43], and it would be possible to use these techniques here.

An initial (direct but inefficient) implementation of the *FindHighestMembership* operation can be given by:

```
FindHighestMembership(T,Concepts,[C,E1,E2]) :- Nodes(Concepts,X1),
                                               member(C,X1),
           MembershipValue(T,C,[E1,E2]),
           not((member(C1,X1),
               MembershipValue(T,C1,[F1,F2]), greater(F1,E1))).
```

where we encode $\forall \, x : s \bullet \phi$ as $\neg \, \exists \, x : s \bullet \neg \, \phi$ in Prolog.

The efficient version of this operation uses a loop:

```
FindHighestMembership(T,Concepts,[C,E1,E2]) :-
           Nodes(Concepts,X1),
           member(C1,X1),
           MembershipValue(T,C1,[E3,E4]),
           greatest_member(T,X1,[C1,E3,E4],[C,E1,E2]).

greatest_member(T,[],[C,E1,E2],[C,E1,E2]).
greatest_member(T,[C1|X1],[C,E1,E2],[C2,E3,E4]) :-
           MembershipValue(T,C1,[E5,E6]),
```

```
( (greater(E5,E1),
    greatest_member(T,X1,[C1,E5,E6],[C2,E3,E4]));
    greatest_member(T,X1,[C,E1,E2],[C2,E3,E4]) ).
```

Hand coding of the system from the specification was carried out, with the type and operation definitions from each class being retained as comments in the (untyped) Prolog code. Implementation was straightforward, with no logical errors uncovered, and was much faster than a specification-free development would have been.

7.6 Comparison with Other Work

A similar methodology is suggested in [188], for the case of inference or diagnostic processes, although maintenance is not treated. Both [177] and [13] see the need for a new software engineering methodology based on rapid prototyping and greater adaptability of applications. We believe that object-oriented specification is an advance on mathematical specification languages such as Z or VDM, in allowing specifiers to structure their specification at a useful level. It allows hierarchical designs to be expressed within the formal language, instead of in informal documentation, thus improving the maintainability and verifiability of the specified systems. Modification and maintenance of specifications is a central factor in their usefulness: even experienced specifiers often need to revise specifications several times in order to obtain a clear and useful description of a system, and in AI, the system to be specified may only be known in some aspects, whilst other aspects are left open to experimentation.

The above design paradigm is close to a hardware view of systems, in which applications are implemented by a multi-layer set of subsystems, each of which makes certain guarantees to higher levels, and places some requirements on these higher levels. This method has been shown to have definite benefits for system security and reliability. It also assists in the rapid prototyping of systems, as has been shown in work on the B formal method toolkit [7].

Development in AI usually takes place in a mathematical language, such as LISP or Prolog, so that the familiarity of software engineers with specification languages in this domain is greater than for those in others, such as commercial data processing. Z^{++} uses algebraic and functional forms of specification, in addition to the set-theory based style of Z, so it may, in this respect, be more usable to software engineers in AI. The tools developed for Z^{++} have all been written in Quintus Prolog and ProWindows [166].

Formalisation of inference processes has been undertaken by Todd and Stamper [188] using Z. Our work generalises this in the sense of providing a framework in which inference processes can evolve, as a result of learning, and in which they can be compared in terms of their relative power. Another area in which a general framework and a set of underlying principles has been elucidated is in uncertain reasoning [103, 158], so our method could be directly applied to this field.

7.7   Conclusion

We have shown how a methodology based upon object-oriented specifications of systems, and transformational refinement of these specifications, can be used to develop real systems. This methodology should help in making development and maintenance of systems more effective. This can be achieved since this specification style allows easier modification of systems, limiting the 'ripple effect' of successive change requests, and allowing teams to work on separate parts of a system, knowing only the common interface requirements. As has been established [143], for the Eiffel language, object or class-oriented languages are suitable for the development of a large library of re-usable routines and modules, removing much work in the repeated redevelopment of standard processes.

7.8   Appendix: A Mapping from Z^{++} to Z

In this appendix we briefly define the Z equivalents of Z^{++} constructs. For a class C:

```
CLASS  C
OWNS
     c
INVARIANT
     Inv_C
OPERATIONS
     m  :  INT  →  OUT ;
     . . . .
ACTIONS
     Pre_{m,C} &
          m  x  y  ==>  Def_{m,C}
     . . . .
END CLASS
```

we define the following schemas:

$$
\begin{array}{|l}
\hline
\_State_C \rule{5cm}{0pt} \\
\; c \\
\hline
\; Inv_C \\
\hline
\end{array}
$$

$$
\begin{array}{|l}
\hline
\_In_m \rule{4cm}{0pt} \\
\; x : INT \\
\hline
\end{array}
$$

In these last two schemas, variables and types will be listed in pairs in the conventional Z style.

We have expanded the definition of the method (a schema predicate) by any necessary equalities for variables of the state that are not changed by the method.

Conditions such as internal consistency can then be expressed in terms of proof conditions on Z schemas:

(i) :

$\vdash \exists\, State_C \bullet true$

(ii) :

$\vdash SPre_{m,C} \Rightarrow pre\ Schema_{m,C}$

and so forth.

Chapter 8

Specification in OOZE with Examples

Antonio J. Alencar and **Joseph A. Goguen**

OOZE, which stands for 'Object-oriented Z Environment', is intended for both the early and the late specification phases of the system life cycle. It builds on the notation and style of Z, and adapts it to fit the object-oriented paradigm. The OOZE implementation is based on OBJ3, and provides not only type checking but also a module database, rapid prototyping, and theorem-proving facilities. OOZE modules can be generic, organized hierarchically, and used for structuring and re-using specifications and code. Modules can be linked by views, which assert relationships of refinement. Module interfaces can be precisely specified using theories. Abstract data types, multiple inheritance, complex objects, overloading and dynamic binding are supported. Data types, objects, classes and modules are clearly distinguished from one another, and a precise and relatively simple semantics based on algebra can be given to the entire language. This paper presents an overview of the OOZE notation along with two brief examples that show how some of its main features can be combined to produce concise but easy-to-read specifications.

8.1 An Overview of OOZE

OOZE is an environment in which many different concepts for system development are combined and clearly distinguished from one another, allowing specifications that are concise, as well as easy to create, understand, update and re-use. OOZE supports both loose, non-executable specifications of objects that are encapsulated in *theories* and executable specifications that can be used for rapid prototyping. By providing animation facilities, OOZE helps to improve communication with the client, and makes it easier to master its mathematical basis. In OOZE, *objects* (which are instances) are carefully distinguished from *class declarations* (which serve as templates for objects). Objects are also organised into *meta-classes*, for ease of identification and to support iteration. Multiple inheritance is supported for both classes and modules. Overloading and exception handling are also supported. All of this can be given a precise semantics based upon order sorted, hidden sorted algebra.

Ultimately, OOZE is a programming environment designed to take advantage of the attractive properties of formal methods while reducing the burden associated with their use. This environment includes not just a syntax checker, type checker, and an interpreter for an executable sublanguage, but also a theorem prover and a module database; all of this is based on facilities provided by the OBJ3 [67] system and 2OBJ [74]. OOZE can also help with subsequent phases of system development, including design, coding and maintenance. As a result, OOZE should reduce the time and cost of formal methods, and also increase confidence in correctness.

Some readers may question the justification for a language inspired by Z that is neither a proper extension of Z nor based upon set theory, but rather upon algebra. The reasons for choosing to modify Z rather than just extend it are several. First, some of the very nice stylistic conventions of Z should be more than mere conventions – they should be enforced. For example, we wish to prohibit introducing new constraints on old data and operations at arbitrary points in a specification; such freedom allows radical violations of encapsulation, and is also contrary to the principles of object orientation, and indeed of good specification in any paradigm. Moreover, it is important to provide proper modules, with generic capability. Finally, the scope conventions for declarations in Z are unnecessarily complex, partly due to the excessive mobility of schemas; this is reflected in the complexities of the semantics given by Spivey [181].

OOZE looks and acts like a model-based language, and indeed, it provides the same meaning for common set-theoretic constructions, such as product and power, as well as for lists, partial functions, total functions, and all the operations upon these that are familiar from Z. Thus, the models of OOZE specifications will be equivalent to models of corresponding Z specifications, when these exist. However, the underlying semantic formalism used to define these models is different: OOZE uses algebra, whereas Z uses a Zermelo–Frankel-like set theory based on axioms given in first-order logic.[1] Unfortunately, it can be very difficult to reason about complex set-theoretic constructions founded on axioms in first-order logic. Reasoning about algebraic specifications can be significantly simpler, and it can also be easier to support mechanical verification in this approach; indeed, it was relatively easy to implement OOZE precisely because of this, based on facilities provided by OBJ. A more complete introduction to OOZE can be found in [3].

---

[1] An elementary introduction to Zermelo–Frankel axiomatic set theory can be found in [55].

8.1.1   Modules

By convention, a Z schema with non-decorated variables represents the state space of some system component, and is followed by another schema defining the initial values for those variables as well as by others defining operations on these variables. But these conventions are not enforced, and it is very easy to write specifications that violate them. Indeed, new relationships among variables can be added anywhere.

OOZE groups the state space schema, initial state schema, and operation schemas into a single unit called a *module*.[2] Only the operations defined in this unit are allowed to act upon the objects of that class. Syntactically, such a unit is an open-sided named box in which the features of the class are defined, with the following general form:

```
┌ Class class-name < ancestor-names ──────────────────────────
│
│   constants
│
│   ┌ State ──────────────────────────────────────────
│   │  class attributes
│   │ ─────────────
│   │  class invariant
│   └────────────────────────────────────────────────
│
│   ┌ Init ───────────────────────────────────────────
│   │  initial values
│   └────────────────────────────────────────────────
│
│   methods
│
└──────────────────────────────────────────────────────
```

where **class-name** is the name of the class and the symbol $<$ indicates that the class being defined is a subclass of one or more previously defined classes, named in **ancestor-names**. The **constants** are fixed values which cannot be changed by any method, and are the same for all instances of the class. The **class attributes** are variables that can take values either in another class or in a data type. The **class invariant** is a predicate that constrains the values that the attributes can take; it must hold for all objects of the class, before and after the execution of methods and in the initial state. *Init* gives the **initial values** that attributes take. **methods** are given in schemas that define operations involving one or more attributes of the same class, and possibly input or output variables; these define the relationship between the state of an object before and after the execution of a method. (Differences between the syntax of schemas in OOZE and Z are discussed in Section 8.1.4.)

---

[2]This structure was inspired by that of Object-Z [47].

8.1.2 Encapsulation of Classes in Modules

In many object-oriented languages, including Eiffel [142], Smalltalk [159] and Object-Z [47], modules and classes are identified, so that only one class can be encapsulated. Because of this, cases where several classes have interdependent representations are not easily captured. For example, consider a class **Private-Teachers** and a class **Independent-Students**, where each class has only one attribute, with a value involving the other class: teachers keep a list of their students and students keep a list of their teachers. Because these two classes are interdependent, it is impossible to determine which should be defined first. If no order is established, then the object hierarchy is not properly enforced. A straightforward solution is to introduce both classes in one module. Hence OOZE modules can contain any number of classes, and can also be generic:

module-name[parameters]

  importing
  imported-modules

  Class class-name$_0$
  $\vdots$

  $\vdots$

  Class class-name$_n$
  $\vdots$

Here **module-name** names the module; **parameters** is a list of formal names with their corresponding requirements on the actual parameters that instantiate the module; **imported-modules** lists the imported modules, and **class-name$_0$, . . . , class-name$_n$** are the classes defined in the module. Note the clear distinction between module importation and class inheritance. The former concerns the scope of declarations; for example, a class cannot be used unless the module that declares it is imported. Note that module importation is *transitive*, so that if A imports B and B imports C, then everything in C is also available in A. See [69, 71] for more detailed discussions of the module concepts used in OOZE, including importation and genericity. They are evolved from those introduced in Clear [22] and implemented in OBJ [67], and are given a precise semantics using concepts from category theory.

8.1.3   Parameters and Theories

It can be very useful to define precisely the properties that the actual parameters
to a parameterised module must satisfy in order for it to work correctly; in OOZE
these properties are given in a *theory*; theories are a second kind of module in
OOZE. In particular, theories can be parameterised and can use and inherit other
modules. The main syntactic difference between theories and other modules is that
axioms in theories can be arbitrary first-order sentences, whereas other modules
are more limited in order to ensure executability. A theory is introduced in an
open-sided box, with its name preceded by the key word *Theory*.

Theories declare properties and provide a convenient way to document module
interfaces. Understandability, correctness, and re-usability are improved by this
feature. Also, theories provide loose specifications of data and objects, and in
conjunction with views they can be used to assert invariants for objects of a given
class. Semantically, a theory denotes the variety of order-sorted, hidden-sorted
algebras that satisfies it. If no new classes are introduced into a theory, then
the variety of order-sorted algebras satisfying it will be its semantics. (See [3]
for further discussion of the semantics of theories.) For example, the following
theory requires that an actual parameter provide a totally ordered set with a given
element:

Theory TotalOrder

$[X]$

$v : X$

$\_ < \_ : X \leftrightarrow X$

$\forall\, x, y, z : X \bullet$

$\qquad \neg(x < x)$

$\qquad (x < y) \wedge (y < z) \Rightarrow (x < z)$

$\qquad (x < y) \vee (x = y) \vee (y < x)$

Here the notation $[X]$ indicates that X is a set newly introduced for this specification.

The formal parameters of an OOZE module are given after its name in a list,
along with the requirements that they must satisfy. The actual parameters of
generic modules are not sets, constants and functions, but rather modules. The
motivation for this is that the items that naturally occur in modules are usually closely related, so that it is natural to consider them together rather than
separately. Moreover, by allowing parameters to be modules, OOZE incorporates
the powerful mechanisms of parameterised programming [69]. In the syntax be-
low, $P_0, P_1, \cdots, P_n$ are the formal module names, while $T_0, T_1, \cdots, T_n$ are theory

names:

$$\text{module-name}[P_0 :: T_0, P_1 :: T_1, \cdots, P_n :: T_n]$$

8.1.4 Method Schemas

In both OOZE and Z, schemas are used to define key aspects of systems. However, in OOZE executable and loose specifications are clearly distinguished – theories are used for loose specifications of objects[3] and modules other than theories are used for executable specifications. Although schemas are used in both kinds of specifications to describe methods that act upon objects, the predicate part of an executable module schema differs from that of a non-executable one, and from a Z schema. While in loose specification schemas and Z schemas the values of variables before and after method application are related by arbitrary first-order sentences, in executable module schemas a more restricted form is used, in which those values are related by conditional equations. Non-executable specification schemas have the following general form:

```
┌─ schema_name ─────────────────────
│  declarations
├────────────────────────────────────
│  first-order sentence
├────────────────────────────────────
│  first-order sentence
├────────────────────────────────────
│  ⋮
└────────────────────────────────────
```

Here, the conjunction of all sentences is taken as the first-order sentence that relates the values of variables when a method is used. Executable module schemas have the following general form:

```
┌─ schema_name ─────────────────────
│  declarations
├────────────────────────────────────
│  equations
│    if  predicate
├────────────────────────────────────
│  equations
│    if  predicate
├────────────────────────────────────
│  ⋮
└────────────────────────────────────
```

---

[3]See Section 8.1.3 for an overview of the use of theories.

Here, the *if* clause can be considered a pre-condition, and the respective equations are required to hold if the condition, expressed by a predicate, is *true*. If the *if* clause is omitted, then the equations must hold in any circumstance.

In both loose and executable specifications, the value of an attribute before method application is indicated by an undashed variable, while the dashed (′) variables indicate the value after. Method inputs are indicated by variables with a question mark (?) and outputs by variables with an exclamation mark (!). Also, **declarations** may contain a list of attributes whose values can be changed by the method. This list is headed by Δ, and attributes absent from it do not change,[4] i.e. the dashed attribute value equals the undashed one. The absence of a Δ-list means that no attribute value can be changed by the method.[5] Unlike Z, these are not mere conventions; they are part of the definition of OOZE, and are enforced by the implementation.

8.1.5 Applying Methods

In OOZE, the following syntax indicates that a certain method acts on a certain object,

$$\text{object} \bullet \text{method}(p_0, p_1, \cdots, p_n)$$

where **object** is an object name, **method** is a method name for the class to which **object** belongs, and $p_0, p_1, \cdots, p_n$ are parameters whose types must agree with those of the corresponding formal parameters. Actual parameters are associated with formal parameters according to the order in which the latter are declared. The method *Init* is an exception, because it acts on no objects, and its syntax is simplified to the form $Init(p_0, p_1, \cdots, p_n)$.

Also, OOZE provides a selection function for each visible attribute of a class, indicated by a dot before the attribute name. So if A is an object of a class that has b as an attribute, then $A \bullet b$ yields the current value of that attribute in A.

8.1.6 Meta-classes

Meta-classes are a powerful concept that makes reasoning and specifying simpler, by allowing specifications that are easier to create, understand and update. The basic idea is to associate to each class of objects a meta-class that provides access to its instances.

---

[4] This feature was inspired by Object-Z [47].

[5] *Init* is an exception to this rule; its signature has no Δ-list, and only dashed variables are available. The anomalous nature of *Init* is due to the fact that it is really a method of the meta-class, rather than the class.

In OOZE, every object has a unique identifier that is set when it is created, and a specification of a class X defines a meta-class $\overline{X}$. $\overline{X}$ has only one instance, with identifier $\overline{X}$, and one visible attribute, called *objs*, that contains a list of all the objects of class X. Note that every time an object is created, its identifier is added to the list kept by its meta-class, as well as to the meta-classes of its ancestors. These meta-classes allow us to define methods that act upon all or part of the objects of a class, by using the built-in meta-class method *Map* having the general form

> meta_object•Map(objects, f)

where **meta_object** is the unique instance of a meta-class, **objects** is a list (or alternatively a set) of objects upon which the operation **f** is required to act (it may be a method or a function).

Often the meta-object can be inferred by the parser from the operation **f**, and in any case, it can be inferred from the class name, so that we could always write $X \bullet Map(objs, f)$ for $\overline{X} \bullet Map(objs, f)$, and usually write just $Map(objs, f)$, or even $Map(f)$.

8.1.7 Animation

Animation is useful for rapid prototyping during the requirement and early specification phases. In order for an OOZE module to be executable, its axioms must have a special form:

$$
\begin{array}{|l}
m \\ \hline
\Delta L \\
p_1 : T_1 \\
\vdots \\
p_n : T_n \\ \hline
a_1' = e_1 \\
a_2' = e_2 \\
\vdots \\
\underline{if} \ P \\ \hline
\end{array}
$$

where $a_1, a_2, \ldots$ are attributes changed by the method m and listed in L, $p_1, \ldots, p_n$ are parameters of m with types $T_1, \ldots, T_n$, $e_1, e_2, \ldots$ are expressions in $p_1, \ldots, p_n$ and the state of the object, including $a_1, a_2, \ldots$, and P is a predicate in the same variables. The *if* clause is optional, and there could even be more than one such clause, each giving a set of conditional equations. These equations have a declarative interpretation, and in fact are referentially transparent. They define a method by its effects on attributes. Alternatively, methods can be defined as compositions of other methods already defined.

8.2   Examples

One of the most effective ways to introduce the features of a formal language is to present brief easy-to-read examples that show how those features are combined to produce specifications. This section presents two OOZE specifications that are concise but, we hope, not too trivial. The first concerns bank accounts, and the second symbol tables. Both examples show how the natural hierarchy that exists among objects in the real world can be represented in the object-oriented paradigm, how objects are easily organised into clusters, and how methods can be indirectly specified by method composition. In particular, the first example shows how the satisfaction relationship that exists between different phases of the same specification can be precisely stated in OOZE.

8.2.1   Bank Accounts

Nowadays competition in the banking industry is intense, so that banks have to make the services that they offer as attractive as possible. It is not only the quality and speed of those services that count, variety also plays an important role. For example, some bank accounts will allow the use of cheque books, while others will pay interest, or provide an overdraft facility.

The example in this section specifies different kinds of bank accounts, organised into a hierarchy where each descendant account builds on its ancestor by offering new features that make it more attractive to potential clients. Five kinds of bank accounts are specified:

- *Current Account* – a basic bank account that offers no facilities other than depositing and withdrawing money.
- *Overdraft Account* – an account that provides an overdraft facility.
- *Premium Account* – an account that pays interest.
- *Cheque Book Account* – an account in which withdrawals can be made by writing cheques.
- *Super Premium Account* – an account that combines overdraft, cheque book and interest facilities.

Figure 8.1 summarizes the relationships that exist among the classes that represent these accounts. Here classes are represented by boxes and inheritance by arrows, where the presence of an arrow from B to A indicates that B inherits from A.

The specification of the bank accounts considered in this example is presented at two different levels of abstraction. Initially some general properties that should hold in all bank accounts are given in an abstract, non-executable specification. After this, a more concrete executable specification that still satisfies the first

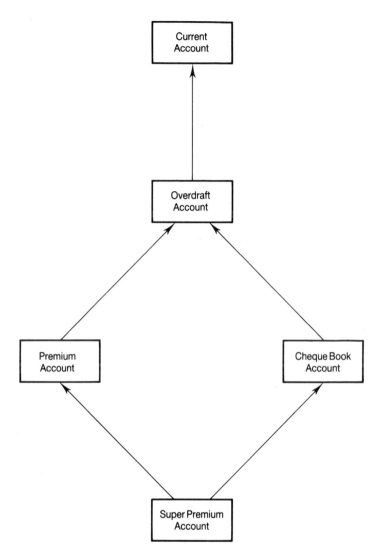

Figure 8.1: The Hierarchy of Bank Accounts

specification is introduced. Finally the relationship between the two specifications is stated precisely.

Abstract Specification
We give a parameterised abstract specification *LooseAccount* for bank accounts, preceded by its parameter requirement theories *Date* and *Money*.

Theory *Date*

[*DATE*]

   Class *Clock*

    $C : Clock$

     Today

      $out! : DATE$

Here, *DATE* is a given set that represents an arbitrary date system, *Clock* is a class of objects, *C* is an object of that class, and *Today* is a method that returns the current date in the date system defined by *DATE*.

Theory *Money*

[*MONEY*]

$MONEY \subseteq R_0^+$

$\forall\, m : MONEY \bullet \lfloor 100 * m \rfloor = 100 * m$

Here *MONEY* is a newly introduced set and R_0^+ is the set of positive real numbers union zero. Observe that the elements of *Money* are constrained to be real numbers with two digits after the decimal point.

Theory *LooseAccount* [*P1* :: *Date*; *P2* :: *Money*]

   Class *CurrentAccount*

    A current account can be modelled with two variables, one that holds its balance, and another that keeps a precise history of the account transactions.

    State

     $bal : MONEY$

     $hist : \text{Seq}_1\, DATE \times \mathbf{R}$

     $bal = \sum\limits_{i=1}^{\#hist} second(hist(i))$

When an account is opened its initial balance is set.

```
┌─ Init ──────────────────────────────────────────────
│ b? : MONEY
├──────────────────────────────────────────────
│ bal' = b?
└──────────────────────────────────────────────
```

When money is paid in, the account balance increases by that amount.

```
┌─ Credit ────────────────────────────────────
│ Δ bal, hist
│ m? : MONEY
├──────────────────────────────────────────────
│ bal' = bal + m?
└──────────────────────────────────────────────
```

When money is withdrawn, the account balance decreases by that amount.
However, debits are limited to the account balance.

```
┌─ Debit ─────────────────────────────────────
│ Δ bal, hist
│ m? : MONEY
├──────────────────────────────────────────────
│ bal' = bal − m? ∧ bal ≥ 0
└──────────────────────────────────────────────
```

```
┌─ Class OverdraftAccount < CurrentAccount ───────────────────────────
```

An overdraft account is a current account with an overdraft limit.

```
┌─ State ─────────────────────────────────────
│ overdraft_limit : MONEY
├──────────────────────────────────────────────
│ bal + overdraft_limit ≥ 0
└──────────────────────────────────────────────
```

When money is debited, the account balance decreases by that amount. However,
the class invariant ensures that it never decreases beyond the overdraft limit.

```
┌─ Debit ─────────────────────────────────────
│ Δ bal, hist
│ m? : MONEY
├──────────────────────────────────────────────
│ bal' = bal − m?
└──────────────────────────────────────────────
```

___Class__ ChequeBookAccount < OverdraftAccount_____

A cheque book account is an overdraft account that allows the use of cheques and keeps a history of the cheques cleared so far.

__State_____
$chist : \text{Seq } DATE \times \mathbb{N} \times \mathbb{R}$

___Class__ PremiumAccount < OverdraftAccount_____

A premium account is an overdraft account that pays interest.

__State_____
$rate : R^{+}$

A super premium account is an account that is both a premium account and a cheque book account.

__Class__ SuperPremiumAccount < PremiumAccount, ChequeBookAccount

Observe that a class invariant in OOZE is a predicate that must hold at every time after the creation of an object. For example, the relationship between the account balance *bal* and the account history *hist* defined by the class invariant of *CurrentAccount* must hold in all models of that specification after the use of the method *Init*, and before and after any use of the methods *Credit* and *Debit*. Therefore there is no need to write these requirements explicitly in the specification of those methods.

Concrete Specification
The parameterised module *BankAccounts* contains a more concrete specification for bank accounts. Its parameter requirements are specified in the theory *ExtMoney* that follows and in the theory *Date* introduced in Section 8.2.1.

Theory ExtMoney —————————————————————————————

> *importing* ————————————————————————————————
> Money

$\|\|-\|\| : \mathbf{R} \nrightarrow MONEY$

$\forall r : \mathbf{R} \bullet$
$\qquad \|\|r\|\| = \lfloor 100 * r \rfloor / 100 \quad \underline{if} \ r \geq 0$

Here $\|\|-\|\|$ is a function that rounds off positive real numbers to be MONEY.

BankAccounts [*P1 :: Date*; *P2 :: ExtMoney*] ————————————————

> *Class CurrentAccount* ————————————————————————————
>
> Every current account has a balance and a history that keeps track of its credit and debit transactions.
>
> > *State* ———————————————
> > $bal : MONEY$
> > $hist : \mathrm{Seq}_1 \ DATE \times \mathbf{R}$
>
> An initial deposit $b?$ has to be provided when a new account is opened.
>
> > *Init* ————————————————————————
> > $b? : MONEY$
> > ————————————————————
> > $bal' = b?$
> > $hist' = \langle C \bullet Today, b? \rangle$
>
> In order to pay money into an account one has to provide the amount of money $m?$ involved in the transaction.
>
> > *Credit* ————————————————————
> > $\Delta bal, hist$
> > $m? : MONEY$
> > ————————————————————
> > $bal' = bal + m?$
> > $hist' = hist \ ^\frown \langle (C \bullet Today, m?) \rangle$

Debits are limited to the account balance.

__ *Debit* _____
$\Delta\,bal, hist$
$m? : MONEY$

$bal' = bal - m?$
$hist' = hist \frown \langle\langle(C\bullet Today, -m?)\rangle\rangle$
   if $bal \geq m?$
_____

Accounts may be closed at any time.

  $Close \equiv \mathsf{Del}(self)$

Given a list of current accounts the auxiliary method *total_deposit* yields the total amount of money deposited in those accounts.

$total\_deposit : \mathrm{Seq}\ CurrentAccount \rightarrow MONEY$

$\forall\,S : \mathrm{Seq}\ CurrentAccount;\ c : CurrentAccount \bullet$
   $total\_deposit(\langle c\rangle \frown S) = c\bullet bal + total\_deposit(S)$
   $total\_deposit(\langle\rangle) = 0$

It is crucial for a bank to keep track of the total amount of money held in its current accounts.

__ *Total_Deposit* _____
$total! : MONEY$

$total! = total\_deposit(objs)$
_____

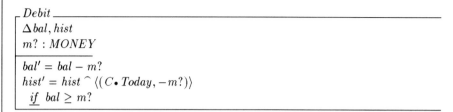

__ *Class OverdraftAccount < CurrentAccount* _____

An overdraft account is a current account with an overdraft limit.

__ *State* _____
$overdraft\_limit : MONEY$
_____

When an overdraft account is created its overdraft limit is set.

__ *Init* _____
$o? : MONEY$

$overdraft\_limit' = o?$
_____

When a withdrawal operation takes place one has to consider the account's overdraft limit.

Debit
$\Delta bal, hist$
$m? : MONEY$

$bal' = bal - m?$
$hist' = hist \frown \langle (C \bullet Today, -m?) \rangle$
  $\underline{if} \ bal + overdraft\_limit \geq m?$

Given a list of overdraft accounts the auxiliary method *total_overdraft* yields the total amount of overdraft credit allowed to those accounts.

$total\_overdraft : \text{Seq } OverdraftAccount \rightarrow MONEY$

$\forall S : \text{Seq } OverdraftAccount; \ o : OverdraftAccount \bullet$
  $total\_overdraft(\langle o \rangle \frown S) = o \bullet overdraft\_limit + total\_overdraft(S)$
  $total\_overdraft(\langle \rangle) = 0$

It is crucial to be able to keep track of the amount of overdraft credit given so far.

Total_Overdraft
$total! : MONEY$

$total! = total\_overdraft(objs)$

Class *ChequeBookAccount* < *OverdraftAccount*

A cheque book account is an overdraft account that allows the use of cheques. It keeps a history of the cheques cleared so far.

State
$chist : \text{Seq } DATE \times \mathbb{N} \times MONEY$

Initially there are no cheques to be recorded.

Init
$chist' = \langle \rangle$

The hidden method *RecordCheque* records both a cheque number *ch?* and its value *m?* if the account balance allows.

RecordCheque [*hidden*]
Δ*chist*
ch? : $\mathbb{N}$
m? : *MONEY*

chist' = *chist* $\frown$ $\langle\langle(C \bullet Today, ch?, m?)\rangle\rangle$ <u>*if*</u> *bal* + *overdraft_limit* $\geq$ *m?*

In order to clear a cheque *ch?* one has to debit its value *m?* from the account balance, and to record its number and value.

ClearCheque
ch? : $\mathbb{N}$
m? : *MONEY*

Debit(*m?*) ; *RecordCheque*(*ch?*, *m?*)

Class PremiumAccount < OverdraftAccount

A premium account is an overdraft account that pays interest.

State
rate : $\mathbb{R}$

Initially the account interest rate is set.

Init
r? : R^+

rate' = *r?*

Interest can be paid in at any time.

Interest $\equiv$ *Credit*($\lfloor\!\lfloor rate * bal \rfloor\!\rfloor$)

A super premium account is an account that is both a premium account and a cheque book account.

Class SuperPremiumAccount < *PremiumAccount, ChequeBookAccount*

Observe that using meta-classes can considerably simplify specifications by allowing easy access and interaction with the existent object of a class. For instance, the methods *Total_Deposit*, *Total_Overdraft* and *Close* were easily specified with the use of meta-classes. Moreover, the meta-class attribute *objs*, the list of the current objects of a class, has been used in the definition of several methods, and the context defines to which meta-class *objs* refers when this is not explicitly stated.[6]   Therefore methods that base their specification on *objs* are automatically specialised when inherited by other classes. For example, the method *Total_Deposit* is defined in the class *CurrentAccount* that is an ancestor of class *Overdraft_Account*, so the inherited *Total_Deposit* yields the total amount of money held in all overdraft accounts.

The meta-class method Del used in the above specification terminates the life span of objects, and removes them from the meta-class list *objs* of the currently available objects.

It is also important to point out that both the abstract and concrete specifications of bank accounts are risky in that they allow withdrawing money that has not been deposited. For example, if too much overdraft credit is given, a bank may have to borrow money to honour debit transactions. Note that a protecting mechanism could have been specified at the very beginning by defining a subclass *CA* of *CurrentAccount* with a tighter class invariant requiring that the total amount of money held in all bank accounts be never negative, and letting this new class invariant be naturally inherited by the new specification of the other accounts.

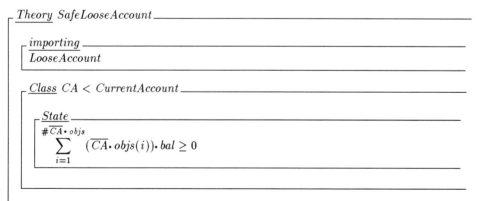

> *Class* $OA < CA, OverdraftAccount$
>
> *Class* $CBA < CA, ChequeBookAccount$
>
> *Class* $PA < CA, PremiumAccount$
>
> *Class* $SPA < PA, CBA$

Here the meta-class attribute $objs$ that appears in the specification of CA is not specialised when inherited by other classes and the eventual availability of cash in one kind of account can be used to compensate shortage of money in others. Note that when a class inherits from others, the class invariant of the descendant class is the conjunction of the class invariants of the ancestors conjoined with any new class invariant predicate defined in the descendant. In particular, the class invariant of the class *CurrentAccount* must also hold for all objects of the class CA.

Refinement
When creating large systems, it is important to relate the different stages of the development process. For example, the *BankAccounts* module satisfies the requirements stated in the *LooseAccount* theory, and it represents a more recent stage of the development of the bank account specification. Therefore there should be a way of describing the refinement relationship that exists between them. In OOZE, this relationship is described by a *view*, a mapping from the features (sets, methods, functions, etc.) in the requirement theory to those in the target module. The view *Account* that follows asserts that the module *BankAccounts* satisfies the theory *LooseAccount*.

> *View Account*
>
> $LooseAccount \mapsto BankAccounts$
>
> ---
>
> $MONEY \mapsto MONEY, DATE \mapsto DATE$
>
> > *Class LooseAccount* $\mapsto$ *CurrentAccount*
> >
> > > *Attributes*
> > > $bal \mapsto bal, hist \mapsto hist$

Methods
Credit ↦ Credit, Debit ↦ Debit

In a view pairs of the form $A \mapsto A$ can be omitted as it is clear what is intended. Also, pairs of the form $A \mapsto B$ can be omitted if A and B are each the first class or given set specified in their respective module. Therefore the view *Account* can be concisely specified by

View Account
LooseAccount ↦ BankAccounts

8.2.2 Block-structured Symbol Tables

An essential function of type checkers, interpreters and compilers is to record the different symbols used in the source program together with information about their different attributes. Symbols such as variable names have to be recorded along with their types and storage allocation, while symbols such as procedure names are likely to require additional attributes that record the number of arguments, their respective types and method of passing.

A *symbol table* is a data structure containing a record for each symbol, with components for the symbol attributes. Although the kind of information stored in a symbol table varies, operations for looking up, updating and deleting the record associated with a symbol will be very much present in any implementation. Symbol tables are crucial for both early and late compilation phases. While the lexical and syntax analysis feed a symbol table with information, the semantic analysis and code generation use that information to check that the source program uses symbols in a correct way, so that proper code can be generated [2]. See Figure 8.2.

More complex operations have, however, to be provided if the source program supports nested block structuring. In this case the source language allows instructions to be grouped in blocks where new symbols can be declared – variable and procedure names, for example. The scope of these symbols is usually limited to the block in which they have been declared, and blocks of instructions may well contain other blocks where new symbols can also be declared. Moreover, it is common to assume that the declaration of symbols in inner blocks takes precedence over those in enclosing outer blocks. Therefore when manipulating a symbol one has to take

source program

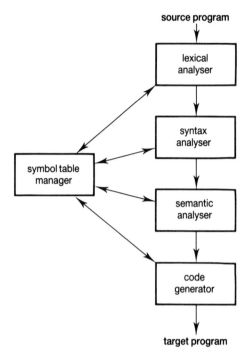

Figure 8.2: Phases of a Compiler

into consideration what symbols can be referred to at that moment. The parts of a program in which a symbol may be referred to are called its *scope*.

Let us take the block structure shown in Figure 8.3 as an example. The outermost block A declares variables x of type integer and y of type char, and these variables may be referred to anywhere within block A. However, block B also declares a variable y, and all references to y within block B refer to the most recent declaration of y, i.e. that made in B. The same reasoning applies to variable x declared in block C and variable y in block D. Note that neither block B nor block C encloses block D, so the variables declared in B and C cannot be referred to within D.

The State Space
A simple way of keeping track of the symbols declared in a single block is to define a partial function st from the set of symbols SYM to the set of values VAL, i.e. $st : SYM \nrightarrow VAL$. Looking up, updating and deleting the information associated with a symbol is made easier by respectively using function application, $\oplus$ (override) and $\lhd$ (domain anti-restriction) on the set of pairs that defines st. Figure 8.4 summarises the main changes that st undergoes if block A of Figure 8.3 is considered in isolation, i.e. without the inner blocks B, C and D. Note that if a

```
┌ Begin A
│    integer x;char y;
│    ...
│   ┌ Begin B
│   │    real y; integer z;
│   │    ...
│   │   ┌ Begin C
│   │   │    bool x;
│   │   │
│   │   │    ...
│   │   │    x := TRUE;
│   │   │    ...
│   │   └ End C
│   │    ...
│   └ End B
│    ...
│   ┌ Begin D
│   │    bool y;
│   │
│   │    ...
│   │    y := FALSE;
│   │    ...
│   └ End D
│    ...
└ End A
```

Figure 8.3: Block Structure

symbol $s? \in$ dom st then $st(s?)$ yields the information associated with $s?$, $s? \lhd st$ deletes $s?$ from st, and $st \oplus \{s \mapsto v\}$ updates st by associating the value v with the symbol s.

Begin A	$\longrightarrow$	$st = \{\}$
integer x;	$\longrightarrow$	$st = \{x \mapsto \text{integer}\}$
char y;	$\longrightarrow$	$st = \{x \mapsto \text{integer}, y \mapsto \text{char}\} = \{x \mapsto \text{integer}\} \oplus \{y \mapsto \text{char}\}$
...	... ...	
EndA	$\longrightarrow$	$st = \{\}$

Figure 8.4: Main Changes in a Symbol Table

However, at a given point in a program a symbol table has to keep track of all symbols declared in each block enclosing that point. This can be achieved by associating a simple symbol table with each block, and organising a list of symbol tables in which tables are added to the list as soon as new blocks are identified. Note that outer block tables precede the inner ones in the list, and at the end of a block all symbols declared in that block can be removed from the symbol table, so the last table in the list can be removed. Also, the correct scope of the symbols declared so far is obtained by overriding the state space of all tables in sequence, starting with the one at the head of the list. If the block structure introduced in Figure 8.3 is taken as an example, Figure 8.5 shows the main changes that a list of nested block symbol tables undergoes. Observe that the correct scope for symbols just before the end of block B is given by $\{x \mapsto \text{integer}, y \mapsto \text{char}\} \oplus \{y \mapsto \text{real}, z \mapsto \text{integer}\}$, i.e. $\{x \mapsto \text{integer}, y \mapsto \text{real}, z \mapsto \text{integer}\}$.

$$\longrightarrow \quad \langle \rangle$$

Begin A $\quad\longrightarrow\quad \{\}$

integer x; $\quad\longrightarrow\quad \{x \mapsto \text{integer}\}$

char y; $\quad\longrightarrow\quad \{x \mapsto \text{integer}, y \mapsto \text{char}\}$

. . .

Begin B $\quad\longrightarrow\quad \{x \mapsto \text{integer}, y \mapsto \text{char}\} \frown \{\}$

real y; $\quad\longrightarrow\quad \{x \mapsto \text{integer}, y \mapsto \text{char}\} \frown \{y \mapsto \text{real}\}$

integer z; $\quad\longrightarrow\quad \{x \mapsto \text{integer}, y \mapsto \text{char}\} \frown \{y \mapsto \text{real}, z \mapsto \text{integer}\}$

. . .

Begin C $\quad\longrightarrow\quad \{x \mapsto \text{integer}, y \mapsto \text{char}\} \frown \{y \mapsto \text{real}, z \mapsto \text{integer}\} \frown \{\}$

bool x $\quad\longrightarrow\quad \{x \mapsto \text{integer}, y \mapsto \text{char}\} \frown \{y \mapsto \text{real}, z \mapsto \text{integer}\} \frown \{x \mapsto \text{bool}\}$

. . .

End C $\quad\longrightarrow\quad \{x \mapsto \text{integer}, y \mapsto \text{char}\} \frown \{y \mapsto \text{real}, z \mapsto \text{integer}\}$

. . .

End B $\quad\longrightarrow\quad \{x \mapsto \text{integer}, y \mapsto \text{char}\}$

. . .

End A $\quad\longrightarrow\quad \langle \rangle$

Figure 8.5: Main Changes in a Nested Block Symbol Table

The Specification

The specification presented in this section defines a symbol table that copes with nested block structuring. The module *SymbolTable* specifies the symbol table state space together with operations for looking up, updating and deleting the information associated with symbols. The theory *SymVal* that follows defines the requirement that an actual parameter to that module should satisfy. First, simpler operations are considered, and then more complex operations are built on the initial ones. The meta-class method **Del** used in the specification of the method *BEnd* terminates the life span of objects, and removes them from the meta-class list *objs* of the currently available objects.

Theory SymVal _____

[*SYM*, *VAL*]

_____

Here, *SYM* and *VAL* are newly introduced sets. The former is the set of all symbols that can be stored in a symbol table, and the latter the set of all unique values, possibly a record, that can be associated with symbols.

SymbolTable[P :: Sym Val]

The state of a symbol table can be modelled by a partial function from symbols to values.

State

$st : SYM \nrightarrow VAL$

Initially the symbol table is empty

Init

$st' = \{\}$

Given a symbol $s?$ its associated value is returned in $v!$.

LookUp

$s? : SYM$
$v! : VAL$

$v! = st(s?)$
  $\underline{if}$ $s? \in \mathrm{dom}\ st$

Given a symbol $s?$ and a new value $v?$ the current value associated with $s?$ is updated.

Update

Δst
$s? : SYM$
$v? : VAL$

$st' = st \oplus \{s? \mapsto v?\}$

A symbol $s?$ and its associated value can be deleted from the symbol table.

Delete

Δst
$s? : SYM$

$st' = \{s?\} \ntriangleleft st$
  $\underline{if}$ $s? \in \mathrm{dom}\ st$

The auxiliary function $\oplus/$ yields a partial function $SYM \nrightarrow VAL$ by overriding the state space of a sequence of symbol tables.

$$\oplus/\_ : \text{Seq } SymbolTable \rightarrow (SYM \nrightarrow VAL)$$

$$\forall\, S : \text{Seq } SymbolTable;\; x : SymbolTable \bullet$$
$$\oplus/(\langle x \rangle \,\hat{}\, S) = x \cdot st \oplus (\oplus/S)$$
$$\oplus/(\{\}) = \{\}$$

Scoping rules have to be taken into consideration when looking up a symbol $s?$. In order to do this the list of all symbol tables created so far, *objs*, is given as a parameter to the function $\oplus/$, and its result is applied to $s?$.

BSearch

$s? : SYM$
$v! : VAL$

$v! = (\oplus/objs)(s?)$
$\underline{if}\ s? \in \text{dom}\,(\oplus/objs)$

At the end of a block the symbols declared in that block can no longer be referred. Therefore the last symbol table created so far is deleted.

$$BEnd \equiv \mathsf{Del}(\text{last}(objs))$$

Scoping rules have to be taken into consideration when the information associated with a symbol $s?$ is updated.

BUpdate

$s? : SYM$
$v? : VAL$

$\text{last}(objs) \bullet Update(s?, v?)$

Note that it is not necessary to define a method that adds a symbol table to the list *objs* of symbol tables when the beginning of a block is found, as this is done by the method *Init*.

A comparison between the above specification and the *Block-Structured Symbol Table* specification, written in Z, that appears in [86] reveals that the OOZE specification is considerably more concise. This is largely due to the fact that OOZE is better fitted to support the object-oriented paradigm. For example, OOZE objects have unique identifiers and are organised in meta-classes, while in Z, and indeed in many languages based upon Z, it is hard to use a class of objects as a template for more than one object. If any collection of objects has to be defined, then a new level of specification in which objects are uniquely identified must be created and the operations specified so far have to be promoted in some way. Furthermore, the above OOZE specification is executable and that written in Z is not. Note that facilities for rapid prototyping can greatly improve communication with the client, and confidence that the desired system behaviour has been captured. Also, the form of the executable OOZE axioms make specifications easier to understand and update in many cases by clearly distinguishing pre-conditions from post-conditions, and this was found to be particularly true in the symbol table specification.

8.3   Conclusion

OOZE is a 'wide spectrum' object-oriented language with both *loose* specifications and *executable* (compilable or interpretable) programs. These two aspects of the language can be encapsulated in *modules* and may be linked by *views*, which assert refinement relationships.

Modules are organised according to an *import hierarchy*, and can also be generic, i.e. *parameterised*. A system of modules, which may be loose and can even have empty bodies, can be used to express the large-grain *design* of a system. A single, very high-level module can be used to express overall *requirements*, via a view to a module that encapsulates the whole system, or at earlier stages of development, just its design or specification.

Rapid prototypes can be developed and precisely linked to their specifications and requirements by views. The use of loose specifications to define interfaces can be seen as a powerful semantic type system [71]. Theorem proving can be provided for OOZE by the 2OBJ system [74], which is itself an extension of OBJ3. OOZE is truly object-oriented, allowing varying number of objects to a class, and complex objects (i.e. object-valued attributes), as well as multiple inheritance and dynamic binding. The precise semantics based on order-sorted algebra that can be given to the entire language supports exception handling and overloaded operations. Objects are organised into meta-classes that allow operations ranging over instances of a class. These characteristics are unique among the proposals[7] for extending Z, and along with its animation and database facilities, make OOZE a very attractive language for developing large systems. More about OOZE can be found in [3].

---

[7]See Chapter 2 of this volume for a survey on other proposals for object-oriented extensions of Z.

Chapter 9

Refinement in Fresco

Alan Wills

In this chapter the formal language Fresco is described, with a focus on its practical application to the refinement of specifications into Smalltalk code, using a proof system. The close relationship between refinement and polymorphism is stressed, and used as a guideline for the construction of inheritance hierarchies in the example given, a system for manipulating complex graphical figures.

9.1   Fresco

Fresco is an interactive environment for building specified and proven re-usable program components in an object-oriented language. (Rather, it is a projected one, since only small pieces of a prototype yet exist. The use of the present tense is grammatically simpler, but should not be understood to imply that any more than a design currently exists.)

The benefits of re-usability promised by object-oriented programming include greater reliability – because components are tried and tested; and more rapid construction – because new products and components are built largely from archived components with a small amount of product-specific 'glue'. There are a number of (soluble, I believe) problems connected with the management, accountancy, legal and distribution aspects of this scenario; but under the assumption that these can be overcome, Fresco is an attempt to address its reliability problem.

If software is to be constructed from library components obtained from everywhere, then we must be sure that the components will fulfil their functions as advertised. But if this means reading and testing them all for ourselves, then we lose much of the supposed benefit of re-use. This is a good motivation for using formal methods. Clearly, formal specification and proof take more resources: but if a component is to be used in many products, then it is worth the extra effort.

The aim in Fresco is therefore to specify object-oriented program components – rather than merely to write specifications in an object-oriented style. This brings practical differences from many of the current object-oriented specification projects:

- Specifications must be able to deal directly with all the important features of a component's interface, and verification methods related to those features must be available. For example, efficiency often dictates that pointers must cross component boundaries, compromising encapsulation: interfaces must document how clients should deal with them.
- Objects in an object-oriented program often work in close cooperation ([95]; [88]), so that it may not be useful to refine and verify individual types in isolation, but rather frameworks of them.
- Polymorphism is important for re-use. The most important kind of subtyping is therefore that in which subtype-members are entirely acceptable in all aspects of their behaviour by clients designed to expect supertype-members. This has a different significance for objects than for immutable values.
- Specification and reasoning must be well integrated with the code.

The following sections discuss these issues in more detail, and their consequences in Fresco's design, which are also summarised in the final section. We begin by looking at an example specification of a group of types, understanding its semantics in terms of formal notions of theorems and theories. Section 9.3 deals with refinement and proofs; Section 9.4 with the special difficulties of reasoning about object-oriented programs. The conclusion summarises the principal features of interest, and assesses the extent to which the objectives have been met.

A discussion of the Fresco view of interchange of software in 'capsules' can be found in [196].

9.2 Specification in Fresco

9.2.1 A type

Shape is the type of objects representing mutable two-dimensional shapes. Every such instance has at least two operations which can be performed on it: you can ask whether it contains a given two-dimensional **Point**, and you can move the whole shape by some **Vector**, which translates the set of **Points** it contains.

```
Shape
─────────────────────────────────────────────────────────
op contains ∈ (Point) Bool
op move ∈     (Vector)
v · [ v∈ Vector :– ∀ p · p∈ Point ⇒
                  (⊙self.contains(p) ⇔ self.contains(p+v)) ] move(v)
```

The description lists the signatures of operations which clients can access; but the most important part is the axiom [...] **move(v)** which details the effect of **move** on the state of the object. The axiom is in the form of an 'opspec':

variables · [*pre-condition* :– *post-condition*] *operation* (*parameters*)

For any match between the variables and specific objects, provided that the client ensures that the pre-condition is met, then the operation will terminate properly and the post-condition will be satisfied. Within the post-condition, items prefixed with ⊙ refer to the state prior to the operation. In this example (unusually) one operation is specified in terms of another. More than one opspec may apply to one operation.

Other theorems may be derived from the axioms of a type, and the entire set of derivable theorems is called the type's theory.

An opspec may be extracted from the context of its type T by

- making **self** the explicit receiver of the operation;
- prepending **self** ∈ T to the pre-condition;
- renaming **self** arbitrarily.

Thus:

v, s · [s∈ Shape ∧ v∈ Vector :– ∀ p · p∈ Point ⇒
$$(\odot\text{s.contains}(p) \Leftrightarrow \text{s.contains}(p+v))] \text{ s.move}(v)$$

In this form, the opspec can be used as a theorem in the proofs of clients which use **Shape**.

The type-membership assertion x∈ T means that x conforms to all the axioms (and therefore all the derivable theorems) of T. x may also belong to many other types. The type-description carries no implication that other operations may not be applicable to members of **Shape**: merely that we do not know anything of how they will behave. The vacuous specification

[false :– true] op

applies to every operation we do not yet know about.

Types and Subtypes

A Fresco type is the set of all objects each of which conforms to a set of theorems about observable behaviour throughout its life. The type defines a set of possible histories of operations on the object; an opspec defines the states in which a given transition may occur, and the relation between the states at each end of a transition.

If H_{ST} is the set of possible histories generated by the type ST, and H_T of T, then if $H_{ST} \subseteq H_T$, we say that ST is a subtype of T, and write ST⊆T.

A client which knows about **Shape** – for example, which keeps a list of **Shapes** and permits users to move them around – will work for all subtypes of **Shape**.

9.2.2 Type Extension

FourSides is the type of objects representing shapes bounded by four straight edges. It is defined as an extension ('::+') of **Shape**: every axiom is inherited. Any theorem derived from the axioms is therefore also true of the derived type. Any client only interested in the movability of all members of **Shape** may therefore make the same assumptions about members of **FourSides**. Fresco type membership is defined by conformance to behavioural theorems, and so for any types A, B

$$A ::+ B \vdash A \subseteq B$$

Model-oriented Specification

FourSides has a model, the four variables p_i, in terms of their effects on which the operations are defined. There is an invariant on the model, which should be true before and after execution of every operation. Its maintenance is only the responsibility of an implementation, and not of the clients.

The model is hidden from implementations of clients, but clients may use it in their own specifications and reasoning. It is sometimes argued that access to the innards of a model breaches the principle of encapsulation; but encapsulation is about permitting implementations to be changed without change of specification, so that more efficient or more powerful code may be introduced. Neither of these is an issue with specifications, however: if a more succinct way of expressing the specification is discovered, it can be used as well as the old one, rather than instead of it. If the specification is to be rewritten to specify something else, then the clients will have to be re-assessed in any case. Encapsulation is therefore a less pertinent issue for specifications alone.

Since it is not our business here to learn geometry, let us assume a predicate nonIntersectingLoop which ensures that the boundaries do not cross; and a predicate in **Point**, withinLoop, which tells whether a point is within the bounds defined by a given tuple of points.

The special variable ↑ is used within a post-condition to signify the object returned by the operation.

Pre-conditions and Invariants

At this stage, we know that setp$_i$ sets its corresponding vertex, but nothing else about what it does or does not do. Note that their pre-conditions duplicate the invariant. If they did not, an implementation would be obliged to achieve the post-condition for any prior state; since it is impossible to guarantee that and be sure of satisfying the invariant as well, the type would be unimplementable.

```
┌─────────────────────────────────────────────────────────────────────┐
│ FourSides ::+ Shape                                                   │
├─────────────────────────────────────────────────────────────────────┤
│ op setp1 ∈ (Point)                                                    │
│ op setp2 ∈ (Point)                                                    │
│ op setp3 ∈ (Point)                                                    │
│ op setp4 ∈ (Point)                                                    │
│ v · [:− ↑ = p.withinLoop ⟨p1, p2, p3, p4⟩] contains(p)                │
│ np · [nonIntersectingLoop⟨np,p2,p3,p4⟩ :− p1=np]setp1(np)             │
│ np · [nonIntersectingLoop⟨p1,np,p3,p4⟩ :− p2=np]setp2(np)             │
│ np · [nonIntersectingLoop⟨p1,p2,np,p4⟩ :− p3=np]setp3(np)             │
│ np · [nonIntersectingLoop⟨p1,p2,p3,np⟩ :− p4=np]setp4(np)             │
├─────────────────────────────────────────────────────────────────────┤
│ var p1 ∈    Point                                                     │
│ var p2 ∈    Point                                                     │
│ var p3 ∈    Point                                                     │
│ var p4 ∈    Point                                                     │
│ nonIntersectingLoop⟨p1,p2,p3,p4⟩                                      │
└─────────────────────────────────────────────────────────────────────┘
```

This VDM-based interpretation contrasts with that of Z-derived notations. In Z, there is no explicit pre-condition: clients have to infer it by considering under what prior states the post-condition and invariant can be achieved. (In this example, the inference is easy and the explicit pre-condition seems a tedious duplication; but experience suggests that this is less so in the majority of more realistic cases.)

The Z approach works well when considering the behaviour of a community of objects all of whose specifications are known to the designer: but for re-use of code, we require a clear separation of the concerns of clients and providers, and so the VDM interpretation is more appropriate.

Subtyping = Substitutability
One of the key features of object-oriented programming facilitating re-use is polymorphism. As software engineers, we are therefore crucially interested in substitutability; and so in Fresco, A is a supertype of B if and only if all objects which have been shown to operate according to the rules determining membership of B will always conform to all clients' expectations of A-members.

In this definition of subtyping, the mutability of objects is important. For example, an immutable rectangle (think of a cardboard one) is undoubtedly a kind of immutable quadrilateral: rectangles conform to all the criteria one could write down to characterise quadrilaterals. But a mutable rectangle (think of four telescopic radio aerials welded at right angles) is not a kind of mutable quadrilateral: you would expect to be able to bend the hinges of the latter, and stretch its edges asymmetrically. So while in the world of immutable values, rectangles ⊆ quadrilaterals, the same is not true of their mutable counterparts.

Quadrilateral ::+ FourSides
np · [:– p2=⊙p2 ∧ p3=⊙p3 ∧ p4=⊙p4] setp1(np)
np · [:– p1=⊙p1 ∧ p3=⊙p3 ∧ p4=⊙p4] setp2(np)
np · [:– p1=⊙p1 ∧ p2=⊙p2 ∧ p4=⊙p4] setp3(np)
np · [:– p1=⊙p1 ∧ p2=⊙p2 ∧ p3=⊙p3] setp4(np)

However, it is possible to find a useful common supertype: FourSides describes all the static and dynamic properties which they have in common.

In an applicative world dealing with immutable values, a subtype is a subset of the value space, and can always be obtained by strengthening the constraints. When dealing with objects, the important characteristics are not the static properties of the object in a particular state, but the set of possible histories – sequences of states – through which an object's operations could take it. Viewed in this light, a subtype is still a subset: but a subset of the possible histories, not of any individual state. To facilitate re-use of program components dealing with mutable objects, we must adopt this notion of subtyping.

The Z-tradition interpretation works well for subtyping of values: a stronger invariant reduces the state space to a subset. The VDM-tradition interpretation works well for subtyping of objects: strengthening the invariant may lead to an unimplementable type, since the real emphasis is on the opspecs.

In Fresco, invariants are therefore regarded as

- irrelevant to clients

- implicitly conjoined with all pre- and post-conditions.

A subtype's opspecs have stronger post-conditions and weaker pre-conditions. Strengthening an invariant may be permissible where the post-conditions are not thereby strengthened to invalidity – that is, if they were previously underdetermined.

9.2.3   Strengthening Opspecs

HVRectangle is a further extension describing rectangles with sides parallel to the axes. Repositioning any corner leaves the opposite one unmoved, but the other two adjust accordingly.

HVRectangle ::+ FourSides

---

np · [:– p1=np]setp1(np) // now no constraint on pre
np · [:– p2=np]setp2(np)
np · [:– p3=np]setp3(np)
np · [:– p4=np]setp4(np)
np · [:– p3=⊙p3]setp1(np) // opposite point is fixed
np · [:– p4=⊙p4]setp2(np)
np · [:– p1=⊙p1]setp3(np)
np · [:– p2=⊙p2]setp4(np)

$(p1–p2).y = 0 \wedge (p4–p3).y = 0 \wedge (p1–p4).x=0 \wedge (p3–p2).x=0$

No new operations or model variables are introduced here, but new opspecs apply to the existing operations. Implementors must prove that their implementations meet all the applicable axioms, and clients may assume any or all of the axioms they know about. Therefore there is a composition rule:

$$\frac{[\text{pre1 :– post1}] \text{ code} \quad [\text{pre2 :– post2}] \text{ code}}{[\text{ pre1} \vee \text{pre2 :– } (\odot \text{pre1} \Rightarrow \text{post1}) \wedge (\odot \text{pre2} \Rightarrow \text{post2})] \text{ code}}$$

A type may extend more than one supertype. There is no guarantee that the result will be implementable, since axioms from the conjoined types may be inconsistent: that is up to the designer. Model variables and operations are correlated by name, unless explicitly renamed (e.g. FourSides[p1\origin]).

9.3   Refinement and Proof

9.3.1   Model Refinement

HVRectangle1 is not defined as an extension of HVRectangle, but is believed to represent a subtype of it. While the operations available to clients are the same, the model variables are different. It will be necessary to prove the subtype relationship.

HVRectangle1
op contains ∈ (Point) Bool
op move ∈ (Vector)
op setp1 ∈ (Point)
op setp2 ∈ (Point)
op setp3 ∈ (Point)
op setp4 ∈ (Point)
p · [p∈ Point :− ↑= origin<p ∧ p<origin + extent] contains(p)
p · [p∈ Point :− origin = ⊙origin+p ∧ extent=⊙extent] move(p)
p · [p∈ Point :− origin=p ∧ origin+extent = ⊙origin + ⊙extent] setp1(p)
p · [p∈ Point :− origin.y=p.y ∧ origin.x=⊙origin.x ∧
(origin+extent).y = (⊙origin+⊙extent).y ∧
(origin+extent).x = px] setp2(p)
p · [p∈ Point :− origin=⊙origin ∧ origin+extent = p] setp3(p)
p · [p∈ Point :− origin.x=p.x ∧ origin.y=⊙origin.y ∧
(origin+extent).x=(⊙origin + ⊙extent).x ∧
(origin+extent).y=p.y] setp4(p)
var origin ∈ Point
var extent ∈ Point

(Assume a relation < on Points: p1<p2 ⇔ p1.x<p2.x ∧ p1.y<p2.y .)

In order to prove subtyping in general, we need to prove that all the axioms AX_T of the supertype T are observed by any member of the subtype ST:

$$ST \subseteq T \quad \Leftrightarrow \forall x \cdot x \in ST \Rightarrow x \in T$$
$$\Leftrightarrow (AX_{ST} \vdash AX_T)$$

The model variables present a slight complication. In the formal semantics of the language (into the details of which we shall not go) model variables are hidden with existential quantification: the history of the visible features is such that there is a history of tuples (such as ⟨origin, extent⟩ and ⟨p1, p2, p3, p4⟩) such that the axioms are satisfied. It is therefore sufficient to demonstrate that any relation between the two sets of variables exists, from which subtyping can be proven. Effectively, the trick is to imagine that the subtype inherits the axioms and variables of the supertype, and that an invariant relates the two sets of variables: given that 'retrieval relation', show that the inherited axioms are all derivable from the subtype's axioms, and therefore redundant.

A suitable retrieval relation for this example is

$$p1 = origin \land p3 = extent+origin$$

(The invariant in HVRectangle constrains p2 and p4.)

9.3.2   Proofs and Theories

The full form of a theorem is

$$[\,variables \cdot \,]\,[\,hypothesis1,\ hypothesis2,\ ...\ \vdash\,]\ conclusion$$

(or it may be displayed in the conventional rule form) where the hypotheses and conclusion may be opspecs, ordinary predicates, or nested theorems. A theorem may be used as a proof rule: if, with a consistent substitution of expressions for variables, known theorems can be found to match all the hypotheses, then the conclusion may be inferred. A theorem may be proven either by matching it in its entirety from such a conclusion or by proving its conclusion within a context in which its hypotheses are assumed.

Each theorem derived in this way should be annotated with a justification pointing to its antecedents. A graph of such justifications is called a 'natural deduction proof' (and can be displayed in many ways).

The generation of a context in which hypotheses are assumed is a localised version of the overall structure imposed on knowledge represented by theorems. A theory is a set of variables and a set of axioms, together with the theorems which can be derived therefrom. We have already met the theories generated by type descriptions. Just as the variables of an individual theorem may be substituted by expressions to specialise the theorem to a specific case, the variables of a type theory – the model variables – may be substituted by expressions to demonstrate applicability to a specific object.

Each theory may be the context within which another is nested: all its variables and theorems are inherited. The outermost types defined by a designer are defined within the context of a standard Fresco theory which inherits information about predicate calculus, sets, arithmetic, the Fresco language, and 'built-in' types and classes.

Fresco's proof support tools impose no chronological order upon the creation of theorems or their justifications. Help in searching a context for theorems to support any other is provided, and consistency and completeness checks can be called upon. Fresco generates 'proof expectations' – theorems which should be verified to support an implementation claim. The publication of unverified code is made difficult, and the same checks are run on imported software.

Model-refinement Proofs
Since withinLoop is not defined here, we cannot verify contains, but we can check its relationship to move. Since that axiom does not refer to a model, the retrieve relation is not needed:

h1	p · [p∈ Point :− ↑ = origin<p ∧ p<origin+extent] contains(p)		
h2	p · [p∈ Vector :– origin =⊙origin + p ∧ extent=⊙extent] move(p)		
1h		v · v∈ Vector	
1	⊢	p · p∈ Vector	**by 1h**

2h1	v ·		origin $=$ ⊙origin$+$v $\wedge$ extent$=$⊙extent
2h2			v$\in$ Vector
2.1h		p ·	p$\in$ Point
2.1.1			⊙origin$+$v$<$p$+$v $\wedge$ p$+$v$<$⊙origin $+$ v $+$ ⊙extent

2.1.1   ⊙origin$+$v$<$p$+$v $\wedge$ p$+$v$<$⊙origin $+$ v $+$ ⊙extent
$\Leftrightarrow$ origin$<$p$+$v $\wedge$ p$+$v$<$origin$+$extent
       by subs-eq from 2h1

2.1.2   ⊙origin$<$p $\wedge$ p$<$⊙origin$+$⊙extent
$\Leftrightarrow$origin$<$p$+$v $\wedge$ p$+$v$<$origin$+$extent
     by Point::Sym+-¡ from 2h2, 2.1h, 2.1.1

2.1   ⊢   ⊙self.contains(p) $\Leftrightarrow$ self.contains(p$+$v)
     by fn-defn from h1, 2.1h, 2.1.2

2   ⊢ $\forall$ p · p$\in$ Point $\Rightarrow$ ⊙self.contains(p)$\Leftrightarrow$ self.contains(p$+$v)
     by $\Rightarrow$ -intro from 2.1

⊢   v· [v$\in$ Vector :– $\forall$ p · p$\in$ Point $\Rightarrow$
     ⊙self.contains(p) $\Leftrightarrow$ self.contains(p$+$v)] move(v)
     by refine from h2, 1, 2

The theorem to be proven is formed by the hypotheses h1, h2 and the concluding line labelled '⊢ '. There are several subproofs (1, 2, and 2.1) which may have local variables and hypotheses: these are necessary for the application of rules containing subtheorems. Non-hypotheses are justified with **by** rulename **from** antecedents. Rules used here include:

refine :	[P1 :– R1] S, (P ⊢ P1), (P, R1 ⊢ R) ⊢ [P :– R] S
subs-eq :	E1 $=$ E2, P[E1] ⊢ P[E2]
$\wedge$ -elim:	A $\wedge$ B $\wedge$ ... ⊢ A, B, ...
$\Rightarrow$ -intro :	(i · P1[i] ⊢ P2[i]) ⊢ $\forall$ i· P1[i] $\Rightarrow$ P2[i]
Point::Sym+-¡ :	p1$\in$ Point, p2$\in$ Point ⊢ E[p1]$<$F[p1] $\Leftrightarrow$E[p1$+$p2]$<$F[p1$+$p2]

'E[e]' stands for any expression with a subexpression e.

Certain rules such as $\wedge$ -elim and its complement, and the commutativity of some common operators, are used so frequently that they are built into the support tool and made implicit.

The following is another proof, this time using the retrieve relation, and with three useful conclusions (lines 4, 5, and 6) dealing with different supertype axioms:

h1	p1$=$origin $\wedge$ p3$=$origin$+$extent		
h2	np · [:– origin$=$np $\wedge$ origin$+$extent $=$ ⊙origin$+$⊙extent] setp1(np)		
1h	np ·	nonIntersectingLoop(np,p2,p3,p4)	
1	⊢	true	**by true-intro**
2h		origin$=$np $\wedge$ origin$+$extent $=$ ⊙origin$+$⊙extent	
2.1		p3$=$⊙p3	**by subs-eq, $\wedge$ -elim from 2h, h1**
2.2	⊢	p1$=$np	**by subs-eq, $\wedge$ -elim from 2h, h1**
3	true		**by true-intro**
4	np · [nonIntersectingLoop(np,p2,p3,p4) :– p1$=$np] setp1(np)		

		by refine from 1, 2.2
5	np · [:– p1=np] setp1(np)	by refine from 3, 2.2
6	np · [:– p3=⊙p3] setp1(np)	by refine from 3, 2.1

9.3.3   Operation Decomposition

Types and Classes
While an object may be a member of many types, it is an instance of precisely one class, which describes its implementation as a list of component variables and a set of methods. It is useful to annotate a class with invariants and opspecs, and so we merely extend the type notation to include method-definition. Class descriptions may be derived from each other, for convenience, but that has little to do with any useful behavioural relationship, and is not dealt with here.

While the definitions of a type and a class may be combined in one type/class description, it is not automatic that a class's instances conform to its 'home' type. Fresco ensures that all methods defined in or inherited by a class are proven to conform to the relevant axioms of the home type. Not all the axioms of a type need be provided for by methods in the associated class – partially implemented 'abstract classes' are allowed. But the proof of a method which creates a new member of a type depends at some point on a theorem of the form

$$\text{C.implements}(T), x \text{ class} = C, T\text{-invariants}[\text{self}\backslash x] \vdash x \in T$$

and the first hypothesis can only be satisfied by a special 'built-in' justification which checks whether proofs exist that all axioms of T are satisfied by the methods of C.

Code Development
Although the abstract syntax and semantics of the coding component of the Fresco language is that of Smalltalk, the concrete syntax is somewhat adapted to fit with the reasoning system. (Nor do we expect to be able to give formal rules for every detail of the language.)

The axiom applicable to setp1 can be satisfied by

```
np · setp1(np) =
            ( p4 · p4 := origin+extent;
                   origin := np;
                   extent := p4 – origin )
```

and the proof is largely documented by annotating the code with pre- and post-specifications. Preferably, the code should be developed from the axiom in stages as advocated in [150].

1	origin+extent = origin+extent	by A=A

2      $[:- \text{p4} = \odot\text{origin}+\odot\text{extent}]$ p4 := origin+extent   **by assign**

3      $[$ origin+extent = origin+extent $:- \text{p4} = \odot\text{origin}+\odot\text{extent}]$ p4:= origin+extent

                                                    by stren from 1, 2

4      $[$ p4 = $\text{origin}_o+\text{extent}_o$

              $:-$ origin=np $\wedge$ p4 = $\text{origin}_o+\text{extent}_o]$ origin:= np

                                                    by assign

5      $[$ p4 = $\text{origin}_o+\text{extent}_o$ $:-$ origin=np $\wedge$ p4 = $\text{origin}_o+\text{extent}_o$ $]$ origin:= np

                                                    by stren from 4

6      $[$ origin=np $\wedge$ origin+p4−origin = $\text{origin}_o+\text{extent}_o$

         $:-$ origin=np $\wedge$ origin+extent = $\text{origin}_o+\text{extent}_o]$ extent := p4−origin **by assign**

7      $[$ origin=np $\wedge$ p4 = $\text{origin}_o+\text{extent}_o$

              $:-$ origin=np $\wedge$ origin+extent =

                        $\text{origin}_o+\text{extent}_o$ $]$ extent := p4−origin

                                                    by stren from 6

8      $[:-$ origin=np $\wedge$ origin+extent = $\odot\text{origin}+\odot\text{extent}]$

              (p4:= origin+extent; origin:= np; extent:= p4−origin)

                                                      by seq from 3,5,7

The following rules are used:

seq: $[$ P :− $M_1[\odot x]$ $]$ S_1,

                       $[$ $M_{i-1}[x_o]$:− $M_i[x_o]$ $]$ S_i ⊢ $[$ P :− $M_n[\odot x]]$ $(S_1; S_2;...S_n)$

assign: $[$ P[e] :− P[v] $]$ v:= e

var-decl: (**var** x ⊢ $[$ P:− R $]$ S) ⊢ $[$ P :− R $]$ (x · S)

An alternative 'in-line' style (like Morgan's) may be used for documenting decomposition proofs, in which [...:−...] represents any code which conforms to that spec, and any spec or code may be prefixed by another spec or set of specs which it refines. Some of the auxiliary proofs are a little difficult to integrate into the code in such a style, though a good browsing tool should be able to expose and hide the proofs as required.

Side-effects

The rules are more complicated when the possibility of expressions with side-effects is taken into consideration – not unusual in object-oriented and non-object-oriented languages. For example:

assignment: $[$ P :− R$[\uparrow, x]]$ E ⊢ $[$ P :− $\exists x_o \cdot$ R$[x, x_o] \wedge \uparrow$ == x $]$ x:= E

Similarly, although we can extract, say

          p, np $\cdot$ $[$r∈ HVRectangle :− r.p3=$\odot$r.p3$]$ r.setp1(np)

it can only be applied directly as a proof rule in a decomposition proof if we know that **p** and **np** match expressions without side-effects. If there are side-effects, then we need:

opcall:
$$
\begin{array}{l}
[\ P :- M_0[\uparrow\ ,\ \odot v]]\ E_0, \\
[\ M_{i-1}[a_{i-1},\ v_0]\ :-\ M_i[\uparrow\ ,\ v_0]]\ E_i\ , \\
[\ M_n[a_n,\ v_0]\ :-\ R[\uparrow\ ,\ v_0]\ ]\ a_0\ .\ op(a_{1..n})
\end{array}
$$
$$
\vdash\quad [\ P :- R[\uparrow\ ,\ \odot v]\ ]\ E_0\ .\ op(E_{1..n})
$$

where a_i represents the arguments after they have been computed, v all the other variables that may be affected, and E_i the argument expressions. (This rule-schema assumes that arguments are evaluated in sequence.)

This complication necessitates two kinds of variables in theorems: those which match variables or pure expressions (or, to look at it another way, the results of expressions) and those which match other expressions with possible side-effects.

As with many features of conventional programming, the complexity of reasoning about side-effects is the clearest encouragement to avoid them. However, it is in the spirit of Fresco to acknowledge that under some circumstances such constructs can be extremely useful: and so we should have the power to cope with them.

9.4   Reasoning about Systems of Objects

9.4.1   Constraint Maintenance

A Constrained Association

The functional focus in an object-oriented program is often not individual objects but cooperating clusters of them. Johnson and Foote [95] suggest that types should be documented in 'frameworks', or interdependent groups whose instances cooperate. The object-oriented design method of [174] lays as much emphasis on the attributes and properties of the connections between objects (and therefore the relations between their classes) as on the objects and classes themselves. The typical problem is to maintain an invariant across a link, and in the first stages of design, it useful to annotate the link with the invariant, deferring the design decision as to how to realise it, or to which class to attribute it:

Subject	v.projects(s)*	SView
s		v

'*' signifies there may be many SViews per Subject. Each SView displays a Subject on the screen (or provides a 'view' in database terms to other interactive devices or other parts of the software), and may possibly be used to invoke modifications of it. When a modification occurs, all extant views should simultaneously reflect the change: that is, the **projects** relation should be maintained.

Because we still wish to be able to add new classes (for example, new kinds of view) after the initial design of the framework, it is essential to be able to define the interfaces between them. Medeiros *et al.* [134] suggest a rule-based programming approach, and [88] demonstrates a 'white-box' notation for this purpose, in which skeleton sequences of operation calls are documented. Fresco uses invariants, opspecs and an effects calculus to achieve a black-box approach.

Suppose that Subject is a type of object representing some problem-specific information, and that there will be several different types of display of Subjects, not all of which are yet specified, and of which SView is to be the common supertype. (If subtypes of Subject are designed later, this exercise will be repeated with them: they will have their own views, which may or may not be related to SView. So our present purpose is not to codify a generic structure for all such relationships.)

We begin the design with a model of Subject, which is the *raison d'être* of this subsystem. There is some stored Data with an invariant, and a typical pair of modification and query operations:

Subject
op mod ∈   (Key, Item) $\Delta\{d\}$ op get ∈   (Key) Item $\Delta\emptyset$ [:− R[k, i, d]] mod(k, i) [:− ↑ = F[k, d]] get(k)
var d ∈   Data d.consistent

Frames

A new piece of notation is introduced into the signatures: op $\Delta\{d\}$ means that, of the fields accessible in the current context, op only alters the value represented by d. So for any other variable x which can be proven to be of type T, x $=_T$ ⊙x could be appended to op's post-condition; and this will be guaranteed in all subtypes. (The equality has to be subscripted with the type name, since equality can be defined with increasing precision in subtypes: there is not always just one definition of = for the content of any variable. This is an interesting issue, discussed further in [197].)

In a subtype, the Δ-list may be narrowed to a subset; or may be extended to include new fields known in the subtype which were not known in the supertype. A null set ($\emptyset$, the default) signifies that no fields known in this type are altered.

'New fields' can include both new model variables of the subtype (such as vv in SubjectV) or fields which a variable's contents are known to have in a subtype which were not known in the supertype. For example, if in some subtype of Subject, the constraint on d were tightened to d ∈ DataSubType, and DataSubType has a field x which Data does not have, then it would be permissible to add d.x to the Δ-list of get.

Characterising the Association with Types

While Subject is sufficient as a model of the information to be stored by this system, further 'hooks' are needed for it to take part in the project's association.

Candidate implementations of such associations include: a third class representing the association; a pointer from one to the other; or two-way pointers. In this example, we choose this last option:

SubjectV ::+ Subject
op addView $\in$ (View) $\Delta\{vv, v\}$ **op** removeView $\in$ (View) $\Delta\{vv\}$ [v $\notin$ vv :- vv = vv $\cup$ {v}] addView(v)   [v $\in$ vv :- vv = vv - {v}] removeView(v)
var vv $\in$ IdSet.of(Sview)   bk-ptr: $\forall$ v $\cdot$ v $\in$ vv $\Rightarrow$ v.s == self

SubjectV contains an extra model variable and invariants to constrain it. IdSet is a generic type of sets of objects of a given type. In contrast to Set, IdSets distinguish their members not by equality of state, but by object-identity. '==' signifies that v.s refers to the object self – not just any object with an equal state. The frame constraint $\Delta\{vv\}$ permits the set of object-identities to be altered, but not the states of the objects referred to.

SView is the skeleton-type of the views we are interested in. It needs to see its Subject, and defines the signature of projects.

SView

op fix $\in$ ()   // restores projection
 op clear $\in$ ()   // tidies when released
 [:- self.projects(s)] fix
 dep-d: $\forall$ a,b $\cdot$ a $\in$ SubjectV $\wedge$ b $\in$ SubjectV $\Rightarrow$
              a.d = b.d $\Rightarrow$ self.projects(a) = self.projects(b)

var s $\in$ SubjectV   **fn** projects $\in$ SubjectV $\rightarrow$ Bool   self $\in$ s.vv

Finally, a further type SubjectVisible is defined, to insist on the contractual constraint; and to introduce an operation which brings all the views of a particular object to the front of the screen.

SubjectVisible ::+ SubjectV
op bringForwardAllViews $\in$ () $\Delta\{v - v\in vv\}$ [:- $\forall$ v $\cdot$ v$\in$ vv $\Rightarrow$ ...] bringForwardAllViews   view: $\forall$ v $\cdot$ v$\in$ vv $\Rightarrow$ v.projects(self)

It is this type that needs to be implemented by a class.

An implementor of mod knows that it is necessary to preserve the invariant labelled view. But if the code which effects the modifications falsifies the projects relation, there are no means within SubjectVisible to restore it. Therefore the designer must look outside, to the views themselves: fix guarantees to restore projects, and so the last act of mod must be to call fix on all members of vv. It does not matter if the details of fix and projects are different for every view, or not yet determined at the time of designing SubjectVisible: what is important is their relationship, and the fact that the implementor of SubjectVisible is obliged to use the operation to restore the relation.

9.4.2 Transaction Types

Callback and Invariants

It was observed in an earlier section that an object either belongs throughout its life to some type or it does not, since type membership is a predicate over an object's history. This is certainly true if we look upon each operation as an atomic transition. But while **mod** is executing, the invariant **view** may be invalid, and so the object is temporarily not a SubjectVisible, in the practical sense that it would be improper to call **bringForwardAllViews**, whose implementation might rely on the views being up to date.

For completely encapsulated objects, this is not an issue, since it would be impossible to call an operation on an object that is already in the process of executing one. But SubjectV and SView stipulate a loop of pointers between their members, and so a call to, say, **fix**, can 'call back' the originating subject. (Such callbacks are prohibited in POOL [5] to avoid this complication.)

For this reason, SView::s ∈ SubjectV, rather than SubjectVisible: this allows fix to get the information it needs to restore the contractual constraint.

This is a good illustration of how invariants can be considered to be abbreviations for common conjuncts among the pre- and post-conditions of the type's operations. An elaboration of the get opspec for any member of SubjectV is

$$[bk\text{-}ptr \wedge \text{d.consistent} :- \text{d.consistent} \wedge bk\text{-}ptr \wedge \uparrow =...\text{d}...] \; \textbf{get}(...)$$

while for any member of SubjectVisible, we have:

$$[view \wedge bk\text{-}ptr \wedge \text{d.consistent} :- view \wedge \textbf{bk-ptr} \wedge \text{d.consistent} \wedge \uparrow =...\text{d}...] \; \textbf{get}(...)$$

(and similarly for **mod**); so the operations are required to preserve those invariants which are true on entry. (Where this is not the required effect, a lattice of multiple supertypes can be used.)

Within a method implementing any operation, it cannot therefore automatically be assumed that **self** ∈ T for any T: such an assertion would have to be proven like any other at any given point in the code.

Propagation of Transaction Status

While **s** ∉ SubjectVisible, we cannot call operations which assume **s** ∈ SubjectVisible either directly in a pre-condition or indirectly in an invariant. Note that the type assertions in declarations are forms of invariant. For example, this type strengthens the requirement on **s**:

ZoomView ::+ SView
op zoom $\in$ (Real) Δ... [:– ...] zoom(r)
var s $\in$　　　SubjectVisible ...

Therefore, while s $\notin$ SubjectVisible, it follows that $\forall$ v · v$\in$ s.vv $\Rightarrow$ v$\notin$ZoomView, and it would be improper for any method in SubjectVisible to call zoom on any of its views, except where it could prove the invariant of SubjectVisible.

Using Transaction Types

So the usefulness of transaction types is to characterise a contract not as a specific sequence of events but as a set of relationships between objects undergoing transitions – which such a sequence should satisfy.

As an aside, the notion of transaction type is also useful when dealing with sequences of interactive operations. A whole sequence of actions – e.g. 'edit a proof' – can be considered to be one operation, at a coarse-grained perspective: before and after operations at this scale, the object must conform to constraints – e.g. consistency – which do not apply during it.

Read-frames

One remaining question is how we know when fix is required. The approach being pursued in Fresco is outlined here, and the issues are elaborated in [197].

removeView does not interfere with view, and could be implemented with

```
SubjectV::removeView(w)=
        (                       vv.remove(w) ;
                        w.clear )
```

(which also takes the unspecified action of tidying the removed view).

dep-d in SView forces all subtypes to define projects in a way that depends only on d. fix is not required, therefore, provided neither of the above statements alters d. Since vv$\in$ IdSet, for which vv.remove(w)Δ{vv}; and since w$\in$ SView, for which clear's frame excludes s, we can conclude that d is unchanged.

Encapsulation by Contract

The cooperation between the members of a contract involves more intimate dealings than available to the public at large. Only SView should be aware of SubjectV: others should use only SubjectVisible. The types of the contract should therefore be grouped together and only those which represent the strongest integrity should be available for use by others.

This situation arises whenever the identity of a component object is passed across an encapsulated boundary (whether of a type or a larger unit). The recipient has to be trusted to deal with the pointer properly. This implies that, whenever such a pointer is passed, either in a parameter or 'upwards', by return from an operation, the donor cannot be proven correct without some documentable assumptions about the behaviour of the recipient. So the verification of such a type must involve type descriptions of *clients*. Those cases in which encapsulation is preserved are specialisations of this more general situation, in which the assumed type of the client can be 'bottom' (that type about which we know nothing). Systems are therefore built out of contracts, rather than types.

The extension of the above treatment to deal with contract-encapsulation is part of the current work on Fresco.

9.5 Summary

The Fresco proof system provides a basis for the verification of object-oriented software modules. The features demonstrated here are:

- The interpretation of the type of an object as a characterisation of the set of possible histories of its state-transitions and responses to operations; and subtypes as subsets of such histories.
- The description of types as theories of pre-/post-specifications.
- Monotonic extension of type descriptions to produce subtypes.
- The use of type as a tool in the description of contracts.

As described in [196], the monotonic extension of type descriptions serves to ensure that, when modifications are made to a software 'capsule', earlier dependents are not invalidated. This supports the distribution of new backward-compatible versions of capsules.

The semantics of expressions in the specification component of the language is the same as that of the programming language, permitting aliasing between expressions and the distinction of an object's identity from the state it represents.

Traditional refinement has been adapted to take account of the imperfect encapsulation of types and encapsulation by contracts – though this has only been outlined here, and is a topic still under development at present.

Chapter 10

SmallVDM: An Environment for Formal Specification and Prototyping in Smalltalk

Silvio Lemos Meira and Cássio Souza dos Santos

We present an environment for specification and prototyping of object-oriented systems in Smalltalk along with a style of specification, which allows the definition of some object-oriented characteristics in VDM. A set of auxiliary tools supports the development of specifications on-line and fast prototyping. The presentation is mostly informal and the mechanism is exemplified by giving an object-based specification of a simple process scheduler. We discuss the benefits of using formal methods, coupled with a good programming environment, in the implementation of object-oriented software systems.

10.1 Introduction

The problems raised by the development and maintenance of large and complex software systems in a competitive and dynamic environment have been studied from various perspectives. The term *'software crisis'* describes this problem and many efforts have been made to overcome it, which has given rise to different paradigms and methodologies of software development. Among many others, formal specification and object orientation address that problem.

Formal specifications allow the construction of more reliable and maintainable systems, as they provide the basis for logical reasoning about design in all stages of the software life cycle. The correctness of the proposed solution may be attested by means of rigorous or formal proofs. Verification and validation of the design are both assisted by formal methods.

The use of formal methods in practice, despite all claims about their advantages, is far from its potential due to the lack of effective tools to support formal development. In addition, most programmers have had only practical education so far and are not qualified to use formal methods.

Nevertheless, the scenery is changing, as foreseen in [89]. Courses on formal specification have started to be normal offerings in computing, as the interest in the subject increases. The need to use formal mathematical methods in industrial applications has driven the development of an increasing number of useful tools.

While definitely not a panacea, as many want to (make) believe, object orientation emerges as an extremely interesting approach to software development. The emphasis on re-usability, along with the unification of many phases of development, has to do with many problems related to the *software crisis*.

The marriage of formal specification with object orientation is not a novelty, but it is known to be unstable. Object-Z [46], MooZ [135] and Abel [40] are some attempts to formalise object-oriented software design. The approaches invariably define a new notation, although some happen to be extensions of existing ones, in order to capture basic concepts such as class and inheritance.

We take a different approach. Starting from VDM, a notation which has achieved a high level of maturity and acceptance, we propose a style of specification supported by a development environment, supporting a development method. The method determines some criteria for the design of object-oriented systems with a fair degree of formalism. The environment, named SmallVDM, has been developed in Smalltalk and supports both the specification and prototyping phases.

SmallVDM is an extension of a previous system [187], where prototypes of model-based specifications were derived in a Smalltalk environment. This work presents a more elaborate and suitable environment, which extends the original Smalltalk environment and makes the specification and prototyping of object-oriented systems an easier task to accomplish. In addition, the original work dealt with model-based specifications, while the current one imposes a style which allows the definition of object-based specifications. As a result, the resulting prototype is more object-oriented and consequently it is more easily derived.

10.2   VDM

VDM was originally developed in the IBM Vienna Research Laboratories, in 1973, and it has evolved to be one of the most well-established methods for rigorous software development. A complete account of the language is given in [96].

VDM is based on first-order logic and set theory. The method suggests the development of software through successive refinements. From a very abstract initial specification, others are derived until, after data and operation refinements, the final implementation is constructed. The consistency, that is, the semantic equivalence between the levels of refinement, must be rigorously verified.

The type system is based on set theory. Types are sets of values. In addition to basic types, such as Integer and Boolean, VDM offers some type constructs and related operations. These types, which include sets, mappings and sequences, are used for data structuring.

A mathematical model is constructed for the software, defining the state of the application and operations over it. Auxiliary functions may also be defined.

An operation is defined by specifying its pre- and post-conditions. Furthermore, operations must indicate which components of the state they read and/or write. Functions do not affect the state.

There is no data encapsulation. A model defines a concrete object upon which the operations actuate, not a data type nor a class that has instances. There are no modularisation mechanisms and re-usability is difficult. One can only re-use functions and pre- and post-conditions in a specification.

Further, we present a partial specification of a process scheduler of an operating system, which is in accordance with the style of specification supported by Small-VDM. The specification incorporates some object-oriented characteristics and is said to be object based.

10.3   Smalltalk

Smalltalk is considered one of the languages most true to the object-oriented paradigm [159]. Its philosophy and implementation are extensively discussed in [77].

In Smalltalk, every object is an instance of a class, including the classes themselves. An executing program consists of a set of objects that communicate sequentially through message exchange. Some other object-oriented languages introduce new concepts to the paradigm, such as that of multiple inheritance, but the basic concepts are all supported by Smalltalk.

Smalltalk is more than a programming language. It is a programming environment, composed of a sophisticated interface, a set of tools such as editors and browsers, and an extensive library of predefined classes from which programmers can derive their own. Although Smalltalk is not very efficient because it is interpreted, this is fundamental to provide the exploratory style of programming embodied in the Smalltalk philosophy, through fast environment interaction. The language is also typeless and some errors may occur during execution.

Smalltalk is also considered a prototyping language. Some of the characteristics mentioned above reinforce that character, although many applications developed for production seem to contradict it.

Some pieces of code generated for the prototype of the process scheduler mentioned in the previous section will be listed in this chapter.

10.4   SmallVDM

SmallVDM tries to combine VDM and Smalltalk into a single framework, making use of what each is able to offer. VDM makes possible the formalisation of the design and contributes a simple model-orientated specification notation. Smalltalk, in turn, apart from being purely object-oriented, presents a sophisticated development environment which is extensible and is ideal for prototyping.

We can define SmallVDM as an interpretation of VDM in a Smalltalk environment that allows rapid construction of prototypes from specifications. This definition suggests two views of the tool: specification animation and formal object-oriented development.

Specification animation was the initial motivation which led us to build a VDM environment in Smalltalk, allowing direct transformation of VDM specifications into Smalltalk code, in spite of the style (paradigm) adopted in the construction of the model and respective operations. Some specifications, such as the semantics of SQL presented in [139], and that of an object-oriented database model presented in [153], were animated in this environment, allowing the validation of specifications in a semi-automatic fashion, as discussed in [153].

Changing the point of view leads to a second interpretation of SmallVDM, this time as a tool for formal object-oriented programming. Now the goal is the construction of an object-oriented system, and the paradigm must be taken into account during the process of formal specification.

As discussed above, VDM was not designed for the specification of object-oriented systems. We believe, however, that it can be used to express many of the characteristics of such systems if some criteria are adopted for the construction of the specification. These criteria constitute a style of specification, which can be enforced by the environment where the specification is developed. On-line development of specifications is the key for ensuring the object orientation and providing re-usability and extensionability.

SmallVDM not only provides animation of object-based specifications but it also assists the specification process, ensuring that no violation of the object-oriented design philosophy occurs.

10.5   Object-oriented Design

Research into object-oriented design has increased as its acceptance grows wider. Many attempts have been made to find new rules for good design and to build tools to support them. Some of these are discussed in [200].

In what follows, we assume the division of software development into three basic phases: analysis, design and implementation. The objects of discussion during analysis are just the same as during design and implementation. That makes the transition from one phase to the next one more natural and straightforward, as the domain of discussion is uniform from the client to the programmer. Further considerations can be found in [99].

The integration of formal design and implementation in the same framework is more directly achieved and that is the approach undertaken by Meyer in the Eiffel programming language, which allows the incorporation of formal requirements in the program code. The contracts established between objects are explicitly expressed as part of the implementation of classes. Eiffel and its philosophy are described in [142].

Objects identified during the analysis of the problem must be defined in more detail in the design phase, which must be language-independent, but not paradigm-independent, so as to provide the best utilisation of object-oriented characteristics.

One can implement an object-oriented design in a traditional procedural language by eliminating inheritance. The implementation of a procedural design in an object-oriented language, however, results in waste.

In the light of those considerations, we conclude that the specification of an object-oriented system must come after high-level design. By high-level design we mean the task of defining in detail the objects of the domain, their interfaces, the classes and dependence relations among them. The formal specification of operations and auxiliary functions will be called low-level design.

SmallVDM does not support the analysis phase. This phase preceds the design and comprehends the identification of the objects in the domain of application, as well as the classes from which these objects will be instances and the hierarchy structure they comprise. Details of functionality and interfaces are postponed to the next phase.

10.5.1   High-level Design

The high-level design phase is supported by SmallVDM in many ways. When working in the environment, one is always in the context of one application. Each application has its own dictionary of classes and classes may be shared by different applications.

The type definitions in the specification are recorded in the environment. Each type gives origin to a class, which is created automatically. A new class is either the origin of a new hierarchy or the extension or specialisation of an existing class. The definition of a type may generate new type definitions. When defining a type, designers are asked to insert the type into the system's hierarchy structure defined up to that moment. If no insertion is possible they are asked to check the global hierarchy of classes, to see whether an insertion is still possible or not. A graphical representation of the hierarchy is available, from which designers may extract all necessary information about the classes and the hierarchy structure itself. The graph of the hierarchy is not necessarily connected, and types can be extensions of types defined in other applications.

The system stimulates the definition of abstract classes (classes having no instances), used to gather characteristics that are common to its subclasses, in order to promote re-usability.

A non-empty set of general concepts must be associated to each new type (class) being defined, helping to identify abstract classes and to position a class in the system's hierarchy.

Informal description of types and their attributes must be given. A type is associated to each attribute of a type (field types in a composite type definition, domain and co-domain types in a map definition, etc.). The environment associates to each class a list of all its clients, i.e. all classes whose instance components may be instances of it. Such a list is very useful when maintaining a class.

In contrast to Smalltalk philosophy, the type definition of attributes is a VDM requirement that is essential for the control of the specification. During the execution of the derived prototype the environment performs parameter type checking in order to detect possible parameter-passing errors in the specification. A final version of the implementation, when errors are no longer expected to occur, may discard type checking, adopting the Smalltalk philosophy again. By then, there should be no possibility of run-time typing errors occurring.

Each class resulting from a type definition is a subclass of one of the following predefined classes of the environment, which implement the types available in VDM for the construction of data structures:

- Mapping
- TypeUnion
- Set
- GivenSet
- Record
- Enumeration
- Sequence

Record implements composite types. The names and types of its attributes are informed to the environment and access methods are automatically generated. In Smalltalk, by default, methods are public and components are private. SmallVDM constrains the access according to the specification (*ext* clauses, specifying which components of the state are used for reading and writing in an operation). Any attempt to disobey the specification is precluded by the environment.

TypeUnion is used to specify polymorphic structures. Whenever such structures happen to be necessary, the set of all possible types in a polymorphic occurrence is used to define a union of types and simulate the (constrained) polymorphism.

GivenSet is used for the representation of basic types, such as Integer and Boolean. The interpretation of these types as given sets makes specifications more natural and homogeneous in the environment, but the original Smalltalk implementation is kept (classes Integer and Boolean for the types mentioned above).

The class *Set* used by the environment is not that in the original Smalltalk image, but a new one incorporating some of the old characteristics, as expected, and extending them with quantification, parameter type checking, etc.

Enumeration is used in the implementation of types with finite domains. These types are defined by the enumeration of the elements in their domains.

The usual VDM operations are defined for each of these classes. The correspondence between some VDM constructions and the environment created in Smalltalk for their implementation is shown below.

VDM	Smalltalk
LOGIC:	

$\forall e \in s \cdot <exp>$	`s forAll:[:e|<exp>]`
$a \Rightarrow b$	`a implies: [b]`
$a \vee b$	`a or: [b]`

SET:

card s	`s card`
$s \subseteq t$	`s isSubsetOf: t`
$a \notin t$	`(t includes: a) not`

MAP:

rng s	`s rng`
$s \lhd m$	`s domainRestriction: m`
$s \ntriangleleft m$	`s domainDeletion: m`

COMPOSITE OBJECTS:

$s(n)$	`n s`
$\mu(n, s \mapsto t)$	`n s:t`

SEQ:

len s	`s len`
$s \curvearrowright [t]$	`s add:t`
tl s	`s tl`

10.5.2   Low-level Design

Although classes can be expressed as abstract data types, VDM does not provide mechanisms for defining them. A VDM model can be seen as an abstract data type, but there is no encapsulation, with models representing concrete objects and not classes which can have instances.

In spite of this, an object-based style can be adopted in order to structure the specification and to create a smooth path to an object-oriented implementation.

The specification is constructed on-line in an interactive environment. Facilities including a syntactic editor and procedures for type and operation definition direct the structure of the specification. ·

As mentioned earlier, a type defined in the specification corresponds to a class in the environment. The methods defining its functionality are specified in VDM notation as *associated functions* of that type. This association is provided by the environment but it is not (formally) reflected in the text of the specification. Internally, however, the environment maintains these associations, as well as the inheritance hierarchy structure and encapsulation requirements. The text of the specification, which is generated by the environment in LaTeX format, reflects informally, i.e. by means of comments, the characteristics which could not be formally expressed.

Associated functions are specified as those whose first parameter and the value returned have the same type and are viewed internally as operations.

Auxiliary functions, which are not viewed as operations, must also be associated to a type, which in this case is the type of their first parameter. A third kind of function, which has no parameter, is associated to the type of the value that it returns and is called a *constructor function*. Examples of these functions will be presented later.

The specification obtained is object-based. The inheritance structure is not formally specified but, as mentioned above, internally maintained by the environment. The specification of a class as a subclass of another is an extension of the superclass specification and the characteristics of the subclasses are attached to their superclasses as if a new and unique class was being defined. The environment provides the separation between the two definitions, keeping re-usability and imposing encapsulation pragmatically.

When defining an operation, the designer must fill in a form where all information necessary for maintenance by the environment is given. This includes the definition of the operation's and arguments' names and respective types, *ext rd* and *ext wr* clauses and the pre- and post-conditions. The environment checks the consistency of the given data with respect to the rest of the system.

The integration of tools such as a syntactic editor and a pretty-printer, which formats the final text of the specification, is intended to stimulate the practice of formal specification by releasing the designer from manual work.

10.6   Prototyping

The prototyping phase corresponds to that of implementation in the analysis, design and implementation schema. Some aspects concerned with implementation, such as efficiency and the definition of sophisticated interfaces for the user of the system are not taken into account when constructing a prototype.

The generation of Smalltalk code from specification is semi-automatic. The predefined types of VDM are implemented as classes in SmallVDM. These classes are the basis for the implementation. The environment generates most of the code, making the implementation process relatively simple.

Pre- and post-conditions are automatically translated and when operations are executed, pre-conditions are tested first. After the execution, post-conditions can also be tested, thus verifying the consistency of the specification with respect to the implementation.

Translation of post-conditions and *associated functions* into methods may involve some transformations which must be carried out by the designer in order to reduce the level of abstraction and to allow automatic coding. These transformations, however, are usually easily performed and may be avoided by adopting a style where more concrete (direct) definitions of functions and post-conditions are built from the very beginning.

The verification of the semantic equivalence between different levels of abstraction is not imposed by the environment. It is up to the designer to verify the consistency of transformations but the system may ensure consistency by testing pre- and post-conditions, as well as type invariants, during execution.

A generic interface is used to test the prototype and there is no need to write code for input and output, which is automatically provided by the environment according to parameter and result types. The internal state of an application can be checked at any time and many versions of the state may be stored to allow different kinds of test to be carried out simultaneously.

10.7   An Object-based Specification

We now present a partial specification of a process scheduler, which is the portion of an operating system that organises the access of processes to processors. The scheduler presented here is based on that of the Minix operating system [186].

Each process has an associated identifier and a process table stores information about them. A process can be in one of the following states: *Ready, Executing* and *Blocked*. The possible state transitions are those shown in Figure 10.1.

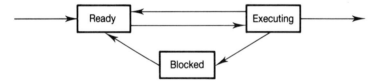

Figure 10.1: Possible State Transitions

There is only one processor and access to it is granted according to priority levels and, for processes with the same priority, according to the order in which they get ready for execution. The scheduler can be modelled in many different ways. Our model is based on two elements, a table of processes and a queue of priorities, as shown below.

10.7.1   Data Type Specification

The first phase of the specification consists of the definition of the type of the objects identified during analysis. Classes are generated automatically for each defined type.

PRIORITY and *STATUS* are defined as enumerations. The type *PRIORITY* is the set of the natural numbers from 1 to n. The constant n must be given a concrete value since the environment cannot operate on undefined values which are, however, preserved in the text of the specification.

$$PRIORITY = \{1, \ldots, n\}$$

The type *STATUS* is the set of the three possible states of a process, as specified in the definition:

$STATUS = \{Ready, Executing, Blocked\}$

IDENTIFIER and *OTHER* are defined as given sets. They may be specified as undefined types but the environment demands their definition. As for constants, the definition is preserved in the text of the specification.

$IDENTIFIER = Integer$

$OTHER = String$

OTHER represents the type of the other components of a process which are not relevant to the scheduler specification. It could be discarded not only in the specification but also in the implementation.

The definition of a type to represent a queue of process identifiers is given below. The operations on objects of that type ensure their behaviour as a queue, where a FIFO (First In First Out) policy is assumed. Its invariant determines that no identifier may occur more than once in a queue of that type.

$IDQUEUE = $ **seq of** $IDENTIFIER$

where

$inv\text{-}IDQUEUE() \quad \triangleq \quad \forall f \in IDQUEUE \cdot \operatorname{len} f = \operatorname{card} \operatorname{rng} f$

PROCESS is a composite type. The *pri* component represents the priority level of the process, *st* is the status of the process and *other* represents other data not relevant to the specification.

$$PROCESS \; :: \quad \begin{aligned} pri \; &: \; PRIORITY \\ st \; &: \; STATUS \\ other \; &: \; OTHER \end{aligned}$$

The definition of a type to represent a table of processes suggests a generalisation. The type TABLE is defined as:

$TABLE(X, Y) = $ **map** $OBJECT$ **to** $OBJECT$

OBJECT is a pre-defined type in the environment. It is the type union of all the types defined in the environment and is used in generic definitions. Other type unions may be defined for that purpose.

The type *TABLEOFPROCESSES* is an instance of *TABLE*:

$TABLEOFPROCESSES = TABLE(IDENTIFIER, PROCESS)$

It is important to note that *TABLEOFPROCESSES* could have been defined as a mapping, without resorting to the definition of *TABLE*. This intermediate type, however, is intended to define an abstract class where many general operations on tables could be defined and re-used later. These operations include insertion and removal of entities, table look-up, etc. With the exception of inclusion and updating, such operations will not be shown here and their existence is taken for granted.

We are aware that inheritance cannot be simulated by type parameterisation [142], but re-usability is achieved and the environment is able to reflect the inheritance structure in the implementation.

There is a queue associated to each level of priority, so there are n queues of process identifiers, with the processes associated to identifiers in those queues all in the *Ready* state. The n queues are grouped in a table which associates priorities to them. The invariant of *TABLEOFQUEUES* asserts that a process identifier cannot occur in distinct queues.

$$TABLEOFQUEUES = TABLE(PRIORITY, IDQUEUE)$$

where

$$inv\text{-}TABLEOFQUEUES() \quad \triangle$$
$$\forall p \in IDENTIFIER \cdot \forall f, g \in IDQUEUE \cdot p \in \mathsf{rng}\, f \wedge p \in \mathsf{rng}\, g \;\Rightarrow\; f = g$$

The state is composed of a table of processes and a table of queues. Its invariant determines that every identifier occurring in a queue will have an entry in the table of processes and that the associated process is *Ready*. It also asserts that there is, at most, one process in execution at any time.

$$
\begin{array}{lll}
SCHEDULER :: & table : & TABLEOFPROCESSES \\
& queues : & TABLEOFQUEUES
\end{array}
$$

where

$$inv\text{-}SCHEDULER(mk\text{-}SCHEDULER(table, queues)) \quad \triangle$$
$$\mathsf{card}\,\{p \in \mathsf{rng}\, table \mid st(p) = Executing\} < 2 \wedge$$
$$\forall p \in PRIORITY \cdot$$
$$\quad \forall id \in queues(p) \cdot$$
$$\quad\quad id \in \mathsf{dom}\, table \wedge st(table(id)) = Ready \wedge pri(table(id)) = p$$

As types are defined interactively, the environment processes the information being given and is able to present them in the VDM format shown above, along with the informal comments added to each type and its components.

10.7.2   Specification of Operations

The limitations of VDM with respect to modularisation led to monolithic specifications. SmallVDM provides modularisation internally, by associating operations, which are defined as *associated functions*: when defining an operation, the designer must first identify the type to which it will be associated.

This is a partial specification, so not every operation of the scheduler will be shown, but the operations depicted illustrate many of the concepts and ideas discussed up to this point.

TABLE

As mentioned above, many re-usable operations can be defined over objects of type *TABLE* but only those for insertion, update and creation will be shown.

> *InsertInTable* (*table*: *TABLE*(*OBJECT*, *OBJECT*)
>   *key*: *OBJECT*
>   *value*: *OBJECT*) *newTable*: *TABLE*(*OBJECT*, *OBJECT*)
> **pre** $key \notin$ **dom** $table$
> **post** $newTable = table \cup \{key \mapsto value\}$

InsertInTable inserts an element in the table. The associated key cannot already have an entry in the table. In *UpdateTable* the key must be in the table so that the associated object can be updated.

> *UpdateTable* (*table*: *TABLE*(*OBJECT*, *OBJECT*)
>   *key*: *OBJECT*
>   *value*: *OBJECT*) *newTable*: *TABLE*(*OBJECT*, *OBJECT*)
> **pre** $key \in$ **dom** $table$
> **post** $newTable = table \dagger \{key \mapsto value\}$

InsertInTable and *UpdateTable* are *associated functions*, i.e. functions that represent operations over a type. The next function is an example of a *constructor function*, which has no parameter and is associated to the type of the value it returns.

> *EmptyTable* *t*: *TABLE*(*OBJECT*, *OBJECT*)
> **post** $t = \{\}$

TABLEOFPROCESSES

The operation that inserts a process in the table of processes and sets its state to *Ready* is specified by

> *InsertProcessInTable* (*table*: *TABLEOFPROCESSES*
>   *identifier*: *IDENTIFIER*
>   *process*: *PROCESS*) *newTable*: *TABLEOFPROCESSES*
> **pre** $identifier \notin$ **dom** $table$
> **post let** $p = SetStatus(process, Ready)$ **in**
> $newTable = InsertInTable(table, identifier, p)$

SetStatus is associated to type *PROCESS* and will be defined soon. The next operation 'executes' the process associated to the identifier passed as parameter.

> *ExecuteProcess* (*table*: *TABLEOFPROCESSES*
>   *identifier*: *IDENTIFIER*) *newTable*: *TABLEOFPROCESSES*
> **pre** $identifier \in$ **dom** $table$

post $newTable = table \dagger \{identifier \mapsto SetStatus(table(identifier), Executing)\}$

PROCESS

SetStatus was used above and defines an operation that changes the *st* component of a process to be that passed as a parameter to the function.

> *SetStatus* (*process*: *PROCESS*
> *newStatus*: *STATUS*) *newProcess*: *PROCESS*
>
> **post** $newProcess = \mu(process, st \mapsto newStatus)$

TABLEOFQUEUES

Constructor functions sometimes need information in order to initialise the object they create. That is the case of *EmptyTableOfQueues*. There is no point in associating it to the type of its first parameter, as if it were an auxiliary function. The designer must be aware of the semantics behind the definitions so as to make the proper associations.

> *EmptyTableOfQueues* () *table*: *TABLEOFQUEUES*
>
> **post** $\forall i \in PRIORITY \cdot table(i) = [\,] \wedge$ **card dom** $table =$ **card** $PRIORITY$

InsertIdInQueue inserts a process identifier in the queue associated to the priority of the process to which the identifier relates.

> *InsertIdInQueue* (*table*: *TABLEOFQUEUES*
> *identifier*: *IDENTIFIER*
> *priority*: *PRIORITY*) *newTable*: *TABLEOFQUEUES*
>
> **pre** $identifier \notin$ **rng** $table(priority)$
>
> **post** $newTable = UpdateTable(table, priority, table(priority) \frown [identifier])$

The next two functions are *auxiliary*, being associated to the type of their first parameter. When many parameters are passed to such functions, some considerations must be made in order to determine which of them best fits in the first position.

> *PriorityOfNextToExecute* (*table*: *TABLEOFQUEUES*) *p*: *PRIORITY*
>
> **pre** $\exists i \in PRIORITY \cdot$ **len** $table(i) > 0$
>
> **post** $p = min(\{i \in PRIORITY \mid$ **len** $table(i) > 0\})$

The function *IdentifierOfNextToExecute* returns the identifier associated to the next process to be executed, while the previous one returned its priority. Both functions use another auxiliary function (*min*) which is associated to the type *PRIORITY*. It returns the smallest integer in the set passed as parameter. As types are sets of values, there is no problem in associating this function to the type *Priority*.

$IdentifierOfNextToExecute$ (*table*: $TABLEOFQUEUES$) *id*: $IDENTIFIER$
pre $\exists i \in PRIORITY \cdot$ **len** $table(i) > 0$
post $id =$ **hd** $table(min(\{i \in PRIORITY \mid$ **len** $table(i) > 0\}))$

The function $RemoveFromQueue$ removes from the table of queues the identifier of the next process to be executed.

$RemoveFromQueue$ (*table*: $TABLEOFQUEUES$) $newTable$: $TABLEOFQUEUES$
post let $p = PriorityOfNextToExecute(table)$ **in**
$\qquad newTable = UpdateTable(table, p, \text{tl } table(p))$

Scheduler Operations
The definition of operations on the state of the application makes use of the operations defined as functions associated to the types of its components and sub-components.

The operation *InitialState* initialises the internal state of the scheduler.

$InitialState$
ext wr *table* : $TABLEOFPROCESSES$
 wr *queues* : $TABLEOFQUEUES$
post $table = EmptyTable() \wedge queues = EmptyTableOfQueues$

The entry of a new process to be scheduled includes its insertion in the table of processes and of its identifier in the queue associated to its priority in the table of queues.

$InsertProcess$ (*identifier*: $IDENTIFIER$
      process: $PROCESS$)
ext wr *table* : $TABLEOFPROCESSES$
 wr *queues* : $TABLEOFQUEUES$
post $table = InsertProcessInTable(\overleftarrow{table}, identifier, process) \wedge$
$\qquad queues = InsertIdInQueue(\overleftarrow{queues}, identifier, pri(process))$

A process is *Executing* when it has access to the processor, passing from the *Ready* to the *Executing* state.

$FromReadyToExecuting$ (*identifier*: $IDENTIFIER$
       process: $PROCESS$)
ext wr *table* : $TABLEOFPROCESSES$
 wr *queues* : $TABLEOFQUEUES$
pre $\not\exists p \in$ **dom** $table \cdot st(table(p)) = Executing$
post let $id = IdentifierOfNextToExecute(\overleftarrow{queues})$ **in**
$\qquad table = ExecuteProcess(\overleftarrow{table}, id) \wedge queues = RemoveFromQueue(\overleftarrow{queues})$

The other state transitions are specified in the same way as *FromReadyToExecuting*, by making use of the functions previously defined.

10.8   Generating the Prototype

Once the system is completely specified, the designer can construct its prototype semi-automatically. Type invariants, pre- and post-conditions are automatically translated to Smalltalk and checked during execution. As discussed earlier, some post-conditions must be transformed into more directly implementable definitions but these changes are easy to perform.

The code generated for some operations specified in the previous section for the process scheduler is now presented.

The operation *InsertProcessInTable*, which was specified as a function, is implemented as a method of class TableOfProcesses. The code derived for the function definition is as follows.

```
InsertProcessInTable:parameters
   | identifier process p |
   identifier := parameters at:1. process := parameters at:2.
   (self dom includes:identifier) not
           ifFalse:[self error:'Pre-condition not satisfied
                              for InsertProcessInTable'].
   p := process changeStatus:(Array with:'Ready').
   self InsertInTable:(Array with:identifier with:p)
```

Pre- and post-condition testing is normally implemented as separate methods in order to make them re-usable. The inclusion of the test of the pre-condition in the method above was intended to ease the presentation.

The first parameter in the specification is removed in the implementation and references to it, whose type determines the class where the method is to be implemented, are transformed into *self* references in Smalltalk (a reference to the receiver of the message itself). The assignment of the value returned by the function in the specification to the object passed as first parameter is substituted by a message sent to that object, as we can verify in the implementation of *InsertProcess*:

```
InsertProcess:parameters
   | identifier process |
   identifier := parameters at:1.
   process := parameters at:2.
   table  InsertProcessInTable:(Array with:identifier with:process).
   queues InsertIdInQueue:(Array with:identifier with:process pri)
```

The methods *InsertIdInQueue*, from class TableOfQueues and *UpdateTable*, from Table, are listed below.

```
InsertIdInQueue:parameters
 | identifiers priority  |
 identifier := parameters at:1.
 priority := parameters at:2.
 ((table at:priority) rng includes:identifier) not
     ifFalse:[self error:'Pre-condition not satisfied
                         for InsertIdInQueue'].
 self UpdateTable:(Array with:priority
                        with:((self at:priority) add:identifier))
```

```
UpdateTable:parameters
 | key value  |
 key := parameters at:1.
 value := parameters at:2.
 (self dom includes:key)
     ifFalse:[self error:'Pre-condition not satisfied
                         for UpdateTable'].
 self at:key put:value
```

10.9   Conclusions

SmallVDM as an animation tool has been successfully used for verification and validation of specifications [153]. Executable programs have been easily derived and tested with the help of a set of tools put together to support a development methodology.

No modification was proposed in the specification language, contrary to many other approaches on formalism in object-oriented design. This possibility, however, is not completely discarded and some attempts to give modularisation mechanisms to VDM are described in [145].

Our approach concentrates initially on the definition of a development methodology based in a established language: VDM offers the language and the development method from specification to implementation through successive refinements.

Programming environments for supporting the programming activity, such as Smalltalk, can be extended to assist formal design and carefully chosen tools can reduce the amount of manual work. The paradigm can be enforced from the specification phase, with software re-usability coming as a consequence of specification re-usability. Classes as modules must be properly managed to facilitate re-use and a good class manager, at the specification level, must provide most re-usability by assisting the definition of new class hierarchies and compartmentalising specifications.

The limitations of VDM for expressing object-oriented characteristics led to the definition of a style of specification supported and imposed by the SmallVDM environment. The experience has proved to be worth while and has indicated some directions towards the definition of a proper formalism for object-oriented systems. The MooZ group, which is working on the definition of an object-oriented extension of Z, as described in [135], and in Chapter 4 of this book, has based some of its decisions on the results obtained from SmallVDM. The final goal is the definition of an environment for supporting object-oriented development starting from MooZ specifications, and many features of SmallVDM are to be re-used. Some of these, such as the syntactic editor for the VDM notation, are under implementation. Most of the environment is already operational and has been used to support the method described in this chapter.

Glossary

While the following definitions adhere to those widely recognised in the object-oriented and formal methods communities, individual authors may interpret them in different ways.

Aggregation: describes a situation in which the existence of an entity requires the existence of certain subcomponents or parts. An example would be a lift system, involving one or more lifts, each with an associated cable. There is sometimes only a subtle distinction between modelling a situation via aggregation or via associations. One distinction which is sometimes used is that an object which is part of another object via an aggregation relationship cannot be removed or replaced during the lifetime of the container object, whereas this is not true for a general association.

Association: an association between two entities or classes is a relation, possibly with cardinality constraints and attributes intrinsic to the relation. An example would be an association *ownership* between home owners and houses, where each element of the association can have attributes such as *starting_date*.

Attribute: a feature of a class or association which consists of a single named variable of a specified type. Attributes may or may not include variables of a class type or of a type derived from a class (such as a sequence of elements of a class). Attributes which are of a class type may be referred to as links or associations.

Class: a template for objects which share common attributes, invariant predicates on these attributes, and operations. A class is usually regarded as a type, of which object instances of the class are elements. Objects can be declared to be of a class type (usually by the notation *object : Class*). The interpretation of this declaration varies, however, depending on the underlying semantics for objects assumed. A class may also be regarded as a theory in a formal language, whose instances are models of its axioms.

Client class: a class which uses an instance of another class (which is then a *supplier* to the using class).

Compositionality of classes: the ability to use one class as a type to define the domain of an attribute of another class. See **client** and **supplier**.

Design: the definition of the architecture, decomposition and components of a system. This development stage can be separated into *logical* and *physical* design steps, with the logical step being concerned with design independent of a particular implementation environment (hardware and software), and with physical design being concerned with implementation of the design in the particular environment.

Dynamic binding: an implementation mechanism which allows the choice of a method definition to be applied to a given object to be made at runtime, based on the class to which the object belongs.

Encapsulation: selective hiding of the local environment (attributes and operations) of a software module (such as an object) from a global environment. This is a key aspect of object-oriented software development, allowing control over the accesses allowed to the private state of modules, and hence allowing changes to a system to be made with reduced impact.

Genericity: the property of a specification component which enables it to be instantiated by different types in order to specify data and behaviour properties in a consistent manner over these different types. In this respect the specification component can also be said to be *polymorphic*.

Inheritance: the inclusion of the features of one class (the inherited class) in another (the inheriting). Inheritance may (but need not) correspond to an 'is-a' relationship between the respective classes: every instance of the inheriting class may be considered to be an instance of the inherited. This form of inheritance is termed *conformant inheritance*. Other forms of inheritance allow, for example, methods of the inherited class to be deleted in the inheriting.

Link: another term for association. In OMT, it refers specifically to an instance of an association, i.e. a particular set of tuples of objects.

Object: an entity encapsulating state and operations upon that state. An object has a persistent state (that is, the values of variables or attributes of that object persist from the last application of an operation upon that object, rather than being re-initialised at each operation invocation). For each object there is a single class of which it is an identified instance, although, depending on the type system adopted, there may be other classes (e.g. supertypes of the identified class) of which it can be regarded as an instance. The effect of operations applied to the object is defined in this identified class (often called the 'owning' class).

Object identity: an intrinsic property of an object, which is preserved over all applications of operations upon the object, and which is not dependent on the values of the attributes of the object (i.e. two different objects can have identical values for all attributes). According to the OMG Object Model:

> *Each object has a unique identity that is distinct from and independent of any of its characteristics. Characteristics can vary over time whereas identity is constant.*

OMG: Object Management Group – a group of some 250 users and developers of object technology, aiming to develop specifications for the portability, re-usability and interoperability of software.

Polymorphism: the ability of a specification or software component to deal with objects or values from a range of types. Both genericity and dynamic binding are examples of polymorphic behaviour which are supported by some object-oriented languages.

Promotion: in Z and Z-related languages, the specification construct which takes an operation OpL on a local state L, together with a *framing* schema F on a global state G, and creates a new operation OpG on G which applies OpL to an element or elements of L selected via F.

Refinement: the process of moving from an abstract specification of a data type or operation to a more concrete specification of the component. Several precise definitions exist, such as that used by Abrial for the B Abstract Machine Notation, and that which is used in Z. There are two main forms of refinement: *data refinement*, in which a relation or function linking the states of the abstract and concrete versions of a class is asserted, and *procedural refinement*, in which the state space of the class remains the same, but operations may be replaced by more deterministic or more robust definitions in the refining class. Usually, procedural refinement is a special case of data-refinement in which the data-refinement relation is the identity map.

Specialisation: the process of restricting the sets of instances of a class by strengthening its invariant, strengthening the pre-conditions of its operations, or by enriching its state, typically to make the class fit more closely to the real-world situation to which it corresponds. An example would be restricting the pre-condition of a *marry* operation to *living* rather than possibly *dead* people. Unlike the OMG Object Model, we do not expect that specialisation will always produce a subtype (for instance, an unshearable square can be considered to be a specialisation of a shearable parallelogram).

Subtyping: if a class C is inherited by a class D, then D is termed a *subtype* if every instance of D can be used as if it were an instance of C. In particular, methods of C should be able to treat instances of D. Examples of transformations which produce subtypes are the addition of new state components which are not affected by existing methods, and the replacement of a method by a procedurally refined one (more deterministic on the old domain, and with an enlarged domain of application). Subtyping can also arise apart from the inheritance hierarchy, via refinement relations between classes.

Supplier: a class C is a *supplier* to another (say, D) if instances of C are referred to within D.

Bibliography

[1] J R Abrial. *Assigning Programs to Meaning.* Prentice Hall International, 1993 (to appear).

[2] A V Aho, R Sethi, and J D Ullman. *Compilers – Principles, Techniques and Tools.* Addison-Wesley, 1986.

[3] A J Alencar and J A Goguen. OOZE: An object-oriented Z environment. In P America, editor, *ECOOP '91 Proceedings,* volume 512 of *Lecture Notes in Computer Science,* pages 180–199. Springer-Verlag, July 1991.

[4] G Alkhatib. The maintenance problem of application software: An empirical analysis. *Software Maintenance: Research and Practice,* 4:83–104, 1992.

[5] P America. Issues in the design of a parallel object-oriented language. *Formal Aspects of Computing,* 1(4):366–411, 1989.

[6] W D Atkinson, J P Booth, and W J Quirk. Modal action logic for the specification and validation of safety. In *Mathematical Structures for Software Engineering.* The Institute of Mathematics and its Applications Conference Series 27, Clarendon Press, 1991.

[7] B Core UK Ltd, Oxford Science Park, Oxford. *B-tool Reference Manual,* 1992.

[8] R Barden, S Stepney, and D Cooper. *Z in Practice.* Logica Cambridge, 1993.

[9] N S Baron. *Computer Languages: A Guide for the Perplexed.* Penguin, 1988.

[10] R S M Barros and D J Harper. Formal development of relational database applications. In *International Workshop on Specifications of Database Systems.* Springer-Verlag, 1991.

[11] V Basili, S K Abd-EL-Hafiz, and G Caldiera. Towards automated support for extraction of reusable components. In *Proceedings of IEEE Conference on Software Maintenance,* pages 212–219, 1991.

[12] I Benbasat and J S Dhaliwal. A framework for the validation of knowledge acquisition. *Knowledge Acquisition,* 1:215–233, 1989.

[13] D Bobrow and M Stefik. Perspectives on artificial intelligence programming. In *Artificial Intelligence and Software Engineering.* Morgan Kaufmann, 1986.

[14] B W Boehm. The economics of software maintenance. In R S Arnold, editor, *Software Maintenance Workshop.* IEEE Computer Society Press, December 1983.

[15] B W Boehm. A spiral model of software development and enhancement. *IEEE Computer,* 21, No 5, May 1988.

[16] G Booch. *Software Engineering in Ada*. Addison-Wesley, 1988.

[17] G Booch. *Object-oriented Design with Applications*. Benjamin Cummings, 1991.

[18] P Breuer and K Lano. From code to Z specifications. In *Z User Meeting 1989*, Workshops in Computing. Springer-Verlag, 1990.

[19] R Buhr. *Practical Visual Techniques in System Design: With Applications to Ada*. Prentice Hall International, 1991.

[20] T Bull. An introduction to the WSL program transformer. In *Proceedings of IEEE Conference on Software Maintenance*, pages 242–250. IEEE Press, 1990.

[21] L Burd. The spiral model and object-orientation: A path towards successful reuse. In *Workshop on Object-Oriented Methodologies*. KBSL, 1992.

[22] R M Burstall and J A Goguen. The semantics of Clear, a specification language. In *Lecture Notes in Computer Science 86*, pages 292–332. Springer-Verlag, 1980.

[23] R Cam and S Vuong. A formal specification, in LOTOS, of a simplified cellular mobile communication system. In S Vuong, editor, *Formal Description Techniques, II (FORTE'89)*, pages 485–499. North-Holland, 1990.

[24] D Carrington, D Duke, R Duke, P King, G A Rose, and G Smith. Object-Z: An object-oriented extension to Z. In *Formal Description Techniques, II (FORTE'89)*, pages 281–296. North-Holland, 1990.

[25] C Carter. Object-oriented analysis and recursive development in safety-critical system development. In *Proceedings of Object Technology '93*, 1993.

[26] E Casais. An incremental class reorganisation approach. In *ECOOP '92 Proceedings*, volume 615 of *Lecture Notes in Computer Science*, pages 114–132. Springer-Verlag, 1992.

[27] CESG. CESG computer security manual 'F': A formal development methodology for high confidence systems, Issue 1.0, CESG, GCHQ, 1991.

[28] K Chadha, C Hunnicutt, S Peck, and J Tebes. Mobile telephone switching office. *Bell Sys. Tech. J.*, 58(1):71–95, 1979.

[29] M Christian. Timing and RSL. Technical report MORSE/LLOYD's/MMC/22/V1, Lloyd's Register, July 1992.

[30] P Coad and E Yourdon. *Object-oriented Analysis*. Yourdon Press Computing Series, 1990.

[31] E F Codd. A relational model of data for large shared data banks. *CACM 13, No.6*, June 1970.

[32] E F Codd. Extending the database relational model to capture more meaning. *ACM Transactions on Database Systems*, 4(4):397–434, December 1979.

[33] D Coleman, P Arnold, S Bodoff, H Gilchrist, and F Hayes. An evaluation of five object-oriented development methods. *Hewlett-Packard Technical Report*, May 1991.

[34] D Coleman, F Hayes, and S Bear. Introducing objectcharts or how to use statecharts in object-oriented design. *IEEE Transactions on Software Engineering*, 18(1), January 1992.

[35] B P Collins, J E Nicholls, and I H Sorensen. Introducing formal methods: The CICS experience with Z. Technical report, Programming Research Group, Oxford University, 1988.

[36] S Cook. Interpreting object oriented models. In *Proceedings of Object Technology '93*, 1993.

[37] E Cusack. Object-oriented modelling in Z. In P America, editor, *ECOOP '91 Proceedings*, Lecture Notes in Computer Science. Springer-Verlag, 1991.

[38] E Cusack and C Wezeman. Deriving tests for objects specified in Z. In J Nicholls, editor, *Z User Meeting 1992*, Workshops in Computing. Springer-Verlag, 1993.

[39] O Dahl. Object orientation and formal techniques. In *VDM'90, VDM and Z - formal methods in software development. Lecture Notes in Computer Science*, volume 428. Springer-Verlag, 1990.

[40] O J Dahl. *Object-Oriented Specifications*. Research Directions in Object-Oriented Programming. MIT Press, 1987.

[41] C Date. The relational model ... is alive and well! Technical report, Codd and Date Co., 1992.

[42] A M Davis. *Software Requirements: Analysis and Specification*. Prentice Hall, 1990.

[43] J Dick. Using Prolog to animate Z specifications. In *Z User Meeting 1989*, Workshops in Computing. Springer-Verlag, 1990.

[44] A Diller. *Z, An Introduction To Formal Methods*. John Wiley, 1990.

[45] D D'Souza. Teacher! Teacher! *Journal of Object-Oriented Programming*, 5(2), May 1986.

[46] D Duke and R Duke. Towards a semantics for Object-Z. In *VDM'90: VDM and Z!. Lecture Notes in Computer Science*, volume 428. Springer-Verlag, 1990.

[47] R Duke, P King, G Rose, and G Smith. The Object-Z Specification Language. Technical report 91-1 (Version 1), University of Queensland, Department of Computer Science, Software Verification Research Centre, May 1991.

[48] R Duke, P King, and G Smith. Formalising behavioural compatibility for reactive object-oriented systems. In *Proc 14th Australian Compt. Sci. Conf. (ACSC-14)*, 1991.

[49] R Duke, G Rose, and A Lee. Object-oriented protocol specification. In *Protocol Specification, Testing, and Verification, X*, pages 325–338. 1990.

[50] E Durr. Afrodite Esprit III Project Technical Annex, 1992. CAP Gemini Innovation.

[51] E Durr. Syntactic description of the VDM++ language, Version 2.0.1, Afrodite Report FI 92-6, September 1992.

[52] E Durr. VDM++: A formal specification language for object-oriented designs. In P Dewilde and J Vandewalle, editors, *IEEE CompEuro 92 Proceedings*, pages 214 – 219. IEEE Press, 1992.

[53] E Durr. Description of the VDM++ language. Technical Report AFRO/CG/ED/SYNTAX/V5.2, CAP Gemini Innovation, March 1993.

[54] R Elmasri and S B Navethe. *Fundamentals of Database Systems*. Benjamin Cummings, 1989.

[55] H B Enderton. *Elements of Set Theory*. Academic Press, 1977.

[56] E Foster *et al.* PoeT: Object engineering in public transport. In *Proceedings Object Technology '93*, 1993.

[57] M Eva. *SSADM Version 4: A User's Guide*. International Series in Software Engineering. McGraw-Hill, 1992.

[58] A Evans. Position paper, Workshop on Formal Specification and Object Orientation, Logica, 1992.

[59] M E Fagan. Advances in software inspections. *IEEE Transactions on Software Engineering*, 12(7), 1986.

[60] A Fitzsimmons and T Love. A review and evaluation of software science. *ACM Computing Surveys*, 10(1):3–18, 1977.

[61] P Flach. Towards a logical theory of inductive learning. In *ILP '91 Proceedings*. Turing Institute, March 1991.

[62] Z Fluhr and P Porter. Control architecture. *Bell Sys. Tech. J.*, 58(1):43–69, 1979.

[63] R France. Semantically extended data flow diagrams: A formal specification tool. *IEEE Transactions on Software Engineering*, 18(4), April 1992.

[64] M D Fraser, K Kumar, and V Vaishnavi. Informal and formal requirements specification languages: Bridging the gap. *IEEE Transactions on Software Engineering*, 17(5), May 1992.

[65] C George, P Haff, K Havelund, A E Haxthausen, R Milne, C B Nielsen, S Prehn, and K R Wagner. *The RAISE SPECIFICATION LANGUAGE*. Prentice Hall, 1992.

[66] C George and S Prehn. *The Raise Justification Handbook*. Technical Report LA-COS/CRI/DOC/7/V4, Computer Resources International, October 1992.

[67] J Goguen and T Winkler. Introducing OBJ3. Technical Report SRI-CSL-88-9, SRI projects 1243, 2316 and 4415, Computer Science Laboratory, SRI International, August 1988.

[68] J A Goguen. How to prove algebraic induction without induction: With applications to the correctness of data type representations. In Wolfgang Bibel and Robert Kowalski, editors, *Lecture Notes in Computer Science*, volume 87, pages 356–373. Springer-Verlag, 1980.

[69] J A Goguen. Parameterized programming. *IEEE Transactions on Software Engineering*, SE-10(5), September 1984.

[70] J A Goguen. An algebraic approach to refinement. In *Proceedings, VDM'90: VDM and Z – Formal Methods in Software Development. Lecture Notes in Computer Science*, volume 428, pages 12–28. Springer-Verlag, 1990.

[71] J A Goguen. Types as theories. In George Michael Reed, Andrew William Roscoe, and Ralph F. Wachter, editors, *Topology and Category Theory in Computer Science*, pages 357–390. Oxford, 1991. Proceeding of a Conference held at Oxford, June 1989.

[72] J A Goguen and J Meseguer. Unifying functional, object-oriented and relational programming, with logical semantics. In Bruce Shriver and Peter Wegner, editors, *Research Directions in Object-Oriented Programming*, pages 417–477. MIT, 1987. Preliminary version in *SIGPLAN Notices*, Volume 21, Number 10, pages 153-162, October 1986.

[73] J A Goguen and J Meseguer. Order-sorted algebra I: Equational deduction for multiple inheritance, overloading, exceptions and partial operations. Technical Report SRI-CSL-89-10, SRI International, Computer Science Lab, July 1989.

[74] J A Goguen, A Stevens, H Hilberdink, and K Hobley. 2OBJ, a metalogical framework based on equational logic. *Transactions of the Royal Society, Series A*, 1992.

[75] J A Goguen, J Thatcher, and E Wagner. An initial algebra approach to the specification, correctness and implementation of abstract data types. In Raymond Yeh, editor, *Trends in Programming Methodology IV*, pages 80–149. Prentice Hall, 1978.

[76] J A Goguen and D Wolfram. On types and FOOPS. In *Proceedings of Working Conference on Database Semantics*, Windermere, Lake District, United Kingdom, July 1990.

[77] A Goldberg and D Robson. *Smalltalk-80: The Language and its Implementation*. Addison-Wesley, 1983.

[78] R Goldblatt. *Topoi: The Categorial Approach to Logic*. North-Holland, 1982.

[79] C Green, D Luckham, and R Balzer. Report on a knowledge-based software assistant. In *Artificial Intelligence and Software Engineering*. Morgan Kaufmann, 1986.

[80] D Gries. *The Science of Programming*. Prentice Hall, 1986.

[81] M T Harandi and J Q Ning. Knowledge-based program analysis. *IEEE Software*, pages 74–81, January 1990.

[82] D Harel. Statecharts: A visual formalism for complex systems. *Science of Computer Programming*, (8):231–274, 1987.

[83] J S Hares. *SSADM for the Advanced Practitioner*. Wiley Series in Software Engineering Practice, 1990.

[84] J Hartman. Understanding natural programs using proper decomposition. In *13th International Conference on Software Engineering, ICSE-13*, pages 13–16, May 1991.

[85] T Hartmann, R Jungclaus, and G Saake. Aggregation in a behaviour oriented object model. In *ECOOP '92 Proceedings, Lecture Notes in Computer Science*, volume 615, pages 57–77. Springer-Verlag, 1992.

[86] I Hayes, editor. *Specification Case Studies*. International Series in Computer Science. Prentice Hall, 1987.

[87] I Hayes. Specifications are not executable. Technical report, Programming Research Group, Oxford University, 1989.

[88] R Helm, I M Holland, and D Gangopadhyay. Contracts: Specifying behavioural compositions in object-oriented systems. In *ECOOP/OOPSLA '90 Proceedings*. Springer-Verlag, 1990.

[89] C A R Hoare. Programming: Sorcery or science. *IEEE Software*, April 1984.

[90] C A R Hoare. *Communicating Sequential Processes*. Prentice Hall, 1985.

[91] J Hogg. Islands: Aliasing protection in object-oriented languages. In *OOPSLA '91 Proceedings*. Springer-Verlag, 1991.

[92] P L Iachini and R Di Giovanni. HOOD and Z for the development of complex software systems. In *VDM and Z, VDM 90, Lecture Notes in Computer Science*, volume 428, pages 262–289. Springer-Verlag, 1990.

[93] D Ince. *Object-Oriented Software Engineering with C++*. McGraw-Hill, 1992.

[94] CISI Ingenierie and MATRA Espace. *HOOD Reference Manual*. HOOD Technical Group, 1990.

[95] R E Johnson and B Foote. Designing re-usable classes. *JOOP*, 1(2):22–35, June/July 1988.

[96] C B Jones. *Systematic Software Construction using VDM*. Prentice Hall, 1990.

[97] C B Jones. An object-based design method for concurrent programs. Technical Report UMCS-92-12-1, Manchester University, 1993.

[98] E Klein, F Veltman, and M Moens. Default reasoning and dynamic interpretation of natural language. In *ESPRIT '90 Conference Proceedings*. Kluwer, 1990.

[99] T Korson and J D McGregor. Understanding object-oriented: A unifying paradigm. *Communications of the ACM*, September 1990.

[100] R A Kowalski. Problems and promises of computational logic. In *Computational Logic Symposium Proceedings, ESPRIT 90 Conference*, November 1990.

[101] K Lano. Validation through refinement and execution of specifications: REDO project document 2487-TN-PRG-1041. Programming Research Group, Oxford University.

[102] K Lano. Integrating development and maintenance in an object-oriented environment: REDO project document 2487-TN-PRG-1050, 1990. Programming Research Group, Oxford University.

[103] K Lano. A constraint-based fuzzy inference system. In *EPIA 91, Fifth Portuguese Conference on Artificial Intelligence*, Lecture Notes in Computer Science. Springer-Verlag, 1991.

[104] K Lano. Z^{++}, an object-oriented extension to Z. In J Nicholls, editor, *Z User Meeting, Oxford, UK*, Workshops in Computing. Springer-Verlag, 1991.

[105] K Lano. Combining object-oriented representations of knowledge with proximity to conceptual prototypes. In *IEEE CompEuro '92 Proceedings*. IEEE Press, 1992.

[106] K Lano. Developing formal semantics for object-oriented specification languages. Technical report, Lloyd's Register, 1993.

[107] K Lano. Functional specification of mapping of MVS and DOS JCL into the JCL Schema. Technical report, Applied Information Engineering, Lloyd's Register, February 1993.

[108] K Lano. The mapping of OS/VS COBOL into the COBOL schema. Technical report, Applied Information Engineering, Lloyd's Register, March 1993.

[109] K Lano and H Haughton. A specification-based approach to maintenance. *Journal of Software Maintenance*, December 1991.

[110] K Lano and H Haughton. An algebraic semantics for the object-oriented specification language Z^{++}. In *AMAST '91 Conference Proceedings*, Workshops in Computing. Springer-Verlag, 1992.

[111] K Lano and H Haughton. Extracting design and functionality from code. In *CASE '92 Conference Proceedings*. IEEE Press, 1992.

[112] K Lano and H Haughton. Object-oriented Z specifications for safety-critical software. In *Workshop on Object-Oriented Methodologies*. KBSL, 1992.

[113] K Lano and H Haughton. Reasoning and refinement in object-oriented specification languages. In *ECOOP '92 Conference Proceedings*. Springer-Verlag, 1992.

[114] K Lano and H Haughton. Representation of concurrent systems in object-oriented specification languages, 1992. Lloyd's Register.

[115] K Lano and H Haughton. Reuse and adaptation of Z specifications. In *Proceedings of Z User Meeting 1992*, Workshops in Computing. Springer-Verlag, 1992.

[116] K Lano and H Haughton. *The Z^{++} Manual*, October 1992. A User-Guide and Reference Manual for the Z^{++} Toolset.

[117] K Lano and H Haughton. Approaches to object identity. In *EROS II Workshop*. LBMS, London, 1993.

[118] K Lano and H Haughton. Integrating formal and structured methods in reverse engineering. In *Working Conference on Reverse-Engineering*. IEEE Press, 1993.

[119] K Lano and H Haughton. *Object-Oriented Specification Case Studies*. Lloyd's Register, 1993.

[120] M Lehman. Programs, life cycles, and laws of software evolution. *Proceedings IEEE*, 68(9):1060–1076, 1980.

[121] M Lehman, M Meir, L A Belady, and A Laszlo. *Program Evolution – Processes of Software Change*. Academic Press, 1985.

[122] A W Leigh. *Real Time Software for Small Systems*. Halstead Press, 1988.

[123] S Leonard, J Pardoe, and S Wade. Software maintenance – Cinderella is still not getting to the ball. In *BSC/IEE Conference on Software Engineering*, pages 104–106, Liverpool Polytechnic, 1988.

[124] R C Linger, P A Hausler, M G Pleszlioch, and A R Heruer. Using function abstraction to understand program behaviour. *IEEE Software*, January 1990.

[125] C Loosley. CASE tools and repositories: The challenge of integration. In *Nord-DATA '92*. DataBase Associates, 1992.

[126] P Lupton. Promoting forward simulation. In *Z User Meeting 1990*, Workshops in Computing. Springer-Verlag, 1991.

[127] V MacDonald. The cellular concept. *Bell Sys. Tech. J.*, 58(1):15–41, 1979.

[128] R Martil. Task analysis results. Technical Report 2487-TN-LR-1039, Lloyd's Register, 1990.

[129] R Martil and S Wells. Maintenance metrics for KBS: Empirical studies. Technical Report KADS-II/TN/T2.4/LR/0054/0.2, Applied Information Engineering, Lloyd's Register, 1992.

[130] I Maung and J R Howse. Introducing Hyper-Z: A new approach to object orientation in Z. In *Z User Meeting 1992*, Workshops in Computing. Springer-Verlag, 1993.

[131] T McCabe. A Complexity Measure. *IEEE Transactions on Software Engineering*, SE-2, Number 4:308–320, December 1976.

[132] D D McCraken and M A Jackson. Life cycle concept considered harmful. *ACM Software Engineering Notes*, pages 29–32, April 1982.

[133] J McDermid. An approach to the specification of real time systems, York University, 1992.

[134] C B Medeiros and P Pfeffer. Object integrity using rules. In P America, editor, *ECOOP '91 Proceedings*. Springer-Verlag, 1991.

[135] S R L Meira and A L C Cavalcanti. Modular object-oriented Z specifications. In *Z User Meeting 1990*, Workshops in Computing, pages 173–192. Springer-Verlag, 1991.

[136] S R L Meira and A L C Cavalcanti. The MooZ specification language. Technical report, Universidade Federal de Pernambuco, Departamento de Informática, Recife - PE, 1992.

[137] S R L Meira, A L C Cavalcanti, J C Fernandes, and S M Holanda. An object-oriented formal specification of a distributed object-oriented programming language. Technical report, Universidade Federal de Pernambuco, Departamento de Informática, Recife - PE, 1991.

[138] S R L Meira, A L C Cavalcanti, and C S Santos. ForMooZ: An environment for formal object-oriented specification and prototyping. Technical report, Universidade Federal de Pernambuco, Departamento de Informática, Recife - PE, 1991.

[139] S R L Meira, R Motz, and J F Tepedino. A formal semantics for SQL. *Intern. J. Computer Math.*, 34:43–63, 1990.

[140] E Merlo, K Kontogiannis, and J F Girard. Structural and Behavioral Code Representation for Program Understanding. In *CASE '92 Proceedings*, pages 106–108. IEEE Press, 1992.

[141] B Meyer. Genericity versus inheritance. In *OOPSLA '86 Proceedings*. ACM Press, September 1986.

[142] B Meyer. *Object-Oriented Software Construction.* Prentice Hall, 1988.

[143] B Meyer. Tools for the new culture: Lessons from the design of the Eiffel libraries. *Communications of the ACM*, 33(9), September 1990.

[144] B Meyer. *Eiffel: The Language.* Prentice Hall, 1992.

[145] C A Middelburg. Syntax and semantics of VVSL. PhD Thesis, University of Amsterdam, September 1990.

[146] R Milne. Transforming axioms for data types into sequential programs. Technical report 221, University of Cambridge Computer Laboratory, May 1991.

[147] R Milner. A theory of type polymorphism in programming. *Journal of Computer and System Sciences*, 17(3):348–375, 1978.

[148] R Milner. *Communication and Concurrency.* Prentice Hall, 1991.

[149] E F Moore. *Gedanken-experiments on Sequential Machines.* Princeton University Press, 1956.

[150] C Morgan. *Programming From Specifications.* Prentice Hall, 1990.

[151] M Moriconi. A practical approach to semantic configuration management. In *Proceedings of ACM Sigsoft 89 Conference on Software Testing, Analysis and Verification*, December 1989.

[152] B Moszkowski. *Executing Temporal Logic Programs.* Cambridge University Press, 1986.

[153] R Motz. Formal analysis of an object-oriented data model. Master's Thesis (in Portuguese), Departamento de Informâtica – UFPE, 1990.

[154] M R Moulding and L E Smith. Formalising a CORE requirements model in the air traffic control domain. In *IEE Colloquium on Software in Air Traffic Control Systems – The Future*, June 1992.

[155] I Mozetic and C Holzbaur. Extending explanation-based generalisation by abstraction operators. In *Proceedings of EWSL '91. Lecture Notes in Artificial Intelligence*, volume 482. Springer-Verlag, 1991.

[156] S Muggleton and C Feng. Efficient induction of logic programs. In *Proceedings of First Conference on Algorithmic Learning*. Ohmsha Publications, October 1990.

[157] G J Myers. *Reliable Software Through Composite Design.* Van Nostrand Reinhold, 1975.

[158] J Paris and A Vencovska. On the applicability of maximum entropy to inexact reasoning. *International Journal of Approximate Reasoning*, 3(1), 1988.

[159] L J Pinson and R S Wiener. *An Introduction to Object-Oriented Programming and Smalltalk.* Addison-Wesley, 1988.

[160] C Ponder and B Bush. Polymorphism considered harmful. *ACM Sigplan Notices*, 27(6), June 1992.

[161] B W Porter, R Bareiss, and R C Holte. Concept learning and heuristic classification in weak-theory domains. *Artificial Intelligence*, (45):229–263, 1990.

[162] L H Putman. A general empirical solution to the macro software sizing and estimation problem. *IEEE Transactions of Software Engineering*, SE-4 No.4:335–361, July 1987.

[163] D R Pyle. Specifying object semantics. In *Workshop on Object-Oriented Methodologies*. KBSL, 1992.

[164] D R Pyle and M Josephs. Enriching a structured method with Z. In *Methods Integration Conference*, Workshops in Computing. Springer-Verlag, 1991.

[165] D R Pyle and M Josephs. Entity-relationship models expressed in Z: A synthesis of structured and formal methods. Programming Research Group, Oxford University, 1991.

[166] Quintus Corporation, 2100 Geng Road, Palo Alto, California, 94303. *Quintus Prolog III: Interfaces and Delivery Tools, release 3.1*, February 1991.

[167] G-H B Rafsanjani and S J Colwill. From Object-Z to C++: A structural mapping. In *Z User Meeting 1992*. Springer-Verlag, 1993.

[168] U S Reddy. Transformational derivation of programs using the FOCUS system. In *Symposium on Software Development Environments*. ACM Press, December 1988.

[169] C A Richter. An assessment of structured analysis and structured design. *Software Engineering Notes*, 11(4):75–83, August 1986.

[170] J Robinson. The need for methods in an object-oriented environment. In *Workshop on Object-oriented Methodologies*. KBSL, 1992.

[171] E Rosch. Principles of categorization. In *Cognition and Categorization*. Hillsdale, 1978.

[172] C Rouveirol. ITOU: Induction of first order theories. In *ILP '91 Proceedings*. Turing Institute, March 1991.

[173] W W Royce. Managing the development of large software systems: Concepts and techniques. In *Proceedings of Wescon*, August 1970.

[174] J Rumbaugh, M Blaha, W Premerlani, F Eddy, and W Lorensen. *Object-Oriented Modelling and Design*. Prentice Hall, 1991.

[175] A Sampaio and S Meria. Modular extensions to Z. In *VDM and Z. Lecture Notes in Computer Science*, volume 428. Springer-Verlag, 1990.

[176] C S Santos. ForMooZ: Um Ambiente Multi-usuário Baseado em Hipertexto de Suporte à Construcao de Especificacões Formais Orientadas a Objeto. Master's Thesis, Universidade Federal de Pernambuco, Departamento de Informática, Recife - PE, 1992.

[177] B Sheil. Power tools for programmers. In *Artificial Intelligence and Software Engineering*. Morgan Kaufmann, 1986.

[178] S Shlaer and S Mellor. *Object-Oriented Systems Analysis: Modelling the World in Data*. Yourdon Press Computing Series, 1988.

[179] S Shlaer and S Mellor. *Object Lifecycles: Modelling the World in States*. Yourdon Press Computing Series, 1992.

[180] M D Smith and D J Robson. Object oriented programming – the problems of validation. In *Proceedings of IEEE Conference on Software Maintenance*, pages 272–281, 1990.

[181] J M Spivey. *Understanding Z: A Specification Language and its Formal Semantics*. Cambridge Tracts in Theoretical Computer Science. Cambridge University Press, 1988.

[182] M Spivey. *The Z Notation: A Reference Manual*, 2nd Edition. Prentice Hall, 1992.

[183] S Stepney, R Barden, and D Cooper, editors. *Object Orientation in Z*. Workshops in Computing. Springer-Verlag, 1992.

[184] P A Swatman. Using formal specification in the acquisition of information systems: Educating information systems professionals. In *Z User Meeting 1992*, Workshops in Computing. Springer-Verlag, 1993.

[185] C A Szyperski. Import is not inheritance - why we need both: Modules and classes. In *ECOOP '92 Proceedings. Lecture Notes in Computer Science*, volume 615, pages 19–32. Springer-Verlag, 1992.

[186] A S Tannenbaum. *Operating Systems: Design and Implementation*. Prentice Hall, 1987.

[187] J F Tepedino, R Motz, and S R L Meira. From model-based specifications to object-oriented prototypes - a method. Technical report, X Congresso da SBC, Vitria, Brazil, July 1990.

[188] B Todd and R Stamper. The formal specification of diagnostic systems. Technical report, Programming Research Group, Oxford University, 1991.

[189] T H Tse and J Goguen. Functional object-oriented design. Technical report, Programming Research Group, Oxford University, 1990.

[190] P Ward. How to integrate object orientation with structured analysis and design. *IEEE Software*, pages 74–82, March 1989.

[191] R Waters. Program translation via abstraction and re-implementation. *IEEE Transactions on Software Engineering*, 14(8), August 1988.

[192] B Wegner. The object-oriented classification paradigm. In *Research Directions in Object-Oriented Programming*, pages 479–560. MIT Press, 1987.

[193] B Wegner. Concepts and paradigms of object-oriented programming. *OOPS Messenger*, 1(1):7–78, August 1990.

[194] P Whysall and J McDermid. An approach to object-oriented specification using Z. In *Z User Meeting 1990*, Workshops in Computing. Springer-Verlag, 1991.

[195] N Wilde and R Huitt. Maintenance support for object-oriented programs. In *Proceedings of Conference on Software Maintenance*. IEEE Computer Society Press, 1991.

[196] A Wills. Capsules and types in Fresco: Program verification in Smalltalk. In P America, editor, *ECOOP '91 Proceedings. Lecture Notes in Computer Science*, volume 512, pages 59–76. Springer-Verlag, 1991.

[197] A Wills. Formal specification of object-oriented programs, 1992. PhD Thesis, University of Manchester, UK.

[198] A Wills. Specification in Fresco. In S Stepney, R Barden, and D Cooper, editors, *Object Orientation in Z*. Springer-Verlag, 1992.

[199] J Wing. A study of 12 specifications of the library problem. *IEEE Software*, pages 66–76, July 1988.

[200] R J Wirfs-Brock and R E Johnson. Surveying current research in object-oriented design. *Communications of the ACM*, September 1990.

[201] K Won. On unifying relational and object-oriented database systems. In *ECOOP '92 Proceedings. Lecture Notes in Computer Science*, volume 615, pages 1–18. Springer-Verlag, 1992.

[202] J Woodcock. Mathematics as a management tool: Proof rules for promotion. In *Procs. CSR 6th Annual Conference on Large Software Systems*. Elsevier, 1989.

[203] J Woodcock and S Brien. W: A logic for Z. Technical report, Programming Research Group, Oxford University, 1991.

[204] J Woodcock and M Loomes. *Software Engineering Mathematics*. Pitman, 1988.

[205] E Yourdon. *Modern Structured Analysis*. Prentice Hall, 1989.

[206] ZIP Consortium. *Z Base Standard, Version 1.0*, 1993.

[207] H V Zuylen. *The REDO Compendium of Reverse-Engineering*. Wiley, 1993.

[208] N Zvegintov. The future of present systems. In *Software Maintenance Workshop*, Centre for Software Maintenance, Durham University, September 1990.

Index